PRAISE FOR
LEADING DIGITAL
STRATEGY

'For businesses to thrive in today's markets they need to engage effectively with digital. This book provides an effective framework that helps leaders drive their digital efforts in the right direction. It offers a blueprint that many leaders will find invaluable.'
Paul Walsh, Chairman, Compass Group; former CEO, Diageo

'Wake up and smell the differences in the digital world we now find ourselves in! Chris and James very successfully educate, challenge and stimulate smart thinking and practical actions. In particular, the excellent "killer questions" poke the reader into a thorough assessment of their business.'
Feilim Mackle, Sales and Service Director, O2/Telefónica UK

'The speed of evolution in digital business is accelerating. However digitally savvy you may be, this is a useful blueprint for business leadership in the digital age.'
Doug Johnson-Poensgen, former Managing Director, Corporate Banking, Barclays Bank

'This is for the executive who sees the opportunity in digital but who is frustrated or daunted by the practicalities of execution. *Leading Digital Strategy* provides us with a response, refreshingly framed in terms of the fundamental management and leadership disciplines required. It is a confidence-inspiring guide that reminds us that it is not technology, but established business best practice that drives success in the digital world. I wish I had read a copy three years ago.'
Alan South, former CEO, IDEO Europe

'Moore's law is not changing what is done in economy, but it is very significantly changing how things are done. For example, if you take modern cars today, more than 50 per cent of the budget for new cars is software. The same principle applies for selling products and services. *Leading Digital Strategy* is a must-read for those who want to stay relevant in the 21st century through strong e-commerce.'
Jan Mühlfeit, retired Chairman, Microsoft Europe

'A must-read for leaders of all levels, *Leading Digital Strategy* provides a clear leadership blueprint to ensure full commercial advantage is extracted from e-commerce strategy. It demystifies an area that most business leaders over thirty don't "get". I believe most boards would benefit from reading this too, as it clearly pinpoints the key questions to ask to ensure value for money and the collection of key customer insights to underpin organizational strategy for the future. It is a handbook you will return to again and again.'
Helen Pitcher, Chairman, Advanced Boardroom Excellence Limited

'A book that demystifies "digital" for business leaders. No longer can senior business leaders afford to simply delegate digital leadership in their business, and this book provides a practical blueprint by which leaders can measure, monitor and drive their business irrespective of their technical knowledge – or lack of it!'
Craig Hamer, Joint Managing Director, Dews Motor Group

'This is a book for commercial leaders who are looking for a blueprint to drive their e-commerce strategy. It pulls together the key drivers for digital success into a handbook that is straightforward and easy to read. It will persuade you that e-commerce is an organizational more than a technical challenge.'
David Langridge, Group Marketing Director, Fitness First

'As business leaders we face ever increasing complexity, including the changing nature of our customers and colleagues, and how they expect to engage with our business. This book tackles both areas, enabling leaders to develop a digital strategy, while successfully challenging us on how to create the right culture to achieve it.'
Steve Murrells, Chief Executive – Retail, The Co-operative Group

Leading Digital Strategy

Driving business growth through effective e-commerce

Christopher Bones and
James Hammersley

KoganPage

LONDON PHILADELPHIA NEW DELHI

First published in Great Britain and the United States in 2015 by Kogan Page Limited
Reprinted 2015 (three times)

2nd Floor, 45 Gee Street	1518 Walnut Street, Suite 1100	4737/23 Ansari Road
London EC1V 3RS	Philadelphia PA 19102	Daryaganj
United Kingdom	USA	New Delhi 110002
www.koganpage.com		India

© Christopher Bones and James Hammersley, 2015

The right of Christopher Bones and James Hammersley to be identified as the authors of this work has been asserted by them in accordance with the Copyright, Designs and Patents Act 1988.

ISBN   978 0 7494 7309 9
E-ISBN   978 0 7494 7310 5

British Library Cataloguing-in-Publication Data

A CIP record for this book is available from the British Library.

Library of Congress Cataloging-in-Publication Data

Bones, Chris, 1958-
   Leading digital strategy : driving business growth through effective e-commerce / Christopher Bones, James Hammersley.
      pages cm
   Includes bibliographical references and index.
   ISBN 978-0-7494-7309-9 – ISBN 978-0-7494-7310-5 (ebk)   1. Electronic commerce.
2. Internet marketing.   3. Strategic planning.   I. Hammersley, James.   II. Title.
   HF5548.32.B656 2015
   658.8'72–dc23
                                                                                  2014050212

Typeset by Graphicraft Limited, Hong Kong
Print production managed by Jellyfish
Printed and bound by CPI Group (UK) Ltd, Croydon CR0 4YY

CONTENTS

ACKNOWLEDGEMENTS

We would not have been able to complete this book without the support and hard work of a number of people who deserve our thanks and recognition.

First and foremost we must thank our team at Good Growth Ltd whose work we are sharing and especially those who took on tasks associated with this book over and above their normal jobs: Hamish Bones, Tushar Dhiman, Mike Duke, Lynda Gillespie, Frank Page, Simon Rix, Dr Nick Shaw, Dr Sam Stevens and Mark Watson. Frank and his team in Good Growth Design need also to be credited with the great process visuals that have brought the concepts and ideas to life. Thanks also go to colleagues Rupert Angel, who has contributed significantly to the thinking about processes and organization, Jane Upton who contributed to our thinking on change and David Rawlings, who lent us his technical expertise as one of the leading practitioners in this field.

We would like to thank the senior executives who agreed to be interviewed and to provide insights into the challenges and opportunities of leading digital businesses: Brett Aumuller from BSkyB, Helen Brand from ACCA, Craig Hamer from Dews Motor Group, Zac Peake from A-Plan Insurance, Hugh Sturges from Berry Brothers and Rudd, Douglas Johnson-Poensgen from Barclays, David Langridge from Fitness First, Tete Soto from Telefonica/O2 and Konstantine Karampatsos from feelunique.com

Credit goes to Jenni Hall and Karen Raith at Kogan Page who did everything as editors to sharpen our prose and to keep us on time and on target with great skill and patience.

We would also like to thank Professor Michael Hartmann, former Deputy Director and now Visiting Professor at Manchester Business School who was generous with both his time and research materials.

We need to acknowledge a debt of gratitude to Dr Karl Blanks and Ben Jesson, respectively Chairman and Chief Executive of Conversion Rate Experts Ltd, our strategic partners and early mentors into the world of website optimization. They have been generous with their time and expertise and have been significant influencers of our early thinking about the practice of effective e-commerce.

And finally to our families for enduring the lack of attention that the writing of such books inevitably brings.

Introduction

Business not as usual

Business as usual is changing. Digital technology is driving the change and as it engages with business organizations, the changes it makes are creating a gap between leaders who are accountable for direction and performance and the technical and digital specialists required to operate effectively in this new world.

This gap arises from a lack of experience in and exposure to the mechanics and practices of e-commerce for many business leaders, and a lack of experience in and exposure to the operation of a commercial undertaking for many digital specialists. In a large number of organizations, this gap has become a breeding ground for underperformance and frustration. Business leaders are frustrated through a low return on investment and a sense of under-achievement, and digital specialists are frustrated by a lack of leadership engagement with and understanding of what they do, which they see as restricting the level of performance that they can achieve.

Whilst over time exposure to commercial operations and engagement with the business imperatives that drive management decisions may go some way to building capability in digital specialists, this in itself will not bridge the gap; nor will it significantly change performance. Performance will only get addressed if business leaders build sufficient understanding of how e-commerce works and how they can harness the full opportunity it presents to grow the whole business.

This book offers business leaders and aspiring leaders in every sector, whether they are focussed on selling direct to the end customer or to other businesses, the opportunity to engage with and understand the digital world and specifically how e-commerce can drive growth. We have a particular perspective that has been developed through working with medium- and large-scale businesses that deliver their products and services through more than one channel. From this work, we infer that the issues with performance have less to do with technology per se (such as the platform) and more to do with organization issues (such as working practices). Whilst it is undoubtedly true that technology and its application is a major challenge in many e-commerce operations, what sits behind this is more often than not an organizational issue. Poor processes, lack of capability, unclear objectives, multiple measures, misaligned structures, competing priorities and a failure to understand key parts of the operation mean that many e-commerce teams fail to deliver to expectations. These are leadership challenges and they require leadership action.

Most leaders in businesses have built an understanding of the business and operating model they run through experience: either directly through experience of working in the business they lead or through their experience in other businesses. Digital technology is changing both the business and operating models and many leaders need to revise their understanding whilst trying to run a business in change, often in a market that is transforming much faster than their business can keep up. This is the challenge of leadership and it gets more and more difficult the larger the organization becomes.

Being in a leadership position is never an easy place to learn, especially where you have little or no direct experience and may feel slightly intimidated by the language and the technology. In these circumstances, some leaders have opted for appointing specialist support and advice that they then rely on to come to their own judgements. This may be the right call, especially if you are genuinely innovating or introducing leading-edge technology; but generally, this is not the best approach where a business' primary use of digital technology, in driving its strategy, is as a route to market. This is what the vast majority of businesses will be doing. Business as usual in the digital world is e-commerce and every leader needs as good an understanding of e-commerce as they do the other routes to market for their products or services. So how can you assess if what you are doing is business as usual or not?

Some broad observations about digital business

There are two ways of thinking about the impact of digital on business. First, in terms of how it manifests itself, and second in terms of the competitive opportunity.

Figure 0.1 sets out a hierarchical model of digital business that defines the activity in one of three groups:

FIGURE 0.1   Digital business segmented by type

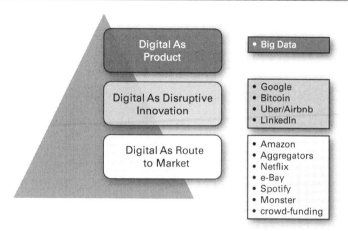

SOURCE: © Good Growth Ltd 2014

- **Digital as a product in itself.** This is where the data itself is the
  product or service, commonly referred to as 'big data'. This part
  is dominated by professional services and some digital services
  businesses who can manipulate billions of data points on behalf
  of very large organizations such as banks, retailers and
  governments.

- **Digital as disruptive innovation.** This is where it makes a market
  that has not existed before using new technology or applying
  technology in a novel way. This is the entrepreneurial part where
  new products and services come into being that were either
  impossible or commercially unviable in the pre-digital age. Whilst
  this is where fortunes can be made (and lost) for the founders and
  early investors, over time these businesses will establish and sustain
  themselves through the tools and techniques required to manage a
  digital route to market.

- **Digital as a route to market.** This is where it is transforming
  the delivery of existing products and services or allowing the
  development of new products and services within established
  markets. This is the world most of us inhabit and the world
  that is facing the most significant levels of change as old models
  break down and new models take their time to establish and work
  effectively. We will use the term e-commerce throughout this book
  to describe this activity.

FIGURE 0.2   The operational challenges in digital business

	Businesses creating innovative/disruptive technology	Businesses going digital in existing/traditional industries
Established	*Examples: Google, LinkedIn, Equinix* Issues: • **Retaining over-qualified employees** • **Fostering constant innovation** • **Retaining customers**	*Examples: Monster, Asos, Booking.com, John Lewis, BestBuy* Issues: • **Manage stakeholder expectations** • **Developing customer confidence** • **Finding employees with industry and digital expertise**
Start-up	*Examples: Kagle, Citymapper, Evernote* Issues: • **Attracting and retaining talented people with non-pay incentives** • **Finding the right time to sell** • **Attracting and retaining customers** • **Balancing between finding funds and growing the company**	*Examples: JustEat, Transferwire, Moo* Issues: • **Breaking into well-established industries** • **Developing customer confidence** • **Finding employees with industry and digital expertise** • **Balancing between finding funds and growing the company**

SOURCE: © K Karampatsos 2014

This model also illustrates why we have chosen to concentrate on e-commerce as the digital leadership challenge. Few of us will work in innovation and even fewer in big data. However, given that virtually every business will use digital as a route to market, we believe that a standard leadership capability in the very near future will be a good understanding of e-commerce.

Figure 0.2 comes from Konstantine Karampatsos[1] who is a leading e-commerce practitioner. It considers digital business in terms of the operational challenges faced by disruptive innovators and businesses using digital as a route to market in established markets.

Both have their disadvantages and opportunities but the issues faced by the vast majority of us working in established markets are classic leadership challenges. They are also becoming the challenges faced by those who are already successful in the disruptive quadrants and will be true for those who will become so in the future. This is the case as, after time, almost all organizations become less creative and more interested in protecting what they already have.

Karampatsos' analysis suggests that despite individual issues particular to a sector or organization there are two that seem to reach across every sector and every size of business: first, the classic one of finding and retaining the right talent with the right sets of skills; and second, getting it right with customers so they respond positively to what a business is trying to do. In our view, whilst the former is always a challenge in an emerging discipline there are some creative solutions available that we share later on in the book. The single biggest challenge however in e-commerce is getting it right for the customer. This is the focus for any digital leader and sits at the core of the thinking behind this book.

Karampatsos calls this 'developing customer confidence' and this description is a good one as the word 'confidence' implies that there is a need to build a relationship. A relationship can only be established properly if it is based on a mutual understanding and where there is a degree of trust existing between the parties. The challenge of e-commerce is to build effective relationships in the absence of any physical human interaction.

This book sets out what it takes to understand the customer and how to use this understanding to build an effective e-commerce operation. It is written to help leaders cut through the noise, the hype and the jargon to be able to make a balanced assessment about current effectiveness and, where required, establish a programme of change to ensure that they are generating the best possible returns.

The challenge of building digital futures

McKinsey's 2014 global survey on trends in digital business[2] highlighted why businesses need to ensure they have effective e-commerce functions. Of the six digital trends they asked about, executives who responded expected the largest share of their digital growth in the coming years would be from digital customer engagement, followed closely by the digital innovation of products, operating models, or business models. The survey reports that the biggest investments are both in the e-commerce area: digital customer engagement and innovations in product, business model or operating model.

Many business leaders also highlighted that they are finding it challenging to create an organization that is well positioned to see digital efforts scaled across the company and achieve the average growth goal reported in the survey of 15 per cent through e-commerce. As can be seen in Figure 0.3 the challenges specifically highlighted in this regard were:

- A failure to understand the value potential from digital (only 7 per cent said their organizations understood the exact value at stake from digital).

FIGURE 0.3   E-commerce challenges

96%
- Poor return on investment

93%
- Don't understand value at stake

90%
- Insufficient talent

60%
- Unaccountable performance management

31%
- Ineffective organization

SOURCE: © Good Growth Ltd 2014

- A failure to extract the value they were hoping for from their investments to date (only 4 per cent reported high returns on their companies' current investments).
- A failure to establish accountability measures and performance (fewer than 40 per cent said their companies have accountability measures in place for their digital objectives, either through measurable targets or performance incentives for relevant employees).
- A failure to establish effective organization structures and flexible business processes (31 per cent, the largest single group of respondents, from large businesses highlighted this as an issue).
- A failure to attract or develop the right talent (9 out of 10 reported having a talent challenge).

These are all leadership challenges: ones that business leaders have to address today if their companies are going to remain effective competitors in their respective markets over the next 10–15 years.

We highlight the findings of this survey not just because it is highly regarded as a barometer of global senior executive views, but also because so many of the findings resonate with our own operating experience as partners to organizations who are working to build effective e-commerce functions. They are all facing an organizational challenge that requires leaders to establish three things:

- An agreed value at stake for the business against which investments will be made and returns expected. This is a commercial imperative not a technology project in a vacuum.

- Clear leadership and management accountability for establishing a business model and an operating model and the most effective processes and structures that can enable these to deliver the expected value.

- A deep understanding of customers and how to attract, engage and retain them in the digital channel.

In our experience, what is missing in many organizations is a model against which leaders can build a common understanding of what is required to deliver these things and a shared programme of change to ensure they get delivered. This book is our response.

How to use this book

We have built this book as a handbook for change. We start off in Chapter 1 with an analysis of the environment and the challenges of leading digital business. Chapter 2 moves on to identify what the most common drivers are for underperformance. Following this in Chapters 3 to 7 we explore the drivers of digital success (customer insight, marketing, operations, organization and leadership), and in Chapter 8 we hear from senior leaders, from a range of different businesses, about how they are responding to the challenges of becoming a digital business.

Each chapter builds on the next to create a clear blueprint for an effective e-commerce operation. Each is constructed to introduce the relevant ideas, tools and techniques and then at the end we offer a framework for leaders to engage with the challenge of how they might assess their own operation. The framework does two things: it presents a series of questions that leaders can ask of themselves and their e-commerce teams that will show the size of the gap between effective operation and current performance and it proposes a set of potential actions that could be taken depending on the answers that are established.

In the last chapter, we pull together the knowledge presented in the previous chapters into an e-commerce leadership model and show how this can drive an integrated plan that will deliver improved performance. One word of advice: leaping to the model at the end, however impatient you are to drive change in your own business, won't be as useful to you as ensuring you engage with the chapters that outline and explain the drivers for success. Understanding the essence of these could enable you to transform your business performance.

Resource bank

This is a very fast-changing environment and whilst much of what is covered in terms of processes, capabilities, organization principles and change leadership will hold true for some time, the book contains some material that will require updating. One example of this will be the recommended tools, another is the listing of commercially important social media sites. To help you we will keep this type of reference material up to date on our website in a section dedicated to the book (**www.goodgrowth.co.uk/digitalstrategy/**). Here you will find the latest versions of key sections, more detailed case studies and an ability to ask questions and get advice from our team. We encourage you to visit these pages and to leave your own feedback and advice for others facing similar challenges.

Some basic nomenclature

There is a glossary at the end of this book; however, as terms change rapidly in e-commerce and various tools use the same terms with slightly different definitions, here is a guide to the key terms we use throughout:

- **E-commerce:** the activity that is responsible for driving commercial performance through a digital channel. This encompasses marketing in the channel, sales, promotions, new digital product development and channel performance measurement and improvement. It does not include responsibility for technology choices or management. We have assumed for the purposes of this book that whilst e-commerce is a key stakeholder in these decisions, the responsibility for them sits within an IT function.

- **Customer in the market:** this is the customer as shopper, not yet committed to a purchase, but actively looking to complete a transaction. This term applies to both 'business to consumer' and 'business to business' markets and regardless of whether the digital channels aim to transact a sale or generate a lead.

- **Customer:** this is the customer as purchaser.

- **Consumer:** this refers to people in the market who may or may not be shopping for your product or service.

- **User:** a customer in the market who is visiting or has visited your website. They can also be known as unique visitors.

- **Session:** a period of time spent on your website. Unlike 'user' it does not discriminate between whether this is several visits by one customer in the market or one visit made by several customers in the market. These can also be known as visits.

- **Platform:** the technology used to support an e-commerce operation.

Notes

1 Konstantine Karampatsos has been Marketplace Manager for Amazon UK, Head of e-Commerce Consultancy for Rakuten UK (Play.com) and Senior Director for feelunique.com, an online beauty products retailer.

2 http://www.mckinsey.com/insights/business_technology/The_digital_tipping_point_McKinsey_Global_Survey_results?cid=DigitalEdge-eml-alt-mip-mck-oth-1406 [accessed 25 August 2014]

21st-century markets

1

EXECUTIVE SUMMARY

We are in the throes of a revolution in how business is done, and driving this revolution is digital technology. However, digital is not just changing the face of business, it is changing the face of how we live. In this chapter we outline the emerging impact on business, on organizations and on leadership and lay out challenges that digital has created for business leaders in the 21st century. We look at the impact in two aspects of business, marketing and organization design, and lay out why understanding the consequences for thinking and practice in these areas will be critical to long-term success. This chapter also expands our core proposition: that whilst digital has developed product and service opportunities for some businesses, for most digital is first and foremost a new route to market, and a new channel through which it can deliver customer service which brings with it the unique capability to listen to customers in the marketplace. It is this dual functionality that business leaders need to understand and learn how to manage to grow. At the end of the chapter we set out a framework for thinking through strategic choices and the role that digital can play in delivering your strategy.

Schumpeter's gale

The opening up of new markets and the organizational development from the craft shop and factory to such concerns as US Steel illustrate the process of industrial mutation that incessantly revolutionizes the economic structure from within, incessantly destroying the old one, incessantly creating a new one... [The process] must be seen in its role in the perennial gale of creative destruction.[1]

So wrote economist Joseph Schumpeter in his book *Capitalism, Socialism and Democracy* in 1942. Built partly on analysis of the impact of the Illinois Central Railroad on the economic landscape of the mid-west, the now famous phrase 'creative destruction' has its champions and its critics, but there is no doubt that the argument he proposes is one that recent changes may be illustrating just as powerfully as the advance of the railroad in the 19th century: the perennial gale driving today's mutation being digital technology.

The impact of the digital revolution on our economic structures is already dramatic. The impact on people is potentially even more so. One commentator describes it as living in 'a world that is changing faster than we can learn'.[2] The pace of change around us seems to be increasing exponentially – driving a sense of incessant revolution through which it is difficult to keep abreast, let alone get ahead, of what is happening. We have difficulty finding time to reflect, make sense and respond. In many aspects of daily life, we hear people talking about being short-term, not being in control and working long hours. The technology that enables our digital engagement now causes as much concern as it does excitement as smarter and smarter devices become available, driving more of us into a world where 24/7 interaction becomes a reality. Recent research has revealed that IT-addictive behaviours are creating serious problems for individuals and organizations alike.[3] One conclusion from this is that our world is at risk of being populated by sociopaths whose ability to form attachments is focussed firmly in the virtual.

The impacts are far from all negative. We have seen dramatic shifts in longevity, not just in the population as a whole, but also in terms of medical conditions that even 10 years previously were seen as death sentences. Since the early 1970s the chances of surviving breast cancer have now increased by 55 per cent.[4] HIV no longer automatically leads to AIDS and eventual death and with effective treatment can be subdued to such an extent that it cannot be transmitted. Genetic research using the latest digital technologies has isolated genes that have until now defined lifespan and life quality and that is already enabling eradication of inherited defects in some specific cases through manipulation of fertilized eggs prior to implantation in the womb.[5]

This is a world defined through the ease by which we can make connections and find information. Newspapers are no longer the primary source of news – individual posts, tweets and uploaded videos can shape our view of events or even make an event news. Our lives are closer to that of Orwell's Winston Smith than we think. Governments too can make connections and access information about us far more readily than when they had to rely on people. Edward Snowden's revelations[6] suggest a world where little is safe or secret, and where Big Brothers are watching, listening, reading and assessing every move we make. Regardless of whether or not we agree on the legitimacy of such activities the fact they can be done is down to the technology that we have adopted with such alacrity over the past few years.

In product terms, we experience significant shifts in functionality and relevance in much shorter timescales than previous generations. As we replace computers, televisions and mobile telephones for example, what replaces them can be a significantly different product with radically different functionality. As communications continue to speed up, so products achieve ubiquity faster and replacement cycles get shorter and shorter. A recent article in *MIT Technology Review* showed that whilst it took almost a century for landline phones to reach saturation in the United States, mobile phones reached this in just 20 years. Furthermore the emerging data trend suggests that smartphones are on track to halve that rate yet again, and tablets could move still faster.[7]

Like it or not, if we are looking for an answer, a product, a service, a home or a source of entertainment we are now likely to turn to the web and start our search there. For an increasing number of us we stay with our search online through to completion. There are now many signs that digital business is redefining markets in nearly every sector of the global economy and in retailing in particular there are now signs that we are living through a period of creative destruction. This book is particularly focussed on e-commerce and in this sphere there are three areas that it is worth considering as we explore the impact and implications of digital technology on modern business: retailing; the sharing economy; and the emerging propositions that look to leap over the top of traditional routes to the customer and 'deal direct'.

The retail sector

The classic example of the impact of e-commerce is of course retailing. A recent study from the United States[9] looked at the impact in retailing over the period 2007–2011 and concluded that the US was 'in the midst of a profound structural shift from physical to digital retail'. The author argued that the drivers of this shift were: the online cost advantage that enabled lower prices with the same if not better margins than offline retailers; wider selection; and increasingly better service. It suggested that, as pricing in the traditional channels would remain under pressure, this would result in increasing numbers of offline bankruptcies which in turn will remove competition from online players and further boost their market share.

The study highlighted figures from the US Census Bureau that suggested that there were two very different patterns going on with respect to e-commerce penetration. In the largest categories – food and beverage, and health and personal care – e-commerce penetration was well below the overall average. These categories are dominated by supermarket and drug stores and here e-commerce has as yet achieved only modest penetration.

The other categories are speciality retail categories that populate shopping malls across the US. They consist of clothing and accessories, electronics and appliances, furniture and home furnishings and media, sporting and hobby goods (media defined as books, magazines, music and videos). All of these demonstrated e-commerce penetration well above the overall average, ranging from a low of 12 per cent for clothing and accessories, up to 24 per cent for media, sporting and hobby goods. It's in these speciality retail categories that e-commerce to date has had its strongest impact and where the pace of online share gain shows no signs of slowing down.

The study highlighted that, for the period in question, the US Census Bureau reported that these four speciality retail categories, representing total sales of just over $600 billion, grew by only $5 billion. That's less than 1 per cent over four years. The e-commerce players increased their cumulative sales in these categories by $35 billion over the time period. This suggests that the cumulative sales of traditional retailers in these categories shrank by $30 billion in just four years.

Regardless of geography there is no doubt that retailing is undergoing a seismic shift. Where once every high street had a bookshop and a music store there are now far fewer who can boast one, let alone both. Large appliance and electronics retail showrooms are also reducing rapidly. The woes of US giant Best Buy have been in the media spotlight for some time and although recent innovations have boosted the share price, sales remain stubbornly on a downward track.[9] In the UK, online retailers overtook bricks-and-mortar operators for market share in consumer electronics in 2011.[10] In January 2014 the UK's Office for National Statistics reported that two-thirds of all retail sales were transacted away from bricks-and-mortar outlets.[11]

The sharing economy

If retail is the classic example then the transformation of the sharing economy is the latest emerging example of the creative destruction power of digital technology. There is nothing essentially new about a sharing economy.

People have swapped assets through bartering as part of the human trading system for thousands of years. People have rented out their property, shared facilities and transport for nearly as long. Prior to digital, this required face-to-face interaction and local knowledge.

With the advent of digital technology, the sharing economy is currently producing explosive start-up growth and has an international impact that is disrupting traditional business sectors such as hospitality, and regulated sectors such as taxi transportation which have to date been protected from change by local governments and, in places, powerful trade unions. The outstanding examples are Uber and AirBnB. Over the last few years these companies have grown from being just another disruptive technology start-up to international names responsible for reshaping the model of the sharing economy from one based on personal knowledge and trust to a global network where systems and compliance reassure and build confidence.

It is fascinating that they are reversing a paradigm that has developed over the last couple of hundred years that the state should pay a role in setting a regulatory framework to ensure service levels and protect the consumer from abuse. We are being invited to trust their systems and quality assurance processes, mostly unregulated, as opposed to the services of those who are regulated. This lack of regulatory protection also applies to the supplier. In a London taxi, for example, if you soil the inside the law holds that you can be charged for cleaning it up. Some of the emerging problems with these models spring from the fact that unlike the traditional sharing economy where personal relationships and trust created a pressure to behave well, in an unregulated world where transaction dominates over relationships, behaving well for some is not seen as part of the contract.

Whilst it may be that they are being overhyped, some experts believe that if successful over the long term these business models have the opportunity to redefine how such things as travel and transportation are bought and consumed.[12] To give you an idea of their scale, as of June 2014 Uber and AirBnB were valued at upwards of $17 billion and $10 billion respectively.[13] These are both interesting examples of how digital technology has enabled entrepreneurs to disrupt and break through.

Uber

Uber was founded in San Francisco in 2009 by Garrett Camp and Travis Kalanick as an antidote to the notoriously bad taxi service in San Francisco and has since grown to well over 100 cities in the US alone and in its last round of funding attracted $1.2 billion.[14]

Uber is essentially a web-based service that connects the passenger with a vetted, private driver who can pick them up and take them where they want to go. With the Uber smartphone application your location is pinpointed with the GPS on your phone. You choose what kind of car you need, check the estimated price of the journey, and then you are told how long you will need to wait for your car to arrive. You can even see where it is on a map, a photo of your driver, their name and a contact phone number.

Unlike with other applications, such as Hailo, that work within the current system and help you 'hail' a cab using technology, Uber uses private individuals who, whilst vetted, are no more trained or informed about the location than they choose to be as individuals. The other significant difference with the traditional business model is that when you arrive at your destination you won't need to hand over cash as the company has your credit card details and you get an e-mail the next day with a breakdown of the costs. You are also not expected to tip your driver.

AirBnB

Shortly after moving to San Francisco in October 2007, Brian Chesky and Joe Gebbia created the initial concept for Air Bed & Breakfast during the Industrial Design Conference held by Industrial Designers Society of America. At the time, roommates Chesky and Gebbia could not afford the rent for their loft in San Francisco so they made their living room into a bed and breakfast, accommodating three conference guests on air mattresses and providing homemade breakfast to attendees who were unable to book a hotel room in the saturated market.

AirBnB is a community marketplace where guests can book living accommodation from a list of verified hosts. Membership of the site is completely free and there is no cost to post a listing. Using a targeted user interface designed to narrow down travelling preferences, AirBnB offers an attractive, cost-saving alternative to traditional hotel bookings and vacation home rentals. Upon finding a desired listing, guests are prompted to sign up for membership, which provides access to contact the host directly as well as provide payment information for a request. Only once the host accepts the transaction and the guest checks in is the credit card charged, along with a 6–12 per cent transaction fee from AirBnB.

By allowing free membership and free access to list properties, AirBnB quickly overcame the initial mobilization hurdle and attracted a dedicated following of guests and hosts. Users were free to browse as they pleased and were only prompted to pay a service charge when a reservation occurred, allowing AirBnB to maximize the number of potential transactions.

Valuing innovation

Since AirBnB was formed it has doubled its listings of 'rooms' every year and has managed to do this across all geographies. From 50,000 room listings in 2011 it has reached 600,000+ in 2014. It is reported that the revenues in 2013 were $250 million and are tipped to double in 2014.[15]

Uber on the other hand isn't as transparent on the numbers, but the fact that it operates in so many cities within four years of incorporation suggests that the top line is growing aggressively. One report is projecting their gross revenue at $10 billion.[16] Whilst it would seem on the surface that the business model is potentially more robust than that of Facebook and Twitter, as both businesses charge fees for completed transactions, there is one thing worth noting that might suggest to some that we are back in the dotcom boom years: neither company has independently published and verified revenue and profitability numbers. In addition, both are facing some quite significant challenges not just from vested interests who are protecting the revenue and profits of the traditional suppliers in these markets, but also from governments who are taking an increasing interest in the revenues that are being generated by the tens of thousands of hosts and drivers who make up the supply side of these new markets.

So if it's easy to set this up using the technology, then competitive offers will enter the market and these early entrants will start to develop their propositions to keep ahead of the competition. If we look at car sharing, the competition for Uber is mostly regional. In America, Uber faces competition from lower-cost real-time ridesharing start-ups such as Lyft and SideCar. To compete at lower price levels and to deal with some of the objections from local governments and the traditional taxicab drivers, Uber has introduced UberTaxi (partnerships with local taxi commissions)[17] and UberX (non-luxury cars such as Toyota Prius hybrids).[18] These moves have led to dissatisfaction amongst existing Uber limo drivers who have seen their earnings decrease.[19]

The problems of disruption

Since their inception, both Uber and AirBnB have been at the centre of multiple controversies. Both these start-ups are battling against regulations and legal hurdles as regulators, local governments, trades unions and tax authorities grapple with the implications of these market changes.

Uber has sparked protests in London, received a cease and desist order in Virginia, waged a price war with the New York yellow taxis, faced a ban in Brussels and Berlin and has been banned in Delhi. With every new city, the regulatory hurdles will pile up and how Uber deals with these will prove crucial to its success.

AirBnB has also had its fair share of issues, from reports of vandalism and burglary to being declared outright illegal. In New York they have faced some serious challenges[20] and in Spain a hefty penalty for breaking the law.[21] What is certain is that although governments, regulators and tax authorities are struggling to catch up, they will do so and what start out as game changers will over time be playing within the same regulatory and tax regimes as everyone else.

Over-the-top propositions

If retail is one of the early adopter sectors and the sharing economy a disruptive innovation, change is also happening elsewhere. In financial services, and especially in banking, digital self-service is automating the local branch out of existence. In the UK the leading retail banks have all announced a significant reduction in their branch networks and a move into customer-driven digital engagement.[22] Travel, insurance, hotel rooms and holidays are now routinely digital interactions and even motor retailing is beginning to show signs of moving from generating leads and offering price comparisons into transacting sales online with the introduction of reverse auction sites such as the UK's Auto eBid. Retailers themselves are moving into this space, with Ford becoming the first manufacturer to set up direct online sales in 2010[23] and others following suit since. One report suggests that by 2020, 4.5 million vehicles a year will be sold in this channel compared with 11,000 in 2011.[24]

This is still retailing however, either direct or through intermediary agg-regators whose proposition is primarily price. What is starting to become more prevalent is what we call 'over-the-top' propositions – a direct engagement by product producers that seeks to undermine traditional product channels and provide their goods direct from the manufacturer. Some manufacturer strategies are clearly direct to consumer: for example Johnson & Johnson's Caring Everyday™ site that offers coupons as direct incentives to consumers to purchase their products;[25] others are less obvious where the producer has become a retailer in their own right such as Diageo's Alexander & James online shop which takes their upmarket products, adds drinks peripherals and uses them to create a premium-priced gift proposition plus 'lifestyle' site.

For an automotive manufacturer, direct sales are arguably easier transitions to manage – after all they tend to own some of their 'bricks-and-mortar' channels so can optimize costs. But over-the-top propositions come with risks, not least that retailers with significant online volumes, square footage on the high street and large portfolio ranges with plenty of competitive choice can make it very tough for a manufacturer who wants to reclaim some of their margin. Channel conflict is a major strategic issue for brand and product owners and each will have to find its way around the potential pitfalls. However, choices that suggest not being in e-commerce are we believe short-sighted as they put the brand or product owner at risk of not being able to build as powerful a customer insight platform as those who own the route to market. Incubator e-commerce operations have a great deal to recommend them in that, as you will read in Chapter 3, they can provide a window on the market that is a source of invaluable data about all customers, not just those who buy your product or service.

But it's not just in physical products that we are seeing changes. The entertainment sector is seeing huge upheavals as services such as Amazon Prime, Netflix, Hulu Plus and Blinkbox deliver programme material that was previously only available through television networks and cinemas. A US report suggested that nearly 60 million US households now consume their entertainment in this way.[26] Given that the route to market is not controlled by television networks and cable companies, but by agnostic telephony and satellite networks, the traditional channels are in a far weaker position to resist the change. All anyone needs is reasonably fast broadband to access media that was previously delivered through channels where watching the advertisement was compulsory (unless you recorded it for later consumption!)

The impact on any proposition whose business model relies solely or significantly on advertising is significant; the impact on distributors who controlled access to desirable product (eg newly released films, major sports events etc) and could therefore 'charge a premium' may well be even more significant. In this sector successful businesses will now either curate content or curate the customer: controlling the distribution channel is no longer where the money will get made.

Modern markets offer near-perfect competition

As a result of the advent of digital technology, modern global markets work across channels rather than within them and leading them successfully requires an 'omni-channel'[27] mindset: one where the proposition will be consistently presented and where this is important (eg in a retail environment) the customer experience will be consistent. What is sometimes less well recognized is that whilst businesses are looking to entice customers to engage with their proposition, in the online channel in particular, the customer will be presented with a large number of, if not all of, the major competing propositions. Indeed recent research has suggested that over 50 per cent of all purchases are now influenced through digital engagement with the market.[28] Modern markets have a very different structure to that for which most organizations have been built over the last century.

FIGURE 1.1   A modern market model

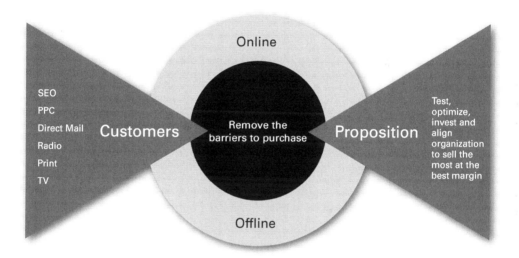

In this market (Figure 1.1), customers are made aware of competing propositions not just through traditional activities off- and online, but also through specific online activities such as those associated with optimizing the outcome of search engine performance for a brand, product or service, paid advertising on search engine or on other websites or direct mail through e-mail. Regardless of how a customer in the market is made aware of products or services that can meet their needs, increasingly they arrive online looking at the outcome of a search request.[29]

A search outcome is now the modern high street and how that outcome is presented to the customer and the experience through which the customer goes will significantly influence his or her decision to buy. But it is more than this. For possibly the first time ever customers in a market can find themselves presented with nearly every option within an economic geography and many options further. It is now their decision as to how much market exploration they are willing to do to find the product or service that is right for them.

The winner in this market is the proposition that has been proven to generate better sales outcomes than any other for the product or service it is selling. These propositions understand the target market and, through doing so, manage to make their propositions the 'least risky' purchase. They do this by engaging with and understanding customer decision making.

The organizations with the winning propositions have understood that their digital channel offers them one thing that other channels cannot. It is a two-way system. Cheaply, quickly and at scale, they use this channel to understand customers at point of purchase. You can have all the historical data you can find in the new world of 'big data', yet it will not give you the insight and access that is possible to engineer through a digital channel. For these businesses, their digital channel is a window into the world of their customer.

Once the behaviour of the customer has been understood and the proposition 'optimized' (ie tested online so that a business is confident that without changing the proposition they cannot sell more within a set period of time), effective businesses can then ensure that the same sales and marketing messages are employed in all other channels chosen by customers looking for their product or service, because they understand that they are talking to the same customer, regardless of channel. It is this opportunity to build deep and rich insight into why customers in the market do and do not buy which lies at the heart of digital business. It is this capability above any other that leaders need to embrace, understand and then use to drive their organizations forward.

In our experience this market model seems to hold as true for 'business to business' (B2B) markets as it does for the more obvious 'business to customer' (B2C). Current analysis shows that the value in B2B e-commerce sales – where the required output is just as likely to be lead generation as a direct transaction – is growing dramatically. In a report from the US in 2013, B2B e-commerce sales were reported as being more than twice the size of B2C e-commerce.[30]

Why most organizations are not fit for purpose

The chapters that follow will explain what it takes to build and sustain an effective e-commerce operation, its management challenges and the leadership that is required to make it 'business as usual'. Through case studies, we will also show how some businesses are adapting their products, propositions, capabilities and their processes to generate dramatically different results.

It is our contention from our work with organizations from radically different sectors, of very different sizes, that there are some key barriers that make it very difficult for leaders to drive change in e-commerce even more than it is in other parts of their organization. It is certainly more difficult to drive change focussed on growth rather than cost reduction. It is more of a 'punt' as there is little, if any, control over the outcome, compared to cost reductions that are far more likely to be internally controlled and therefore more certain to come through. However, this doesn't explain the problems we have experienced with many e-commerce operations. This has become an area where businesses seem to be more willing to accept failure at considerable costs than they are in any other part of their business. We believe that part of the reason for this is that they continue to see it as a technology problem, when, at its heart, it is an organization one.

Humans are essentially social animals and we create organizations to help us regulate our relationships. From earliest times we have lived, worked and indeed competed in tribes.[31] Within these tribes we created structures that signposted the distribution of power, influence and therefore decision making. Very early societies were small enough to be collaborative in the way they made decisions, but by 7000 BC, as larger and more complex societies emerged, so did much more organized structures and whilst there were cultural differences the structure and roles within them were clear to all.[32]

Once established, these structures very quickly became ingrained and indeed in some places some of these early systems are still in evidence today. Jared Diamond, writing about traditional societies and their impact on today, observes: '"Modern" conditions have prevailed, even just locally, for a tiny fraction of human history. All human societies have been traditional for far longer than any society has been modern'.[33]

Diamond argues that billions of people around the world still live in traditional ways and these ways of life persist within even the most modern societies. For example, he reports that many disputes are still resolved informally rather than by going to court in the Montana valley.

Social structures are very difficult to change and they tend to develop slowly through the generations, adjusting as education, technology and economic circumstances evolve. Revolutionary changes in social structures are still rare and have often come as a result of significant upheaval in the physical or economic environment or though the triumph of one tribe over another in conflict. Our social structures have been historically conservative and are almost always based around an established understanding and acceptance of a hierarchy.

The organization of productive work has followed a similar pattern. The original craft guilds of the cities of Europe, who operated the master and apprentice model, were probably one of the earliest organizations to establish a formal management model, and apprentices today, whilst not indentured, still attempt to learn their 'trades' through working for an experienced practitioner. With the rise in industrial activity, especially as manufacturing overtook agrarian activity as the primary driver of trade for 'developed' economies, so we became absorbed with looking for the optimal way of organizing ourselves around this new approach to generating wealth.

The emergence of the modern organization

While the earliest theories of organization came out of the Napoleonic Wars in Europe in the early 1800s, in the US the rapid growth of the railways in the 1850s presented one of the first large-scale non-military organizational challenges as it became clear to investors in the larger lines that they were not making money. One response to these concerns came from Daniel McCallum, general superintendent of the Erie Railroad, who concluded that the reason his line and other large lines were in financial distress was a problem of management.

McCallum installed a management system to replace the one manager who he believed was over-loaded. He re-organized the railway into geographical divisions of manageable size. Each was headed by a superintendent responsible for the operations within his division, who were required to submit detailed reports to central headquarters, from where senior management coordinated and gave general direction to the operations of the separate divisions. Lines of authority between each superintendent and their subordinates and headquarters were clearly laid out. In recording these lines of authority on paper, McCallum created what might have been the first organizational chart in business.[34]

As the other great railways copied this structure, so as a sector they were able not just to thrive and become some of the most successful corporations of the time but also to drive the transformation of the economy. Railways provided a first organizational model for operating large firms. This is probably best illustrated through the rise of the US meat-packing firm Swift & Co in the 1870s and 1880s.[35]

Swift was a wholesale butcher in New England who moved west to Chicago in the 1870s. Getting the meat from where it was reared in the mid-west to markets in the east was an inefficient process that depended on the uncoordinated services of small, specialized local firms. The railways provided part of the solution with the introduction of refrigerated carriages but this provided more challenges, as refrigerated meat required refrigerated storage facilities at the other end. Once the products reached these markets it faced significant local resistance from local suppliers who tried to stop Swift's meat reaching the market, claiming that it was unhealthy. This in turn launched one of the first large-scale advertising campaigns and as this succeeded in persuading consumers that Swift meat was indeed safe the company expanded further. This required the securing of dependable supply and the company moved to organizing stockyards to purchase large numbers of animals on a regular basis. Finally they were one of the first firms to exploit the whole manufacturing process, making use of animal by-products through the production of leather, glue, fertilizer and soap.

Swift & Co is probably the first example of a vertically integrated company; whilst it was not a cattle producer the company took over at the point of sale and controlled the buying, packing, shipping and marketing. The organizational innovation was that instead of creating geographic divisions, as the railways had done, and where everyone was doing the same thing in a different place, Swift created units (called divisions just as in an army), each responsible for a different step in the process of getting the meat to the consumer. They had divisions for marketing, meat-packing, purchasing, shipping, sales and advertising. Each of these divisions was headed by a manager to whom subordinate managers reported. Each divisional manager in turn reported to and received directions from headquarters.

Scientific management

These early developments were popularized in the 20th century through the works of Taylor and Fayol[36] and became described universally as 'scientific management'. Scientific management is the foundation stone for modern organizations: the organization and structuring of work activities into logical segments, each segment being clear on its role in the whole and the whole being directed top down through a pyramid of power. There are a number of assumptions behind this model that are important to draw out:

- those at the top have a broader and more strategic view;
- those at the top have greater knowledge and experience;
- those in the middle are there to operationalize decisions using their expertise and experience;
- those at the bottom are sufficiently skilled to carry out their tasks but add no value to decisions made further up the structure.

These assumptions work well when the fundamentals are unlikely to change quickly, enabling the establishment of processes and routines that remain stable and can be passed quickly and simply to new recruits as they come into the structure. In this situation operational experience is a competitive advantage. Having seen something before, you can predict an outcome with considerable certainty and therefore guide others as to their actions and reactions.

Whilst there have been variations on a theme over the years – matrix and network organizations being two of the more recent – the basic model of a hierarchy where activity happens at the bottom and decisions are taken at the top remains the predominant approach to the organization and management of work.

Since the end of the Second World War many modern management techniques in developed economies have been created to take account of the changes in education, social structures and attitudes that have driven demands from those at the bottom to be more involved in shaping their work. Over time, as levels of intermediate management have been stripped away and automation has removed many transactional activities from the bottom of these pyramids, so jobs at every level now require more self-management than those in similar structures a century earlier. Regardless, however, of how much an organization has adjusted, the core principles still remain stubbornly in place. If you doubt this, take a closer look at a call centre – it is as structured and hierarchical as any of Henry Ford's assembly lines.

This is the organization paradox: we continue to organize and manage activity developed for a world where changes to markets, communications, social structures and values happened at a pace where lessons learned and adjustments made continued to have validity for some time after they happened. But, due to the adoption of digital technology, this world is less and less relevant. Advances in all areas of our lives are coming faster and combining to create changes that can shift, create or destroy a market in months rather than years.

However, the way we organize is not just the random adoption of a particular model by shareowners, their senior management or the consequence of a business school education. There is something fundamental about the way we think about and engage with organizations. The desire to live in a defined and stable structure is part of the human condition. We want to know where we stand in the tribe, we want others to know and we find the prospect of any change to this imposed by others unsettling at best. Many of us do not want to be responsible, we are willing to defer to others, let them take the lead. We who populate structures are often the drivers of the greatest resistance to changing them. Yet change they must if we are going to continue to ensure that they are as productive as they need to be to survive in this new digital age.

The impact on sales and marketing effectiveness

Whilst we can see significant innovation that has an impact in products and services driven by changes in behaviour by customers in the market, it is more difficult to spot correspondingly effective innovation in the way in which these products and services are taken to market and the way in which managers are handling customer (as opposed to brand) communications. Indeed there is a whole industry springing up around 'digital marketing' and e-commerce that is offering all sorts of prescriptions for the measurement of effectiveness of sales and marketing communications in the digital channel.

Measurement of the effectiveness of marketing investment has been one of the great challenges of the past 100 years. Amongst others, Unilever founder, Viscount Leverhulme is credited with the saying: 'Half the money I spend on advertising is wasted. The problem is I do not know which half'.[37] Since then global advertising budgets have spiralled ever upwards. Total global advertising spend in 2013 was set to top $500 billion with internet spend growing from 5 per cent in 2005 to 21 per cent in 2013, making it the second largest area of spend worldwide after television.[38] This figure does not include any costs associated with processes, technologies and resources required to build and execute this investment.

Leverhulme's conundrum still holds true for most businesses today. What is even more intriguing is that, despite dramatic and obvious changes in routes to market and customer behaviour, this spend is still mainly being addressed in the same way and by using the same models as 30 years ago. For example, a recent article from strategy consultants Booz Allen[39] highlights four marketing strategies for the digital age which look suspiciously similar to those applied before the dotcom boom: brand-led, customer experience-led, traffic-led and innovation-led.

Therefore, when spend goes 'online' traditional paradigms quickly resurrect themselves. Just as in more traditional channels, money is spent on driving traffic, rather than on driving sales, so money is spent on display through expensive website designs, where there is no robust evidence that sales and investment in website design correlate; and it is spent on social media. This latter investment has all the signs of a bubble market, and although the latest statistics suggest some improvement in effectiveness, the ultimate issue for an e-commerce operation is still there: does it really generate a sale?

Generally, the conversion rate for an online advert to get a customer to 'click' and engage with the proposition is still very low – experts currently report about 0.07 per cent of all online adverts generate a customer response.[40] The latest available statistics on the commercial impact of social media spend suggest that for Facebook in particular, which had been reporting a performance of 0.05 per cent in 2012,[41] there has been a significant increase with reports varying from 0.20 per cent[42] to over 1 per cent towards the end of 2013.[43]

However, this correlates with a move towards enabling advertising to appear as part of the newsfeed. This has had two effects. First, mobile users of the social networking site can now see commercial messages where they could not before (this is significant as nearly 50 per cent of daily users access the mobile site);[44] and second, whilst Facebook has a strict limit on commercial newsfeed items, their users are responding to an advert that is posing as news content. A closer scrutiny of the numbers also suggests that these dramatically enhanced response rates include media and entertainment items and it may well be that customers are more willing to hear the latest about a new film or album in this way compared to a product or service. Pure retail numbers are improving but far less aggressively.[45] Whilst this activity may generate an interest, there is very little evidence that paid-for advertising on social media is generating significant sales.

Alongside a considerable body of evidence that many people do not want commercial enterprises to be part of their everyday social lives, there has to be a question about the sales effectiveness of buying space on these types of sites. A UK report from YouGov[46] showed that over half (55 per cent) of online shoppers say a store with a presence on a social networking site made them trust the retailer less, while just over a quarter (27 per cent) said that it made them trust it more. The report revealed that many e-consumers segregate their online shopping and social habits. Almost 4 in 10 (39 per cent) like to keep their social media and shopping activity separate, with around the same proportion (42 per cent) believing that networks such as Facebook and Twitter are for friends, not retail.

The report highlighted the finding that the youngest online shoppers (16- to 24-year-olds) are the keenest to keep their social networking activity separate from their shopping activity. More than half (57 per cent) don't like sites such as Twitter and Facebook to be linked with their purchasing history and three in five (61 per cent) like to keep their social networking and online shopping activity separate.

Two further pieces of work in 2014 in the US, by Gallup and the National Bureau of Economic Research[47], also suggest that business leaders might want to reflect on the rush to spend on social media. In a poll of *ca* 18,000 US consumers, Gallup reported that 62 per cent said social media had no influence on their buying decisions and the National Bureau of Economic Research stated that 'brand key-word ads have no measurable short-term benefits'. Whilst we flag these issues, it is not because we think that social media should be ignored or dismissed. We believe that social media can play a role in driving sales, but we are convinced that it can never be a strategic response in itself. We will look at marketing in more detail in Chapter 4.

Just as in marketing, the basic sales models employed by many traditional companies have yet to change dramatically. They still assume that customers in the market will manage their choices through intermediaries. This under-pins the survival of a 'point-of-sale' model where intermediary incentives are used to drive traffic to a specific product or service. Products and services are promoted at point of purchase and customers incentivized through price, be it a loss leader to encourage them to shop in a particular outlet or a discount on an additional purchase to attract them to a particular brand.

Whilst the old sales structures have changed, the principles have not. The major supermarkets may well be serviced through a central account structure but sales development managers are still employed to cover geographic territories calling on smaller retail outlets with the objective of getting them to buy additional stock which in turn they are expected to press on their customers. The whole incentive structure of sales divisions in many major companies is based on this system.

This isn't just a private sector issue. In recent years, in many countries people have been confronted on the streets by charity representatives asking if they would be willing to sign up for a regular donation to a particular cause. The widespread use of this approach and the very insistent style of requests has led to this approach being described as 'chugging' – charity mugging. The insistence comes from the method of employment of those doing 'the ask'. No volunteers for the cause here, but incentivized salespeople. It is the face-to-face equivalent of a cold call from a call centre.

Despite the rise in online giving over the past few years the response of charitable organizations is to ape the approaches of their commercial cousins and invest in brand/cause advertising and face-to-face selling using incentivized intermediaries. Recent reports have shown that both the overall value generated online and the average value of online donations are increasing.[48]

Regardless of sector, it would seem that something is holding established organizations back from responding to some fundamental changes to their markets. This failure to engage at one level is understandable. Whilst cash from sales and investors and financiers is still there, what incentive is there to make changes that require different behaviours, especially if they are required from the very top to the bottom of the organization? At one level this might well explain how, for example, Sears, the US department store group, has had nearly seven years of revenue decline and yet despite a few disposals of activities at the margin of its business, it continues to manage its core in very similar ways to 10 years ago with continuing disappointment in results.[49] This organizational inertia is what has seen big names like HMV and Habitat amongst others depart from the UK high street.

There is a fault line between many of today's organizations and the markets in which they operate that will drive business failure. The winners have already worked out what it is and those who are inquisitive and willing to change are exploring what it means for them. At the heart of this problem is the inability of the organization to engage with the customer at every level despite the fact that digital technology provides just this opportunity.

A brave new world that needs embracing

This change is one of the significant leadership challenges for businesses today. It is one we have to embrace and galvanize others to achieve. To do this we have to become as fluent in e-commerce as we are in finance, sales and marketing. Regardless of the challenges we face, unless we as business leaders engage with and understand this new world we will never be able to set the appropriate performance criteria, judge which is the right strategy or even more importantly appoint the right people to drive it. We will remain unassimilated digital immigrants dependent on others to interpret and guide: and, like any immigrant, unable to assess how expert our guide really is.

Like any new environment, the digital world is not an easy one for immigrants. It has its own language, culture and traditions. Its natives are generally younger and have very distinctive attitudes to work, careers and development that are often quite at odds with those that apply in the leadership echelons of most organizations. This generation, often referred to as 'generation Y' and 'millennials', have value sets that differ significantly in some important aspects from those who manage them. A recent and extensive PWC study[50] highlighted these distinctive elements about what they call 'millennials':

- **They are not convinced that it's worth disrupting their personal lives for work when the demands are excessive.** They value work/life balance, and the majority of them are unwilling to commit to putting their work ahead of other aspects of their lives, even with the promise of substantial compensation later on.

- **They want greater flexibility at work.** They want more choice. But so do many of us and in this survey the results suggested that this has equal importance at all levels – so much that people would be willing to give up pay and delay promotions in order to get it.

- **They want to work in a strong collaborative team culture that creates opportunities for interesting work including international roles.** They place a high priority on workplace culture and environment that emphasizes teamwork and a sense of community. They also value transparency (especially as it relates to decisions about their careers). They want the support of their supervisors, and also want the chance to explore overseas positions.

- **Many stereotypes about them are untrue.** Despite a reputation perhaps to the contrary, they have grown up not expecting their organizations to provide job security. Despite a natural aptitude for electronic forms of communication, e-mail and social media platforms are not always their communication vehicles of choice. Also, despite a common perception otherwise they are as equally committed to their work as their bosses.

- **Whilst the same basic drivers of retention exist for them as others, their relative importance varies.** They have a greater expectation to be supported and appreciated in return for their contributions, and to be part of a cohesive team. Flexibility in where and how much they work is also a key driver, unlike older generations who placed greater importance on pay and development opportunities.

None of this suggests, however, that an e-commerce operation should be managed in any different fashion from other functions or activities. In organizational terms, this means that we need to apply the same disciplines as those applied to any other activity: targets, performance measures, processes and cost management. We need to be able to sort out the important information from the plethora of data points. We need to be able to understand and assess the capabilities required for success and to establish which of these we think are critical to strategy and should be retained in-house as a source of competitive advantage.

As leaders we have to build an understanding of what 'good' looks like and what levels of commercial performance we should expect. All the leaders we have worked with, and many of those we have met in building our framework, have one thing in common: they were dissatisfied with their commercial performance and wanted to change it. We may have to learn to do this differently from the way we were managed 20 or 30 years ago, but we still have to do it if we are going to deliver success.

The leadership agenda

This is the first leadership agenda. This section pulls together the key points and sets out an agenda for change that could help you transform your e-commerce performance. There will be some sections, where you can 'tick the box' and move on and others where you will have much more work to do. We offer it as a model based both on our consulting experience and as online retailers in our own right.[51]

These sections are divided into two parts: killer questions and leadership actions. The killer questions are what we believe you need to ask of yourself or others and ensure you get accurate answers. They will help you assess where you are and what needs your attention. We think they are more likely to put the organization 'on the spot' and help you from being diverted by people answering the questions they wanted you to ask. The leadership actions are a more general list of the sorts of actions you might want to consider in building an agenda for change in your e-commerce operations. They are designed to act as a set of prompts and thought provokers rather than a prescription.

Part One: Setting a strategic framework

At this stage, you should focus on defining the strategic agenda. As stated earlier, this book looks at e-commerce specifically which we would split into two core operations: the acquisition of new customers, and the engagement and retention of current ones.

Killer questions

- How is digital technology impacting your market?
- What is the competitive response? Is there a competitor you think has got it 'more right' than you and if so why?
- What is your business doing to respond and how effective do you think this is?
- What are your business goals?
- What role does e-commerce play in achieving these?
- Is that role expected to change over the next few years and if so how?
- How is your business organized today?
- How is e-commerce positioned against other channels?
- How important do you believe consistency of proposition and customer experience across every channel is to the achievement of your goals?
- How close are you to achieving this today?
- What are the biggest barriers to improving e-commerce effectiveness in the business today?

Leadership action

This is the strategic analysis stage. Actions that would help you could include:

- Try to describe the impact of digital technology on your sector and on your competitive position.
- Think about how you are organized today as a business – are you producer- or customer-centric and if the latter, how would customers see this in the marketplace?
- List the major challenges and issues facing your e-commerce operation; try to identify what is process, what is capability, what is technology, what is cultural and what is structure?
- Try to scale the opportunity – how big is the gap in your view between current e-commerce performance, business expectations and absolute potential if all barriers were addressed?

Notes

1 Schumpeter, JA (1994) [1942] *Capitalism, Socialism and Democracy*, Routledge, London

2 Obeng, E (1997) *New Rules for the New World: Cautionary tales for the new world manager*, Wiley, Oxford

3 Lapointe, L, Boudreau-Pinsonneault, C, Vaghefi, I (2013) Is Smartphone usage truly smart? A qualitative investigation of IT addictive behaviors, http://www.computer.org/csdl/proceedings/hicss/2013/4892/00/4892b063.pdf [retrieved 28 January 2014]

4 http://www.cancerresearchuk.org/cancer-info/cancerstats/types/breast/mortality/uk-breast-cancer-mortality-statistics[#]trends [accessed 22 February 2014]

5 http://news.bbc.co.uk/1/hi/health/7792318.stm [accessed 22 February 2014]

6 http://www.theguardian.com/world/edward-snowden [accessed 22 February 2014]

7 http://www.technologyreview.com/news/427787/are-smart-phones-spreading-faster-than-any-technology-in-human-history/ [accessed 22 February 2014]

8 http://jeff.a16z.com/2014/01/15/the-tipping-point-e-commerce-version/ [accessed 26 January 2014]

9 http://business.time.com/2013/07/15/best-buys-unlikely-return-from-the-dead/ [accessed 22 February 2014]

10 http://www.channelregister.co.uk/2012/03/06/uk_consumer_electronics/ [accessed 22 February 2014]

11 http://internetretailing.net/2014/02/online-sales-rise-by-8-9-in-january-driven-by-strong-clothing-and-department-store-sales/ [accessed 22 February 2014]

12 http://www.forbes.com/sites/tomiogeron/2013/08/07/is-airbnb-the-next-ebay-uber-the-next-amazon/ [accessed 29 July 2014]

13 http://venturebeat.com/2014/06/19/uber-and-airbnbs-incredible-growth-in-4-charts/) [accessed 29 July 2014]

14 http://venturebeat.com/2014/06/19/uber-and-airbnbs-incredible-growth-in-4-charts/) [accessed 29 July 2014]

15 http://techcrunch.com/2014/04/18/airbnb-has-closed-its-500m-round-of-funding-at-a-10b-valuation-led-by-tpg [accessed 29 July 2014]

16 http://www.businessinsider.com/uber-revenue-2014-6[#]ixzz37jaLpL7r [accessed 29 July 2014]

17 http://www.ibtimes.co.uk/ubertaxi-service-launched-ahead-london-black-cab-protest-1452167 [accessed 20 July 2014]

18 http://techcrunch.com/2012/07/01/uber-opens-up-platform-to-non-limo-vehicles-with-uber-x-service-will-be-35-less-expensive/ [accessed 20 July]

19 http://techcrunch.com/2013/03/15/see-uber-this-is-what-happens-when-you-cannibalize-yourself/ [accessed 20 July 2014]

20 http://www.businessweek.com/articles/2014-06-19/airbnb-in-new-york-sharing-startup-fights-for-largest-market [accessed 29 July 2014]

21 http://blogs.elpais.com/trans-iberian/2014/07/a-take-on-airbnb-in-barcelona.html [accessed 29 July 2014]

22 http://www.ft.com/cms/s/0/dde8c642-10b8-11e3-b291-00144feabdc0.html [#]axzz2u4JepWhM [accessed 22 February 2014]

23 http://www.telegraph.co.uk/motoring/car-manufacturers/ford/7855971/Ford-is-first-car-manufacturer-to-sell-its-cars-on-internet.html [accessed 29 July 2014]

24 http://www.verdictretail.com/online-new-car-sales-by-manufacturer-owned-sites-will-grow-rapidly-through-to-2020/ [accessed 29 July 2014]

25 http://www.caringeveryday.co.uk/offers-coupons[#]baby-and-kids [accessed 29 July 2014]

26 http://www.businessinsider.com/amazon-prime-versus-netflix-versus-hulu-plus-2014-4 [accessed 29 July 2014]

27 Whilst omni-channel started out in retail, it is a helpful strategic term in that it requires a business to think from a customer perspective not from a producer or retailer one. The best description we found that seemed to cut through the consultant speak was this one: 'For a company to be truly omni-channel, they really do have to plan, execute, measure and optimize their efforts through every customer touchpoint,' said one panelist, the director of digital customer experience at a major retailer. 'They have to optimize and align a consistent voice, an offer strategy and product assortment mix. They have to think about a strategic approach to both selling and servicing the customer, no matter the channel.' http://www.adconiondirect.com/wp-content/uploads/2013/08/Winterberry-Group-White-Paper-Omnichannel-Audience-Engagement-June-2013.pdf [accessed 29 July 2014]

28 http://www.shopify.co.uk/blog/14210261-10-slideshare-presentations-on-the-future-of-omni-channel-retail, presentation No 7, the future of retail [accessed 29 July 2014]

29 A search request for a specific brand or for a general product category results in competing products being displayed. The only way a business can ensure that potential customers are not presented with the alternatives is to encourage people to locate their website directly through entering the web address in their search bar or through bookmarking or by providing links in their direct e-mail.

30   Hoar, A, Evans, PF, Johnson, C and Roberge, D (2013) *Building a World-Class B2B eCommerce Business*, Forrester Research

31/32 http://catalogue.pearsoned.co.uk/assets/hip/gb/hip_gb_pearsonhighered/ samplechapter/0205835503.pdf [accessed 30 July 2014]. We found this a fascinating resource but in the way we came across it, it is without title or author(s). We would be delighted to add these to the credits here if anyone recognizes the book from which this chapter is taken.

33   Diamond, J (2012) *The World Until Yesterday: What can we learn from traditional societies?*, Allen Lane, London

34   Chandler, AD Jr (1962) *Strategy and Structure: Chapters in the history of the American industrial enterprise*, MIT Press, Cambridge, MA

35   The story of Swift is described in detail in Chandler's book

36   Taylor, FW (1911) *The Principles of Scientific Management*, Harper and Brothers, New York and London; and Fayol, H (1949) *General and Industrial Management*, 1949, Pitman (original work published in 1916 with the title *Administration Industrielle et Générale*)

37   This saying is commonly attributed to both marketing pioneers William Lever and John Wanamaker. At the time of writing there seems to us to be no authoritative source to prefer any one claim over another.

38   http://adage.com/article/global-news/10-things-global-ad-market/245572/ [accessed 22 February 2014]

39   http://www.strategy-business.com/article/00241?pg=all [accessed 22 February 2014]

40   http://digiday.com/platforms/facebook-ads-are-killing-it-but-why/ [accessed 30 July 2014]

41/42 http://www.internetretailer.com/2013/10/17/facebook-ads-click-through-rates-soar-q3 [accessed 30 July 2014]

43   http://digiday.com/platforms/facebook-ads-are-killing-it-but-why/ [accessed 30 July 2014]

44   http://newsroom.fb.com/company-info/ [accessed 30 July 2014]

45   http://www.internetretailer.com/2013/10/17/facebook-ads-click-through-rates-soar-q3 [accessed 30 July 2014]

46   http://yougov.co.uk/news/2014/02/26/consumers-cool-social-networks-online-shopping/ [accessed 9 April 2014]

47   Reported in *Private Eye* No 1370 11–24 July 2014

48   http://www.charitydigitalnews.co.uk/2014/07/28/uk-online-giving-on the rise-according-to-blackbaud/ [accessed 30 July 2014] and http://philanthropy.com/ article/Online-Giving-Totals-Rise-by/138167/ [accessed 30 July 2014]

49 There are many articles on Sears and its woes. See http://blogs.wsj.com/ moneybeat/2013/08/22/for-sears-the-dangerous-downward-spiral-continues/ [accessed 30 July 2014] and http://www.bloomberg.com/news/2014-01-09/ sears-holdings-falls-after-forecasting-fourth-quarter-loss.html [accessed 30 July 2014]

50 http://www.pwc.com/gx/en/hr-management-services/publications/nextgen-study.jhtml [accessed 30 July 2014]

51 See www.hammersleyandbones.com – a business that supplies premium designer kitchen equipment from Italy to the UK market

Identifying the e-commerce opportunity

2

EXECUTIVE SUMMARY

Whilst some businesses have very successful e-commerce operations, many others are not able to get this right. Many describe their efforts as a continuous record of investment and change with little, if any, significant improvement in channel performance and even sometimes performance that continues to travel in the wrong direction. This chapter explores the major reasons behind this, including the unhelpful focus on the website rather than the organization, the immaturity of the digital marketing discipline and how it can get detached from the commercial imperative of the rest of the organization, the difficulty facing leaders and practitioners in separating out the insightful expert from the charlatan, and the ease with which the activity and the outcome can be quickly conflated. It offers leaders a checklist for their own organizations against which they can assess how much might need to change for them to deliver a step change in performance.

Why your new website is unlikely to fix the problem

How often are your criticisms of your company's online commercial performance answered either by a reassurance that the problems will be addressed by the new website which is currently under construction, or by a statement that without you agreeing to invest more in your website they cannot be addressed? And, how convinced are you that this is really the answer?

If you are on your second or third iteration of these conversations you are probably less confident that anything significant is really going to happen. Yet for some reason, despite this being a relatively common experience, organizations seem to feel compelled to continue to invest significant amounts of cash in their digital teams in the hope that 'this time things will be different'. Nevertheless, it should be clear to any of us, expert or not, that a website will not have much chance of coming up with the optimal commercial outcome if it hasn't been constructed on proven assumptions, clear goals and tested expertise.

The real answer to your questions about the commercial performance of your website lies less with the technology and more with the organization. Unless the organization can articulate the precise questions that customers are asking of all propositions in the marketplace and then develop and test a range of hypothetical responses until it finds the one that best answers those questions, then your e-commerce channel will continue to underperform, regardless of how much you spend on it. The only answer that counts here is the one given by customers to your invitation to transact – be that transaction a monetary one or something else, such as requesting a quote, downloading a white paper or registering an interest in a course.

What we have seen over the past three years is that poor performance tends to be associated with a focus on the answers to many different questions, rather than the core commercial one. It is this lack of a clear commercial mindset applied to digital activity that has made it so much easier for organizations to conflate investing in design and technology with investing in a commercial proposition. Indeed, when you search for an answer to the question 'how much should I spend on a website?' what you get back broadly speaking is 'how much do you want to spend?'

Therefore, you can spend a great deal of money on a new website, it can look attractive and be completely on brand, but fail to achieve its commercial objective. In some ways we shouldn't be surprised about this. After all it is one of the great risks of any marketing investment; but this isn't a marketing activity, it is a commercial one. The website in an e-commerce channel is the equivalent of a retail store, a stand at a trade exhibition, a platform at a conference or a networking opportunity. It is both the 'place' and the 'person' of any sales engagement. At its best, it should be able to replicate your most effective customer engagement, whether it is selling or servicing. E-commerce has its marketing activity, but the technology, its functionality and how it communicates with customers in the marketplace should be firmly focussed on meeting those customer's needs, not those of the brand marketing department or any other group.

There are few retailers, or professional services firms, manufacturers or any other business that would delegate the design and development of their sales engagement solely to a combination of marketing and technology specialists. We want their input, we value their expertise but we would want strong commercial leadership, input from the best salespeople and in-depth data about customer behaviour in our current engagement and where that needs improvement. So why are so many businesses willing to do precisely this delegation when it comes to their online engagement?

The e-commerce credibility challenge

You hear the phrase 'digital expert' a great deal in businesses, particularly from senior leaders who have appointed people so that they don't have to understand the detail. Often, though not exclusively, described as digital marketing, the nomenclature 'digital' is a very broad term and, depending on the organization, can embrace everything from online sales execution through web design, online marketing and into web development. Like any immature function, there are few consistently recognized standards, practices or capabilities and organization models. Often businesses have chosen to source this expertise from outside using agencies and in so doing have accepted externally established standards and practices into their organizations with-out challenge or question. They have also often as a result built little or no expertise into their own structures, making it more and more difficult to judge performance with any real confidence.

Many leaders, in making the decision to appoint a 'lead' digital expert, have stepped away from engaging in this new world and in so doing have, perhaps unwittingly, abdicated the responsibility for driving the perform-ance of the channel. Whilst they may set commercial goals, they expect their 'expert' to manage and achieve them and because they don't under-stand the detail, are unable to challenge decisions or set the pace and direction. There are very few disciplines, possibly only the highly technical and scientific, that you can find in a business where senior leaders don't have sufficient appreciation to give direction and make informed assessments of perform-ance; what intrigues – and concerns – us is why in so many organizations treat 'digital' as wholly separate and as though it has the same requirement for technical expertise as the supervision of nano-technology research. Given this is now 'business as usual' and possibly has been for some time, putting it in an organization ghetto and not building an organization-wide capability carries with it an enhanced risk of performance failure.

This becomes an even greater matter of concern when you take a look at two of the current dynamics of the talent pool in the field. First, there is a shortage of available resources with the experience or expertise.[1] This is driving up salary costs in many markets. Second, there is an emerging crisis of credibility. A UK survey of senior leaders in the digital marketing industry in 2014 reported over a third of respondents stating they found it difficult to justify immediate return on investment from digital versus longer-term, brand-building activities, 21 per cent said they had no ability to interpret or attribute analytics data, whilst 14 per cent of those questioned claimed they lacked sufficiently robust research to justify digital channel investment.[2]

There is a difference between the development and information technology skills required for exploitation of digital as a whole and the 'digital marketing' skills required to exploit its commercial potential. There is no doubt that the speed of development is putting huge pressure on the supply of advanced technical skills and this is opening up new markets in skilled labour in places like India where many western-based businesses have opened up digital operations centres. It is in the digital marketing area, however, where it is clear that there is a mounting level of concern.

Leadership wariness and lack of knowledge has in many cases encouraged organizations to treat this area as a pure science where knowledge is the sole defining criterion for expertise as opposed to an applied practice where your perceived expertise comes from an assessment of the outcomes of the application of what you know. We have lost count of the number of times a senior commercial leader has introduced us to a commercially inexperienced colleague with the line that they are the 'expert' in digital and then relied on their judgement as to whether or not they took one action over another.

For any new activity not to be received with some degree of scepticism would be highly surprising, but these findings and those in other reports suggest a degree of cynicism about 'digital marketing'. One possible explanation for this comes from an evaluation of breadth and depth of experience of the current senior talent pool. Research undertaken by our own team from 500 LinkedIn profiles[3] from around the world shows the average time in job for people who hold leadership roles responsible for online activity (Table 2.1).

The first thing to say is that this is a male-dominated function: nearly 70 per cent are men. The second is that to find this degree of data consistency is remarkable. Regardless of gender or geography the median and mode averages for time in previous job are virtually the same. The third is how short a time these people have been in their current role and stayed in their previous one.

TABLE 2.1   Length of time (in months) served in current and past role for e-commerce leaders

	Current Job			Previous Job		
	Mean	**Mode**	**Median**	**Mean**	**Mode**	**Median**
Male	28	12	21	28	24	24
Female	28	12	21	28	24	24
United Kingdom	32	12	21	29	24	24
North America	29	12	21	28	12	24
Rest of world	24	12	20	26	24	24

What lies behind this? First, many of these profiles suggest that previous job and current job are quite similar. They have the same type of role, possibly in a different sector or size organization. Over 90 per cent of job listings reported a similar job being held before the current one. Second, they suggest a relatively narrow career experience profile with a minority (c 35 per cent) having any significant commercial experience. And third, they are relatively inexperienced in comparison to, say, similar level leaders in other functions who have an average reported time in work post-education of c 12 years.

So the concerns about traction, performance and impact in e-commerce may be linked to the problem that, for obvious reasons, many of the resources employed in the field are likely to have a narrow experience base with little or no commercial exposure and a career model which is driven by a perceived shortage of expertise in the market as a whole. This in turn is driving an unfortunate stereotype which, if not addressed, could impact on competitiveness and performance. One senior executive described this to us as: 'Arrive in a new company, gain commitment to invest in a new website, overspend, deliver it late with less functionality than promised, watch the numbers fail to meet the business plan and sometimes even go backwards, blame external factors and move on to the next job where the model is repeated or move into an agency where you advise others to repeat exactly the same process'.

This being fair comment or not (and we think not), there is no doubt that the current experience of many in digital marketing is not ideal. The failure of leaders in organizations to understand and establish the appropriate priorities for the levels of resource and investment they are willing to commit creates environments that often seem very highly pressured and, in some extreme cases, look more like sweatshops or 19th-century cotton mills than Silicon Valley. As a result, e-commerce teams and their supporting technology organizations are often stressed, unable to create time to step away and think strategically, are driven by the most urgent priority, inwardly focussed, have high levels of turnover and lengthy lists of things to do that are important but never get done because they are not urgent.

This is a wasteful process and it destroys value not just for the organization but also the individual. For all other areas of activity, we expect people to whom we give responsibility for making decisions that can directly impact business performance to have a good understanding of the business as a whole. In many businesses, leaders insist that people with brand responsibility have had experience in sales or account management, some expect them to have had operational, production or service delivery experience as well. At a minimum, they expect them to understand the commercial and cost drivers of the business, the key goals and how what they do fits into the operating model. What strikes us about this emerging discipline is that by not applying the same standards regarding experience of the business, the balance between narrow functional and wider commercial expertise is skewed towards the functional.

The organization as a root cause

Often, an underperforming website is a symptom of an underperforming organization where, despite a clear and well-thought-out strategy, its people coalesce around processes, policies and practices that conspire to undermine its ability to achieve its goals. This isn't mismanagement: this is mis-organization.

The inclination to blame the technology, rather than the processes, policies and practices that created it, is the age-old trap of the poor workman blaming his tools. In the traditional channels through which organizations transacted, leaders were able to spot this trap pretty effectively, partly through having had direct experience of working with the tools themselves and partly through their position in the organization itself.

In digital channels many leaders find themselves at a disadvantage: few have direct experience of working with the tools themselves and the way in which the channel presents itself and reports its activities is often opaque to the uninitiated. We've already made the point that to address the shortfall in their own experience and understanding of e-commerce, leaders appoint 'experts' on whom they rely not just to develop and deliver an effective website but also to be the source of benchmarking and external validation. These experts may well understand how to manage the technology, but do they understand the market and the customer sufficiently to ensure that it is focussed on the right questions? And even if they do, are they explaining and engaging the rest of the organization in a way that enables it to respond and support such that the channel can perform?

If this isn't happening what you will see is *mis-organization*, ie significant investment in capital and resources in order to achieve commercial goals being fed into platforms, web design and sales execution and performance analytics that fail to deliver. In traditional channels, organizations would have acted swiftly to change activity, processes or people at the first sign of persistent under-delivery; in digital channels we seem to be more willing to make the same mistakes again and again and repeat the cycle with the same inevitable outcome. Expertise only takes us so far. What differentiates the superior performers is that they have realized that their digital channel is the same as any other. To make it work well requires customer insight and application of specific channel expertise to the real problems and opportunities.

Mis-organization is rather like a complex disease in that the diagnosis comes from a combination of symptoms rather than just one single and obvious sign. It is the business equivalent of ME rather than a broken bone. The obvious cause for concern is poor commercial performance but to work out whether the challenge is mismanagement or mis-organization needs an assessment of five key drivers, as shown in Figure 2.1.

Taking each driver in turn they impact a business as follows:

- **Failure to engage the customer:** we use the word engage here carefully. Many businesses ask their customers to rate them, like them, follow them and give them feedback; far fewer engage them in a way where they can understand what they are saying and why. What this leads to is the establishment of a 'customer agenda' that isn't really a customer-set agenda, but one that is established internally on information of variable quality.

- **Constant changes to sales execution:** changes to sales executions are in themselves neither good nor bad. They can, however, be costly, time-consuming and they will definitely have a commercial impact. Many e-commerce teams seem to make changes against an internal

FIGURE 2.1 The drivers of mis-organization

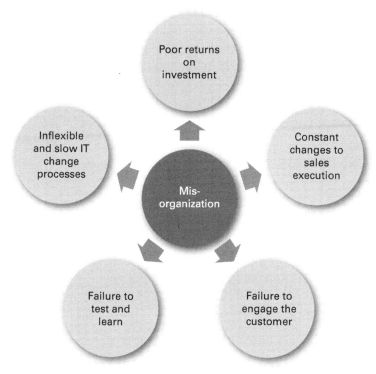

agenda or even as a response to competitor activity. Whilst once in a while these may get lucky and deliver a commercial improvement, many will have no impact on the top line and some may well accompany a decline in revenue. There will always be 'good' reasons provided when the last-mentioned two outcomes arise, but there will always be the question of what would have happened if we had made a different change or made no change at all.

- **Failure to test and learn:** we will repeat this in the manner of a mantra throughout the book. Not having the right insight is unfortunate; not testing proposed changes to see if there is or is not a positive impact is downright careless. And just because someone tells you they are testing does not mean that they are testing effectively. We have come across all sorts of testing strategies, few of them really effective. Testing internal ideas is better than nothing, but unless you are testing against real customer insight then it will not drive your business forward to its full capability.

- **Inflexible and slow IT change processes:** it would be unfair to single out IT here as a blocker to e-commerce effectiveness; however, some of the processes and structures the function has adopted to help deliver a stable and 99.9 per cent reliable systems platform do not necessarily help an organization that needs to respond rapidly to changes in the marketplace. LEAN and 'Agile' and other standards have their place, but ensuring you have flexibility and responsiveness for small changes and a way of fast-tracking successful testing outcomes into full operation are critical for success.

- **Poor returns on investment:** you might initially think this as an outcome from the four drivers above and in one sense it is. It is the consequence of not having an effective e-commerce operation, but once it exists as an outcome it becomes a driver of mis-organization in itself. Frustrated commercial senior leaders faced with continuing underperformance will do what they always do under these circumstances and push for greater and faster change. This puts the system under pressure and encourages short-cuts which mean that the responses are less likely to be based in deep customer insight and even less likely to be tested.

These five drivers work in combination to create a vicious circle in many e-commerce organizations that damages morale in the team and confidence in the business. For example, the longer the sales execution fails to deliver expected revenue, the more business leaders want to see it changed. If IT change processes are restrictive and inflexible, so pressure for change builds up; and when changes are finally made (no doubt at some cost) and they still fail, so the pressure for change increases even further. These changes fail because they in turn are either not being driven by insight into customer interactions at point of transaction, or are being driven by poor quality insight, and they have not been put through a rigorous process of testing prior to implementation.

The following chapters lay out how to address each of these drivers and reduce the risk of e-commerce underperformance, but here are three high-level pointers that will help you through the analysis at the end of this chapter:

- There are a few subtle differentiators in this list of drivers where people in your organization can give you answers and make it sound like they know what they are doing. As with any new language, however, getting people to simplify and clarify their responses will ensure that you get the right answers to your questions. Digital marketing has built up its own jargon and has quickly created a language that tends to shroud its activity in a technical mystique that makes performance management a real challenge. In these circumstances mis-organization can prosper and business performance suffer as a consequence because leaders are unable to spot problems early.

- Make sure you get specific answers to specific questions. Your e-commerce team may well 'survey' but they might not be surveying in the way required to build an effective insight platform. Make sure you really understand the 'what' and the 'how'. Mis-organization arises when people think that what they are doing is the right thing, but actually what they are doing is ineffective and more than likely to misinform key decisions.

- When you hear words like LEAN or Agile in reference to IT processes and change be sure you are clear what this really means. If your IT team is putting every small change to your e-commerce engagement through their process designed to deliver safe and effective major changes then, however 'quality assured' this may be, it is probably not really fit for purpose. Mis-organization can be the result of doing the right things in the wrong places.

Have consultants got better answers?

One of the results of senior management frustration with e-commerce performance has been the development of a strategic consulting proposition that offers leaders the reassurance of an informed assessment of their digital strategy and resource allocation. Most of the major players in management consulting have entered this market, some with e-commerce outsourcing offers of their own. Spotting the propositions that can add value is important. The characteristics of thinking and activity that can add value are:

- a recognition that to sell effectively you need to understand the customer in the market;

- working to processes for successful execution driven from understanding customers at point of purchase and then testing responses;

- an insistence on every potential change being tested and proven to increase sales prior to implementation;

- an ability to distinguish the importance of deep data.

Success in e-commerce comes with the drive to understand the customer and a focus on developing the most effective sales response. Whilst there is a place for models and propositions that help leaders establish the role that digital technology can play in driving their businesses forward, there are two areas of consulting advice that we believe need to be treated with caution.

The first is significant investment in technology in the face of evidence that the current technology is not delivering returns. We would advise any leader looking at this problem to ensure that everything possible had been done to make the current technology work effectively before committing to another investment that is more than likely to deliver the same under-performance. Whilst it is true that platforms can come to the end of their useful life, it is equally true that many platforms fail to deliver because they are not made to work well. The second is the use of random data points to prompt action, especially when much is being made of data correlations where there is little if any evidence of causation.

Take the fascination with social media and the use of this phenomenon as a justification for driving change. In 2012, Accenture published an assessment of digital business models where it cited the following as a reason to act: 'There are now more than 1 billion social media users worldwide, including 256 million in China alone. And that has serious implications for business. A recent study by market research company AYTM showed that 58 per cent of Facebook users have "liked" a brand, and that 39 per cent of Twitter users have tweeted about one'.[4]

This may be true; however, it is equally true that the single biggest challenge facing Twitter and Facebook is to link activity on their platforms directly to sales. In fact, this is recognized by an August 2014 survey of social media marketers where 52 per cent said that it was difficult to prove return on investment (ROI) for social media marketing and 35 per cent said it was difficult to cut through the clutter.[5] Indeed, the difficulty is that the blog, on which this research was reported, suggested that the following were the best ROI measures available:

- audience size and growth – as a measure of brand awareness and exposure,
- mentions – as a measure of campaign impact;
- engagement – a measure of campaign response;
- social impressions – a measure of activity;
- reach – another measure of impact.

From this recommendation it is useful to note that only the first three of these are relatively easy to establish, although all social platforms have a different definition of engagement, and the two where we might be getting closer to hard numbers are, according to the expert who wrote the piece, incredibly difficult to get at. In our understanding 'return on investment' means precisely that: what was the financial return for spending the cash? None of these measures get close to answering this question and until social media platforms can do this, and do it in a way that is consistent and allows for a clear comparison of effectiveness, then whatever you spend in this area is a punt. That's not to say don't do it, but do it with your eyes wide open and don't get fooled by anyone telling you that there is a proven ROI.

It is also useful to remember when you do meet the social media enthusiasts to bear in mind the point we have already noted in Chapter 1 that there is evidence to suggest that over 40 per cent of social media users actively dislike having commercial enterprises in what they consider to be their social space.[6]

The dangers of data

We have already talked about data itself being a product of the digital economy and, whilst we are not focussing on big data per se, it is important to touch on some of the issues as well as the opportunities in the context of thinking through your e-commerce effectiveness.

There is a trend in some parts of business to be obsessed with data regardless of its utility. In 2013, in an opinion piece for *The Economist* online, McKinsey introduces what they call 'on-demand marketing', which includes a response to the 'Veruca Salt' doctrine that they believe is driving consumer behaviour towards 'I want it and I want it now' responses in all channels.[7] This assertion in itself is debatable. For example, in our retail work whilst being 'in stock' and fulfilling deliveries is critical to sales success, we have seen little evidence that getting it to the customer more quickly is a defining competitive edge for the majority of customers. It is clearly important for a segment of the market but there is no robust evidence to suggest that this is considerably more the case now than it was 20 years ago. The right product at the right price point sold in the right way with clarity over shipping time wins nearly every time over any other combination.

We highlight this report because it is a good example of what is now a standard consulting argument for multiple, layered and complex data reporting:

> Most direct-sales companies (retailers, banks, travel services), for example, measure the performance of their spending by analysing what consumers do just

before making a purchase, eg googling a product. That level of analysis is too narrow because it doesn't take into account the advertising, social media chatter, and other media that also influence the consumer during his/her decision journey. In the world of on-demand marketing, marketers will need to develop a broader understanding of the complex series of interactions that make up the entire consumer decision journey.[8]

This is a good example for us of selling services rather than value. There is no doubt that online channels can give you far more data and there are many products and tools out there that can cover endless data points. But, buying these arguments doesn't just keep consultancy square footage rentals going upwards in smart business districts; even more worryingly it can ensure that you drown your organization in data and in doing so blind it to information that is critical to success. This is one of the biggest challenges that any e-commerce team faces and it is part of a wider problem that the 'big data' promoters still need to resolve as they push harder and harder to sell their services into business.

Tim Harford, one of the UK's leading statisticians, makes the point in an article in the *Financial Times* that the big data movement misses the importance of understanding causation and issues of potential sampling bias – just because the sample is big, doesn't necessarily make it representative.[9] He gives a couple of great examples that are memorable reminders about the need for understanding the complexity that surrounds data in the digital age.

First, he uses Twitter to explore the argument used by many in digital marketing that it is possible to draw conclusions from it en masse on the basis that if N=All (ie the sample is so significant you can assume it is representative of all) then the conclusions that can be drawn are per se representative of the public mood. However, other research shows that Twitter users are not representative of the population as a whole. Harford quotes the Pew Research Internet Project in 2013, which reported that US-based Twitter users were disproportionately young, urban or suburban, and black. There are two conclusions that can be drawn from this. The first and general point is that N=All is often an assumption made by those drawing conclusions from large sources rather than a fact about the data; the second point in terms of e-commerce is just because you feature in social doesn't necessarily mean that it is good for you commercially.

Harford's second example of risks of accepting that N=All from the same article was the City of Boston's *Street Bump* smartphone app, which uses the phone to help identify potholes. According to Harford city authorities are on record as saying that the 'data provides the City with real-time information it uses to fix problems and plan long-term investments'. Harford concluded:

what *Street Bump* really produces, left to its own devices, is a map of potholes that systematically favours young, affluent areas where more people own smartphones. *Street Bump* offers us 'N=All' in the sense that every bump from every enabled phone can be recorded. That is not the same thing as recording every pothole. As Microsoft researcher Kate Crawford points out, found data contain systematic biases and it takes careful thought to spot and correct for those biases. Big data sets can seem comprehensive but the 'N=All' is often a seductive illusion.[10]

There are some great case studies out there, be they Amazon, Tesco supermarkets in the United Kingdom or Target supermarkets in the United States, where stories abound about the power of their algorithms and their ability to make money through using these to predict purchase patterns from past behaviour. The truth behind these, however, seems to be much more straightforward – given the data they hold on so many of their customers they have to get it right some of the time. In other words for every time they get the right voucher or recommendation, they fail far more times. In our (equally unrepresentative) experience Amazon just presents us with more of what we have just bought, whether or not we liked it or want to take our interest further and our own Tesco supermarket vouchers are rarely used.

As Harford reminds us: 'none of this suggests that such data analysis is worthless: it may be highly profitable. Even a modest increase in the accuracy of targeted special offers would be a prize worth winning. But profitability should not be conflated with omniscience'.[11]

There will no doubt be a rush into 'big data' activity in many businesses but to be profitable and to grow faster than your competitors does not necessarily require the data factories that are now being sold as the solution. There is an alternative to this approach that can provide a business with data that provides insight into purchasing behaviour. We call this deep data and define it as the combination of multiple data sources, qualitative and quantitative, that can generate informed insight about the customer in the market. Deep data still won't give you the answer, however; it gives you the insight to generate a hypothesis that you can test and through testing learn more about the customer in the market.

Your digital channel gives you both access to deep data and the opportunity to test and learn in real time very quickly and cheaply. If you have a fair amount of traffic then it can do this with a sample size of customers looking at that time for that product or service which can give you considerable confidence in the result. If your test produces (statistically) significantly more sales than your current execution then if you change your execution to the test, sales will grow. To do this well doesn't need a lot of staff or incredibly costly technology. It needs commercial sense, an open mind and a very disciplined process. Getting this right should be at the centre of any e-commerce strategy.

The leadership agenda

Part Two: Assessing the commercial opportunity

This chapter has dealt with the problems of a new discipline moving through a second phase of development (in our view the dotcom boom was the first). As it develops (admittedly at different paces in different businesses) in many organizations it is facing a challenge of commercial credibility. It is difficult for leaders to identify the source of the problem as quite often consultancies and agencies are just as much a part of it as the capabilities of the teams themselves.

We are more and more convinced that this situation arises not because businesses employ incapable people, far from it, but because they are mis-organized. They are using good people to do things that are not necessarily effective in ways that are inefficient or inappropriate. In any other discipline experienced senior leaders would spot this, although perhaps not at first. In a new discipline, made opaque to senior leaders through technology and jargon and often handed to an 'expert' to direct, it can be nearly impossible to spot. However, spotting it is essential if you are to break the cycle of underperformance.

Over the next chapters we will set out how we believe businesses can ensure that they can reduce the risk of not having the right operating, technical and organizational framework in place so that their leaders do not cede control to 'the experts' and allow other agendas to drive decision making over the commercial one.

The killer questions in this chapter are the best we have found that indicate a diagnosis of mis-organization.

Killer questions
Poor returns on investment

- Are you experiencing low/no sales growth in the digital channel?
- Have you seen repeated investments in the channel failing to reach promised outcomes?
- Are you hearing channel performance being attributed to technology issues or competitive responses?

Constant change to sales execution

- Are you seeing regular small changes made to website sales execution?
- Are you seeing inconsistent customer engagement over time?
- Are you being presented with re-designs and changes to presentation based on 'expert opinion' and not tested on real customers in real time?

Failure to engage the customer

- Are there no opportunities for customers to feedback online?
- Is your online engagement through a 'tick box' poll?
- Are you seeing no cross-channel interaction where best offline sales executions are used online and vice versa?

Failure to test and learn

- Is there no structured process that takes customer insight and tests potential responses to find the bestselling one?
- Are you seeing the testing of solutions based on 'expert opinions' rather than solutions based on 'customer feedback'?
- Are you seeing that testing is always of small differences rather than a mix of small and big alternatives?

Inflexible and slow IT change processes

- Are you applying the same processes to change in the online channel as to change in major systems?
- Is there a long list of improvements and changes awaiting execution?
- Are you running change processes in a timescale that drives the prioritization of the urgent over the important?
- Are you applying complex and costly performance analysis and testing solutions?

Leadership action

If you are answering 'yes' to anything over 25 per cent of the points above then you should worry; 50 per cent and above and you should be very worried. There aren't many immediate actions you can take at this stage that you can be sure won't make things worse. Getting this right takes time and is a significant change challenge in its own right. There are, however, some key things you can consider doing that will help you as you move forward:

- Build a senior management consensus that change is needed – you can do that by sharing this analysis and asking colleagues to add and develop it so you have a shared understanding.

- Ask the e-commerce team to map out what they do and how they do it and find them someone from outside to help them do it. An organization development (OD) person from your HR team, if you have one, would be fine or a systems analyst – someone who can help them lay out for you and colleagues what is going on and the resources involved in making it happen.

- Read on – in the next two chapters this book creates a model against which you can benchmark your own operation and in the three after that it lays out what we believe are the elements of an effective e-commerce operation.

Notes

1   http://blog.onlymarketingjobs.com/talent-shortage-continues-to-affect-marketing-and-media-sector/ [accessed 1 August 2014]

2   http://wallblog.co.uk/2014/03/27/is-the-digital-industry-unprepared-for-further-rapid-growth/

3   This was an online random sample CV analysis using publicly available data on 500 individuals with job titles such as head of e-commerce, e-commerce director, digital director, head of online sales and marketing, head of online etc. The geographic split was: UK 272 people, USA 43 people and rest of the world 185 people. Of the 500, 68.6 per cent were male and 31.4 per cent female.

4   Jackson, J, Grange, O and Millan, K (2012) From Analog to Digital: How to transform the business model, *Outlook*, report from Accenture, http://www.accenture.com/us-en/outlook/Pages/outlook-journal-2012-from-analog-to-digital-how-to-transform-business-model.aspx

5   http://searchenginewatch.com/article/2358553/Want-to-Measure-Social-ROI-Start-with-These-5-Cross-Channel-Metrics

6   http://yougov.co.uk/news/2014/02/26/consumers-cool-social-networks-online-shopping/ [accessed 9 April 2014]

7   http://www.economistinsights.com/marketing-consumer/opinion/demands-demand-marketing [accessed 7 April 2014]

8   http://www.economistinsights.com/marketing-consumer/opinion/demands-demand-marketing [accessed on 7 April 2014]

9/10/11 Harford, T (2014) Big Data: are we making a mistake?, *FT Magazine*, 28 March

Putting customers first

3

EXECUTIVE SUMMARY

Putting customers first is an age-old mantra. The trouble is that often, despite every good intention, the voices of customers are unlikely to make it into any of the key decisions that businesses take. In so many businesses the organization takes over, functional agendas drive priorities and current capabilities and technologies act as constraints on thinking about, let alone responding to, customer needs. The digital channel offers leaders the opportunity to cut through the internal noise and get right to the heart of the customer agenda, not just to the concerns of their own customers. This chapter explores customer insight, how it can be used to test ideas and executions, how it can be generated through an e-commerce operation, why it applies to customers in every channel and how businesses can think about sales engagement and optimize its effectiveness at every stage of the sales funnel. It offers leaders a benchmark sales funnel model against which they can judge their own e-commerce effectiveness and a structure for and approach to a decision-making process that puts proven growth in revenue and margin based on customer insight ahead of any other criteria for digital investment.

Customer insight

Whilst brand owners and producers may use the term 'customer' to differentiate their route to market partners from the end consumer, in the online marketplace we define the person transacting (which can range from buying, through enrolling in a service, to a simple registering of interest) as the customer.

It is the potential to understand the actions of the customer and their eventual decision to transact – or not – that sits at the heart of what differentiates an effective growth organization. Building this insight, and then using it to drive growth across every channel, can create a significant and disproportionate advantage against the competition.

Our research team reviewed 20 academic papers from the leading journals in the field[1] discussing the role of the customer in the digital world and whether there was any evidence to suggest that the same customer shopped differently on and offline. The constant conclusion was that whilst shopping behaviour might change – for example shopping for longer online before deciding to purchase – what customers are looking for in making that purchase does not change. In other words, regardless of channel, the same customer is looking to make their decision against the same buying criteria.

This understanding has opened up the opportunity for businesses with multiple routes to market to exploit their online channels not just for driving sales but also for building insight into customer buying criteria in their market: what we call triggers to purchase. Even more importantly this provides business with the opportunity to add to its data sources. Until recently, the best source of predictive customer behaviour data was mining historic purchase data and using this to predict future purchasing interest. Alongside this business leaders can now access 'real-time' data gathered at point of purchase, not just about customers who have 'bought' but just as importantly about customers in the market who have chosen *not* to buy.

However, what differentiates the most successful businesses from their competitors is not just their ability to create the right data sets and mine them for relevant information but how they go about using them to understand customer behaviour and identifying the optimal proposition that encourages more of them to transact, whether that be a purchase, a sign-up, a call, a request for a quote or any other action. What sits at the heart of successful digital businesses is the ability not just to build great insight but to design and test for the most effective response.

Test and learn

The opportunity to track customer outcomes, understand the reasons behind them and then act with far greater certainty than is offered by traditional market research comes from two aspects that are unique to the online world:

- the opportunity cheaply and quickly to collect a significant mass of data; and

- to use this data to test alternative propositions and learn from the results before making significant investment decisions on marketing communications and product development.

Testing online offers a far greater certainty to business leaders in assessing marketing communications, pricing points, sales propositions and product appetite than the testing strategies available to date, as it can provide a simult-aneous comparison between competing options in the same market at the same time under exactly the same conditions. This comparison is measured against a pre-set probability standard (normally .95) and the collection of sufficient data from the marketplace to provide the level of confidence required in a successful test result such that it can be adopted as the pre-ferred approach going forward, with a then considerable degree of certainty as to the outcome in the market.

The issue of the probability of an outcome increasing directly in proportion to a critical mass of data has long been understood. It was one of the defining principles of the 19th-century 'scientific' approach to understanding the human condition and was championed by writers such as the philosopher and explorer William Winwood Reade[2] and it even shaped a whole literary tradition through the writings of Sir Arthur Conan Doyle. When Sherlock Holmes, the world's greatest consulting detective, explains how he made the successful choice on whether to go up or down the bank next to the River Thames in pursuit of a suspect, he recommended Reade to Dr Watson as the originator of his logic and goes on to describe his argument: 'While the individual man is an insoluble puzzle, in the aggregate he becomes a mathematical certainty. You can, for example, never foretell what any one man will do, but you can say with precision what an average number will be up to. Individuals vary, but percentages remain constant.'[3]

Because it is based on this understanding of probability, utilized intelli-gently, online analytics can provide business leaders with significant data samples that can very quickly (and cost-effectively) provide the insight from which strong hypotheses can be developed about customer behaviour. It can also unleash the potential for improved performance through changes to communication of the proposition, or to the proposition itself.

Our approach to online analytics avoids the big data trap discussed in Chapter 2 by first providing qualitative as well as quantitative data, and second, through applying the traditional scientific methodology to address hypotheses: test and learn in controlled conditions. This looks for tests to prove the outcome and, only when the outcome is replicated consistently, take action. Online technology now gives businesses the opportunity to test and learn by enabling them to take a proportion of their customer traffic through a different presentation (revised sales copy, revised headlines, revised 'call to action' etc) or even a different proposition and judge the outcome. This is called 'split testing' and enables a virtual laboratory test to be conducted between two pages in exactly the same environment against the same competitive activity. Sufficient mass of traffic through the test page gives a high probability that the result will be replicated; not just if presented to all online customers but, given the same shopper and same trigger findings, also to every customer regardless of channel.

An advantage of these test results over traditional market research is that they gain insights from all customers in the market who 'visit' a proposition, not just those who buy from them. This offers the business in-depth understanding of why customers choose to buy competing products and services, what triggers to purchase they satisfy and whether this creates opportunities for growth.

Deep data not just big data

The implication for growth is exciting: by understanding why people are buying your product online, and optimizing the proposition through a test-and-learn strategy, you will reduce the number of people who currently 'fail' to buy and be able to market and invest more to acquire additional customers. However, there is one significant assumption: that your organization has the capability to develop powerful hypotheses about customers in your market. We have long argued that businesses have failed to appreciate the difference between a hypothesis and a thesis. The classic definition of a thesis[4] is that it is *a theory that is put forward as a premise to be maintained or proved* whilst a hypothesis[5] is *a proposed explanation made on the basis of limited evidence as a starting point for further investigation.* Much of what is proposed in businesses about customers is a hypothesis communicated as a thesis with supporting 'proofs' on which leaders are asked to act. The problem with this is that a thesis by definition is an argument based on proof. It should be able to be acted upon with some degree of confidence. If you present a hypothesis in this way, the business may act confidently on limited evidence. Taking decisions in this way significantly increases the risk of failure to achieve the desired outcome.

This is what sits at the heart of many of the digital difficulties described in Chapter 1. If you act confidently (and often expensively) on limited evidence you are more likely to destroy value than create it. A process that

FIGURE 3.1   The data sources for a digital hypothesis

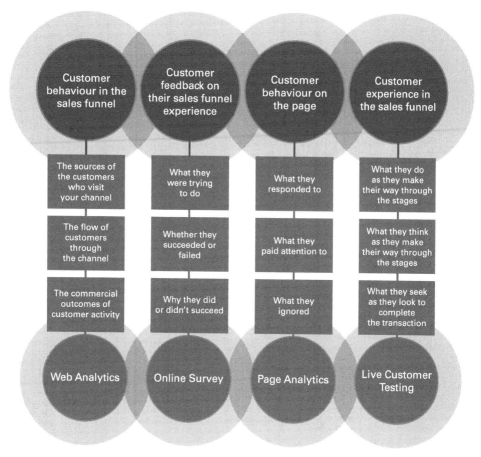

Customer behaviour in the sales funnel

Customer feedback on their sales funnel experience

Customer behaviour on the page

Customer experience in the sales funnel

The sources of the customers who visit your channel

What they were trying to do

What they responded to

What they do as they make their way through the stages

The flow of customers through the channel

Whether they succeeded or failed

What they paid attention to

What they think as they make their way through the stages

The commercial outcomes of customer activity

Why they did or didn't succeed

What they ignored

What they seek as they look to complete the transaction

Web Analytics

Online Survey

Page Analytics

Live Customer Testing

SOURCE: © Good Growth Ltd 2014

generates deep understanding and then tests alternative responses to it to identify the most successful is far more likely to generate success. At this stage you have proof against which you can invest with confidence.

Hypotheses are built in the digital channel through blending four sources of customer data and finding the crossover points where they combine (two, three or all four) to suggest customer behaviour trends. Figure 3.1 describes these sources and what they need to provide.

Chapter 6 goes into greater detail about what should be happening in an e-commerce team, and the tools required to provide these sources of data, but broadly speaking this data comes from four types of tool applied in a way that asserts the primacy of the customer:

- **Web analytics:** these are sourced from software wrapped around your website and can measure the flow from search term through to completed transaction. They need to be set up correctly to ensure your commercial imperatives are being tracked and that the most significant customer journeys through the sales funnel are being measured.

- **Online surveys:** these are separate software packages. The most effective ask 1–4 questions, do not poll customers to rate your views of the issues but rather offer open-ended free-text format opportunities for engagement.

- **Page analytics:** these are software packages that are often described as 'heat mapping tools'. The best of these can show interest, engagement and attention. Other tools will look at form effectiveness, the positioning of the page when it is first presented on the customer's screen to see what is initially visible and whether the important elements (such as a 'buy now' button) really stand out.

- **Live testing:** we believe that user testing as currently practised has a relatively limited use as it normally uses 'testers' often in artificial conditions. Live testing recruits real customers online and records their journey through the sales funnel visually and verbally.

Hypothesis creation

Hypothesis creation is one of the most critical digital capabilities you need to build in your business and in our experience it is the one most businesses lack. It requires a cross-functional team to work together to build a full understanding of the different available data sources and to synthesize these into the best possible description of current customer behaviour in the channel. We use a team that comprises digital and qualitative analysts, commercial product owners, the design lead responsible for creating alternative executions (copy and design), a project leader and, to facilitate these individuals through the process, a process expert. The process we use is described in Figure 3.2.

The key to successful execution of this process is facilitation to enable the synthesis of the different 'stories'. The key to a successful hypothesis is that it gets the business to act. By act we mean agreeing to address the issues raised through a process of test and learn. In our experience the only way to do this is to ensure that the hypothesis does not define a solution. Its function is to build a consensus around the problem that has to be solved.

FIGURE 3.2 The digital hypothesis process

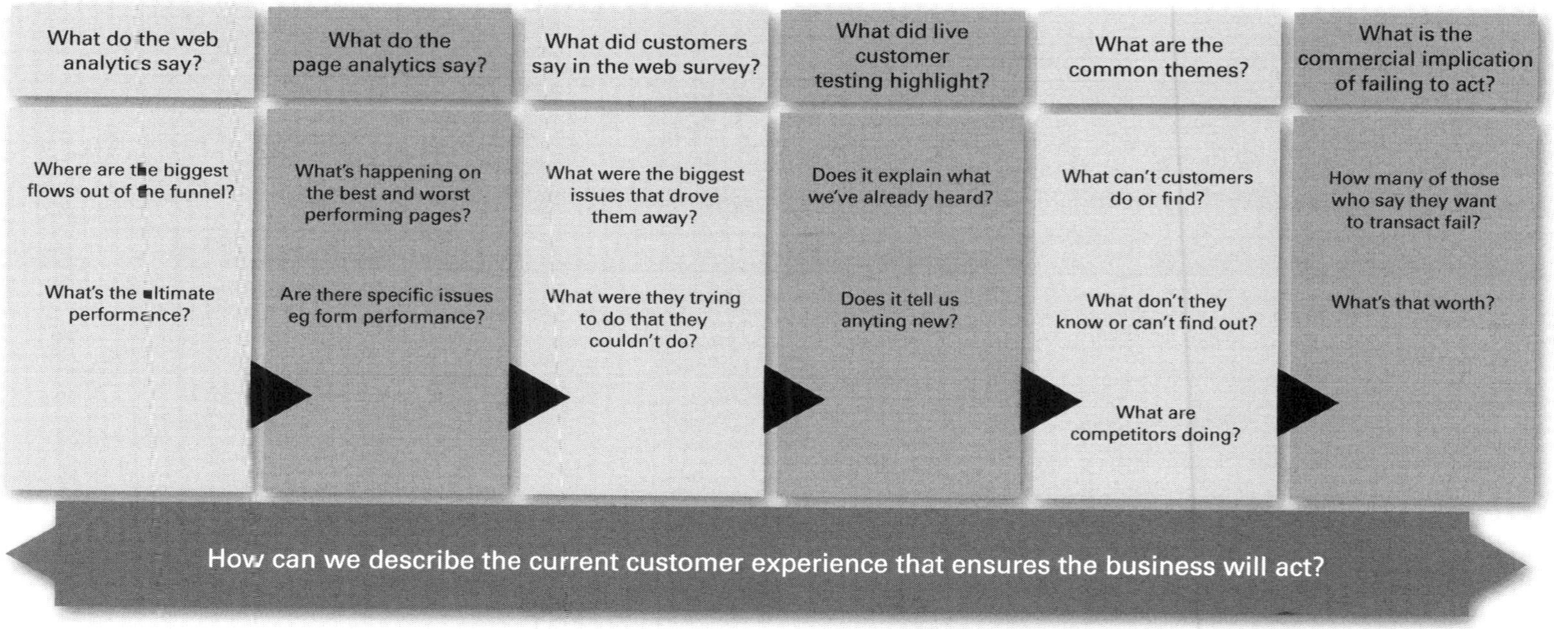

What do the web analytics say?
Where are the biggest flows out of the funnel?
What's the ultimate performance?
What do the page analytics say?
What's happening on the best and worst performing pages?
Are there specific issues eg form performance?
What did customers say in the web survey?
What were the biggest issues that drove them away?
What were they trying to do that they couldn't do?
What did live customer testing highlight?
Does it explain what we've already heard?
Does it tell us anyting new?
What are the common themes?
What can't customers do or find?
What don't they know or can't find out?
What are competitors doing?
What is the commercial implication of failing to act?
How many of those who say they want to transact fail?
What's that worth?
How can we describe the current customer experience that ensures the business will act?

SOURCE: © Good Growth Ltd 2014

The final part of the process that leads to a test is the development of a design response. In this we argue that there needs to be some important differences from the usual approach to developing a web page. First and foremost we include the designer in the whole hypothesis process. Having the person who will turn the analysis into an effective execution as part of the process builds depth of understanding into the design response and enables a conversation to take place between those responsible for commercial performance, those who manage the feeds into the different customer data streams, the e-commerce product lead(s) and the design team. This can often lead to an iterative creation of an early 'wireframe' in the room, building shared understanding of how design and copy can combine to test and learn. This can be best described/understood through a case study.

CASE STUDY   The Open University

In 2013, the UK-based Open University (OU) engaged us to work with them to improve recruitment to their flagship distance-learning MBA programme. In the aftermath of the global financial crisis, the MBA market had suffered considerably. Whilst the OU had fared better than many, with accreditation by all three global quality assurance bodies putting their business school in the top 1 per cent of all institutions worldwide, it was not recruiting at the levels it had sustained prior to 2008.

The decision to purchase an MBA is a long one, taking roughly 12–18 months on average and seems to break down into three phases. These include a research phase, a phase where the key alternatives are identified and then a final phase of about six months where the preferred alternative is settled upon and other elements such as financing are secured. The OU wanted to concentrate its focus on those customers in the market who were in the final six-month phase. As yet undecided customers who 'clicked' the OU's MBA proposition were sent to a single page that encouraged customers to request a prospectus and in so doing share contact details which were then used to fuel an e-mail and telephone sales campaign to drive enrolment.

Our synthesis identified a large number of customers who failed to engage with any of the potential actions on the page as they felt that the information available was inadequate and there was no compelling reason to consider an MBA from the OU, as opposed to any of its major competitors. In reality, the page (Figure 3.3) was not engaging and whilst there was no competitor in their segment of the MBA

FIGURE 3.3   The Open University 2012 MBA sales page

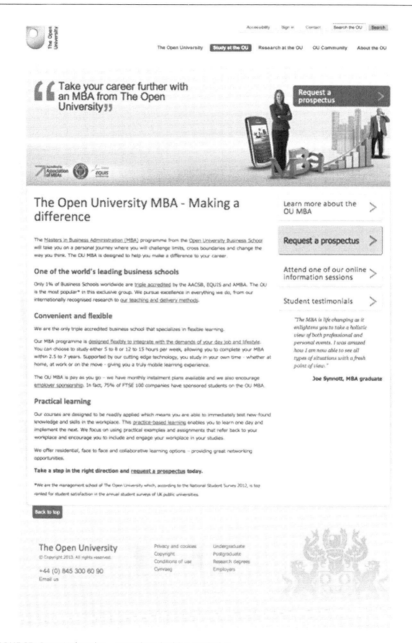

market doing a significantly better job, there were examples we could point to of better selling.

Our shared hypothesis was this:

*We believe candidates who are looking to choose the OU to start within six months are not reserving as fast as they can because the critical differentiating information which says **why the OU** and **what does the OU offer** is spread across pages or is **not available** which causes people to delay, explore other sites or give up as they do not have the answers they need to move ahead.*

This generated the test execution displayed in Figure 3.4.

Figure 3.4 only shows the top of the page. The whole landing page was 2.5 times longer than the original and had supporting information for each of the six sub-headings under the banner headline.

The design responded to six key needs that distance-learning MBA customers told us they had as they were making the critical decision on whether or not to enrol in a particular school:

- a quick glance overview to show the most critical decision-making information in an easy-to-read way;

- testimonial quotes to support key points providing reassurance from current students on the questions they had;

- a video on the home page which covered the programme and key selling points that were addressing major questions;

- data points to support the OU's expertise in distance learning which is very important for prospective students looking to buy this way of obtaining the degree;

- logos of sponsoring companies and rankings to provide credibility and reassurance that this was a recognized qualification;

- a design that reinforces the quality experience that comes from the OU's unrivalled expertise.

The page also offered opportunities to take actions, including enrolment by telephone and attending virtual and physical events, that were proven to convert a high percentage of prospects. The test was soon far more successful than the original page and was quickly implemented as the preferred approach with re-testing of minor changes and additional calls to action. Its implementation resulted in a 33 per cent increase in enrolment in 2013 and an even greater improvement in 2014.

FIGURE 3.4   The Open University 2013 MBA landing page

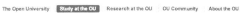

The Open University | Study at the OU | Research at the OU | OU Community | About the OU

The OU distance learning MBA. Where excellence comes as standard.

You're about to make a life-changing decision for your career prospects, so don't compromise. Find out why more people sign up for the OU distance learning MBA than any other triple accredited degree.

Call us to reserve your place now
0845 366 6031

Speak to us on a **webinar**

Meet us at a **local event**

Request a **prospectus**

True flexibility	Clarity of pricing	Proven quality	Pioneering	Course details	Requirements
Only the OU enables you to complete your MBA at a pace that suits you – within a 7 year timeframe.	An OU MBA costs as little as £14,250 with no hidden extras. Or you can begin your MBA with a monthly payment option of £386.27.	The Open University Business School is the UK's largest MBA provider with triple accreditation.	For more than 40 years, the OU has been at the leading edge of distance learning.	The OU MBA offers world-class education and support in a learning experience unlike any other.	Discover your eligibility to start your OU MBA.
FIND OUT MORE	FIND OUT MORE	FIND OUT MORE	FIND OUT MORE	FIND OUT MORE	FIND OUT MORE

At a glance

 MBA format Blended programme - residential, online and peer collaboration

 37 Average age of course members

 Tutor/Student ratio 1:16

 14 Average years of work experience

 Programme duration 30/84 months

 Ratio statistics 36% female / 64% male

 Fees* £14,250

 Countries represented Average 126

 Sponsorship 40% of our students are company sponsored

 Programme rating The most popular triple accredited MBA in the UK

 Watch this video to find out why one of the world's biggest telecoms companies sponsor their employees to take the OU MBA

 Many organisations, including 80% of FTSE 100 companies, have sponsored employees with the OU
BT NHS IBM

 As featured in:
FT THE INDEPENDENT The Economist

 Your nearest World Class Learning Centre

True flexibility

Our MBA has been designed flexibly to integrate with the demands of your job and lifestyle. Choose an OU MBA and you can study anywhere in the world to suit your professional and personal commitments – and wherever you are, we're close to you with 13 national or regional offices across the UK as well as many across the globe.

The OU is the only triple accredited business school that specialises in flexible learning. During stage 1, you study between 12-15 hours per week. You then have the flexibility of studying fewer hours in Stage 2 by choosing fewer modules to study at the same time. This allows you to complete your MBA within 2 and a half to 7 years.

Supported by our cutting edge technology, you study in your own time - whether at home, at work or on the move - giving you a truly mobile learning experience. The OU MBA is a distance learning programme with exceptional levels of support. These come in the form of face-to-face tutorials, residential schools, online tutorial sessions and access to tutors at all times. You can also access online forums with a large number of students at various stages of their MBA and interact with them.

Call us to reserve your place now **0845 366 6031**

Speak to us on a **webinar**

Meet us at a **local event**

Request a **prospectus**

> "I am a Chartered Architect and, at the time I embarked on a MBA, I was a Director of a large professional consultancy firm. I wanted the opportunity to study at my pace and not be tied down to a short time span to complete the course. The OU MBA gave me that flexibility and had the variety of modules in place that allowed me to put together a course of study to suit my needs."
> **Basil Sawczuk**, OU MBA Graduate

SOURCE:
© Good Growth Ltd 2014

BACK TO THE TOP   NEXT

Whilst a hypothesis process builds a shared understanding of the problem and creates a shared 'issue' all agree has to be resolved, it will not drive the business decision on what is to be tested, what success is and whether to 'mainstream' the experiment at the end of the test period. To do this successfully requires a process that has to be understood and accepted across several functions as the way a business establishes the priority issues, tests solutions to them, builds a business case for making the change and establishes a priority order for changes to be made based on the scale of available return.

Customer to Action®

We believe that the most successful growth organizations make a clear strategic choice to drive their decision making from a deep understanding of their customers. This is not a choice about data. It is a choice about their organization. Chapter 6 will look in greater depth at the organization issues, but in essence we believe that growth organizations:

- adopt simple and straightforward processes that ensure the voice of the customer is clearly presented in key decisions relating to product and service development, delivery and communication;
- invest in and develop analytical capabilities that ensure what is presented to them is as accurate as possible;
- exploit their online presence as a channel through which customer insight can be gained and build the technical capability to support this;
- operate fluid boundaries between all their sales channels to optimize communication of their proposition and to distribute the most effective communications to every customer regardless of the channel they use.

All organizations have processes that are the shared way in which people work together to get things done. In 2011, it struck us that whilst there are many accepted processes in businesses – often associated with technology brought in to automate and lower the costs of internal transactions – there were none that addressed one of the single biggest points of failure: the risk of failing to keep in touch with the market. The more we researched, the clearer it became that business processes were often set up in such a way that they militated against customer engagement. The bigger a business gets, and therefore the more it relies on processes to get things done, the more customers have to fit in with organizations that deliver their products and services, rather than the other way around. This is not the way to run a successful business.

To be a growth organization you need to stay closer to the customers in the market than any of your competitors. To find out what works best in a fast-changing world, businesses have to meld the 'test-and-learn' capability provided through online interactions into their process that allocates and prioritizes commercial investments. This will enable them to adopt an external orientation to investment decisions that drive growth. Given that the online customer is the same as the customer on the phone or in person, these processes are just as powerful at testing offline activities (marketing, sales executions, pricing etc) as the equivalent online activities.

We define this process as Customer to Action®. Figure 3.5 illustrates how this links across key business processes.

This process has four parts:

1 **Hypothesis and testing:** as we described earlier, this is the pre-requisite stage for all decisions on resource allocation. This is iterative, as you do not move past this stage until you have a successful outcome of a test-and-learn cycle.

2 **Actionable data:** this analysis stage involves the collation of the outcomes of the test (real customer behaviour) alongside data from your operating systems that tell you what the costs associated with the current way of working are and therefore how much benefit there may be to the organization from mainstreaming the test.

3 **Performance improvement proposal:** this is a planning stage where the potential improvement from either more revenue or lower cost to serve is put into the business' usual investment assessment appraisal, the cost to making the change is factored in and a return projection generated.

4 **Compelling business case:** this is the presentation and approval where the test outcome with its associated costs of change is reviewed and then prioritized against other online projects. For projects that require more than just an e-commerce/digital team activity to deliver this is fed into whatever IT priority-making process exists where IT support is required to ensure the change is made. The priority process is simple; do whatever generates the most money fastest first, and then turn your attention to those actions with a longer-term payback.

FIGURE 3.5   Customer to Action®

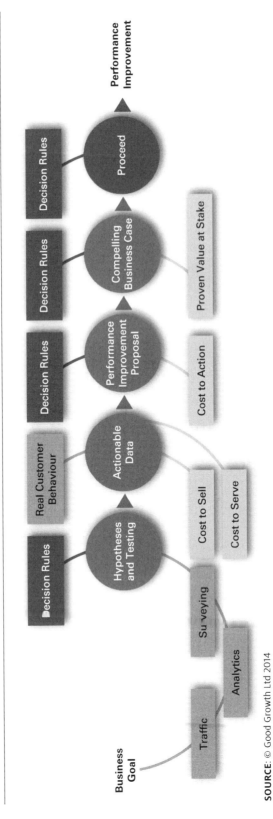

SOURCE: © Good Growth Ltd 2014

To deliver this successfully, growth businesses need to build the capability to collect, collate and analyse customer data and to manage their change processes to test and mainstream marketing communications, not just in their online channel but across all channels.

Any process is more effective if there are clear 'decision rules' agreed across the business or at least those parts of it critically involved in the successful execution of the process. A decision rule is often set through policies that define for any organization what it will or will not do under certain circumstances. For example, in a recruitment process many businesses set a minimum standard for achievement in numerical and verbal reasoning tests for graduate entry programmes.

In e-commerce some policies will be essential, eg pricing, commercial terms etc, and there will also be other policies such as branding guidelines that will be critical if they exist. In addition to these, we believe that e-commerce processes should also create decision rules that impose a structure on data, both on what data is required at every stage and on how it is gathered and presented. We say this from experience – e-commerce can generate literally thousands of data points and if leaders are not careful they can find themselves overwhelmed with data points and fail to see the wood for the trees.

We have come across e-commerce reporting in two major organizations that runs into tens of pages, hundreds of performance measures and thousands of data points. It became clear as we unpicked their internal processes that in both cases the key figure required for any assessment of commercial performance – conversion to sale of users who enter the site from the key sales landing page (sometimes this is the home page but often it can be a shop landing page on a larger site) – was not being tracked, or if it was, was not being highlighted or reviewed.

To help leaders think through exactly what they need and when they need it, we have developed the decision rule checklist displayed in Figure 3.6. In our experience, if you get this agreed by all involved in the decision before you set out on the stage involved, it will ensure that you get there first time.

Adopting this process model can also regulate and focus technology investments required to service customer needs in the marketplace. Over time it will move from driving a change agenda for the current proposition and platform into an innovation agenda where changes to proposition and/or functionality will start to become priorities for the customer. E-commerce developments can often be driven by digital technology enthusiasts whose interests are less with the customer and more with the technology and what it could do.

FIGURE 3.6   Decision rules checklist

Decision: What do you want to do?

Agree what to survey and how

Need (Data)

What is the best data source?
What degree of specificity do we require?
What points of comparison will aid the process?
How do we present the data?
Who is responsible for collating, presenting and sharing the data?

Rules

Whose opinion do we need in the room?
Are there any other brand, corporate or operation policies that need to be accounted for?

Action

How do we agree actions, milestones, targets?
How do we report back?

SOURCE: © Good Growth Ltd 2014

Whilst there is no doubt that customers will often not be able to spot or ask for technology that can transform their experiences, listening carefully and building a robust insight platform can help a business judge when there is a business reason to introduce technology change. If we understand the customer requirements well we can determine whether the latest technology advance will or will not deliver returns. The world is, after all, littered with apps that don't deliver either for the customer or for the business.

Customer to Action® is a process model and has been built to be tailored to fit different sectors, business drivers and IT change processes. Of the last, it is clear that there is an increasing convergence between Agile methodologies and the adoption of LEAN manufacturing principles to software development[6] and this is likely to continue as changes in markets continue to increase in pace and businesses strive to find a balance between quality assurance and speed to test and learn. For one large IT function we tailored a version of the Customer to Action® model to fit a LEAN development framework (Figure 3.7) that worked through applying Agile techniques such as Scrums to traditional LEAN structures such as Kanban boards.

The activities we describe above fit comfortably into the LEAN model (Figure 3.8).

FIGURE 3.7 Customer to Action® tailored to fit the LEAN model

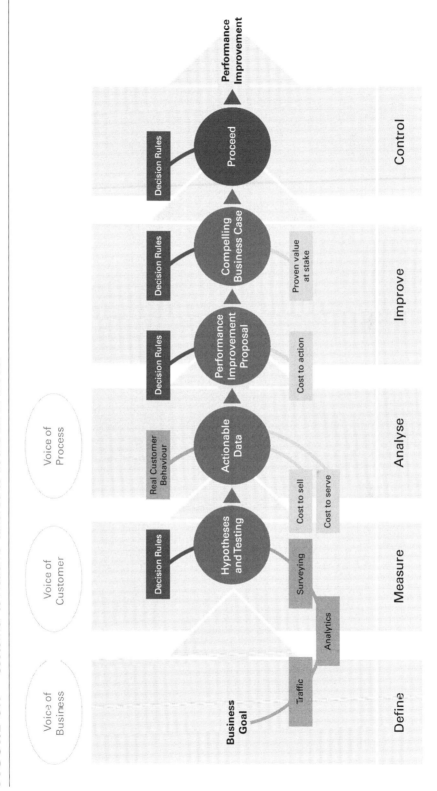

Performance Improvement

Decision Rules — Proceed

Decision Rules — Compelling Business Case

Proven value at stake

Decision Rules — Performance Improvement Proposal

Cost to action

Real Customer Behaviour — Actionable Data

Cost to sell

Cost to serve

Decision Rules — Hypotheses and Testing

Surveying

Analytics

Business Goal

Traffic

Voice of Process

Voice of Customer

Voice of Business

Define   Measure   Analyse   Improve   Control

SOURCE: © Good Growth Ltd 2014

FIGURE 3.8 Process activities in a LEAN framework

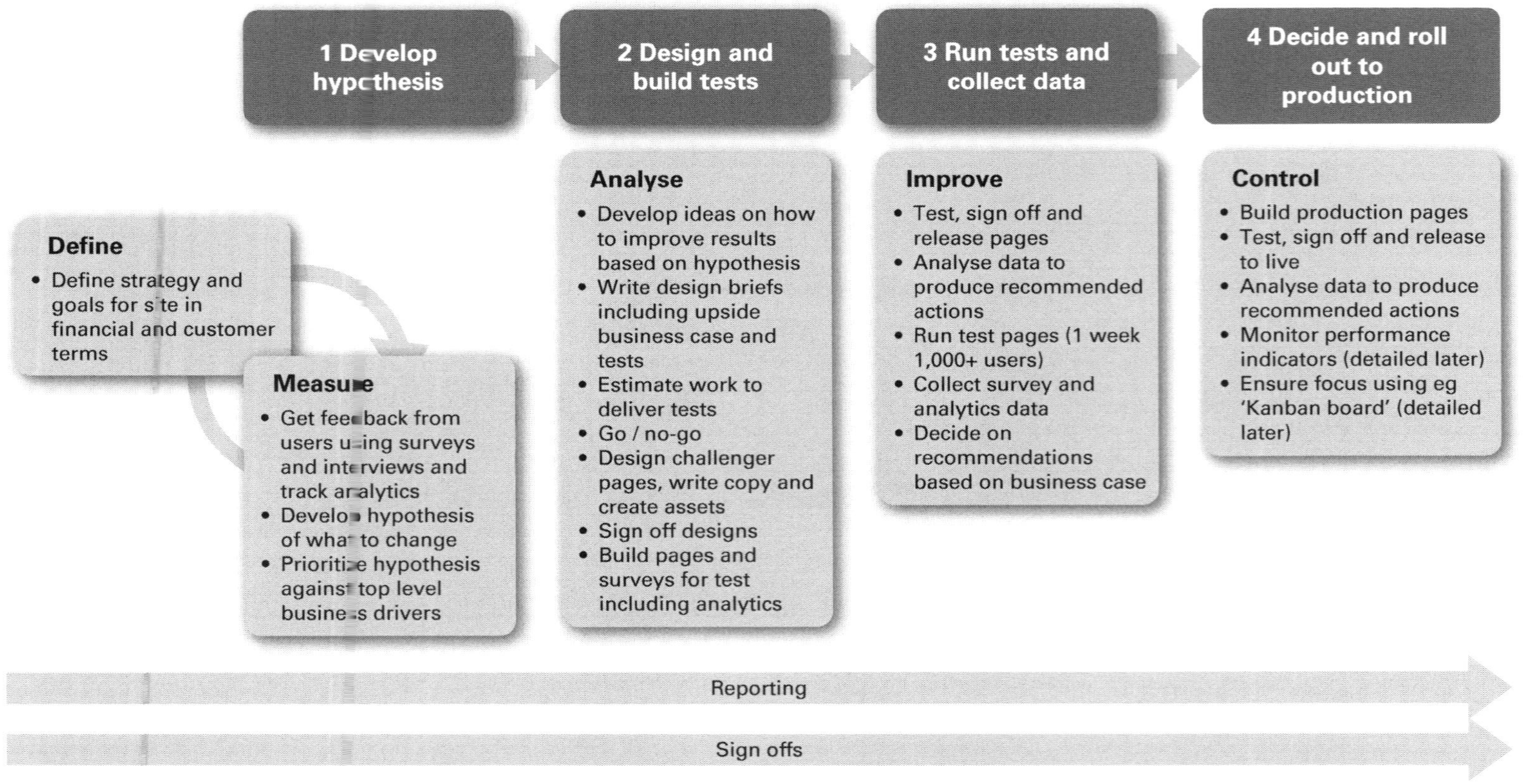

1 Develop hypothesis

Define
- Define strategy and goals for site in financial and customer terms

Measure
- Get feedback from users using surveys and interviews and track analytics
- Develop hypothesis of what to change
- Prioritise hypothesis against top level business drivers

2 Design and build tests

Analyse
- Develop ideas on how to improve results based on hypothesis
- Write design briefs including upside business case and tests
- Estimate work to deliver tests
- Go / no-go
- Design challenger pages, write copy and create assets
- Sign off designs
- Build pages and surveys for test including analytics

3 Run tests and collect data

Improve
- Test, sign off and release pages
- Analyse data to produce recommended actions
- Run test pages (1 week 1,000+ users)
- Collect survey and analytics data
- Decide on recommendations based on business case

4 Decide and roll out to production

Control
- Build production pages
- Test, sign off and release to live
- Analyse data to produce recommended actions
- Monitor performance indicators (detailed later)
- Ensure focus using eg 'Kanban board' (detailed later)

Reporting

Sign offs

SOURCE: © Good Growth Ltd 2014

FIGURE 3.9   The Customer to Action® Kanban dashboard

Hypothesis to test	Tests in design	Tests built and live	Test data analysed	Test validated and in build

SOURCE: © Good Growth Ltd 2014

And the process can be monitored and controlled through a Kanban dashboard (Figure 3.9).

The key to any process control is to set a limit for the number of activities at each stage in the process. In our view, whilst it is quite possible to have several hypotheses ready to test at any one time, we believe that to ensure businesses avoid the perennial e-commerce problems of a long list of changes to the website waiting to be made and limited development resources constantly under pressure to deliver them, the process limit should be no more than two activities running at any of the other stages. If you don't impose a control structure like this, the urgent starts to drive out the important and not only is future value not created, today's value starts to get destroyed.

Who owns the digital channel?

What also has to change is not just the 'what' of the process but also the 'how'. To make these decisions effectively, ie at speed, incurring least possible cost and with the greatest chance of a positive outcome, two further conditions need to be fulfilled: clarity of ownership and cross-functional involvement. Ironic as it may sound, despite this being one of the biggest areas of growth and investment in today's organizations, the one thing that is almost always a matter of debate is 'who owns the website'.

Historically the debate is split between marketing and IT. A 2009 study[7] from the US suggested that marketing or a combination of marketing and IT resources managed the website in nearly 70 per cent of all respondents. This probably made sense if the sole purpose of the web was a function of one of hose departments, but as the web becomes more commercially central there needs to be a reappraisal of the way these assets are owned and managed.

A key driver is your vision for the digital channel. From a business perspective, does it exist only as a communications channel? If so, marketing may be the best group to manage the site. But it's more likely that the web serves more than one function:

- **Sales:** either direct sales where customers transact on the site or indirect sales where the site helps to move prospective customers through the sales cycle such as second-hand car sales or buying complex products such as life assurance.

- **Customer service:** sites that support existing customers either through self-service features (eg account management) or a knowledge base that supports traditional offline customer service (eg fact sheets for medical conditions).

- **Recruitment:** sites that attract job candidates or encourage enrolment (eg in higher education or professional associations).

Whilst there may be other functions (eg media or investor relations) that are important, the primary commercial objective needs to lead and functions should play a partnering role, just as they do in the traditional offline channels. The digital channel should be treated as an organizational entity and, whilst there should be parts of the site that have clear ownership in other functions (eg job recruitment in HR) the core site and its associated technology, processes and revenue and capital budgets should be seen as 'owned' by the channel organization. Chapter 7 will deal with the organizational implications of this.

The second condition is to make the process of driving performance through the channel a cross-functional one from the outset. It is so much easier to remove artificial barriers and deal with functional silos if all key functions are involved from the beginning in understanding the data, building the insight platform, creating a hypothesis, driving the test and learn and validating the outcomes such that the priorities for change have broad ownership. This ownership can only really come from involvement.

The sales funnel

The other required framework is a common understanding of what makes an effective sales funnel. For a business to operate successfully in this market

FIGURE 3.10   Good Growth sales funnel benchmark

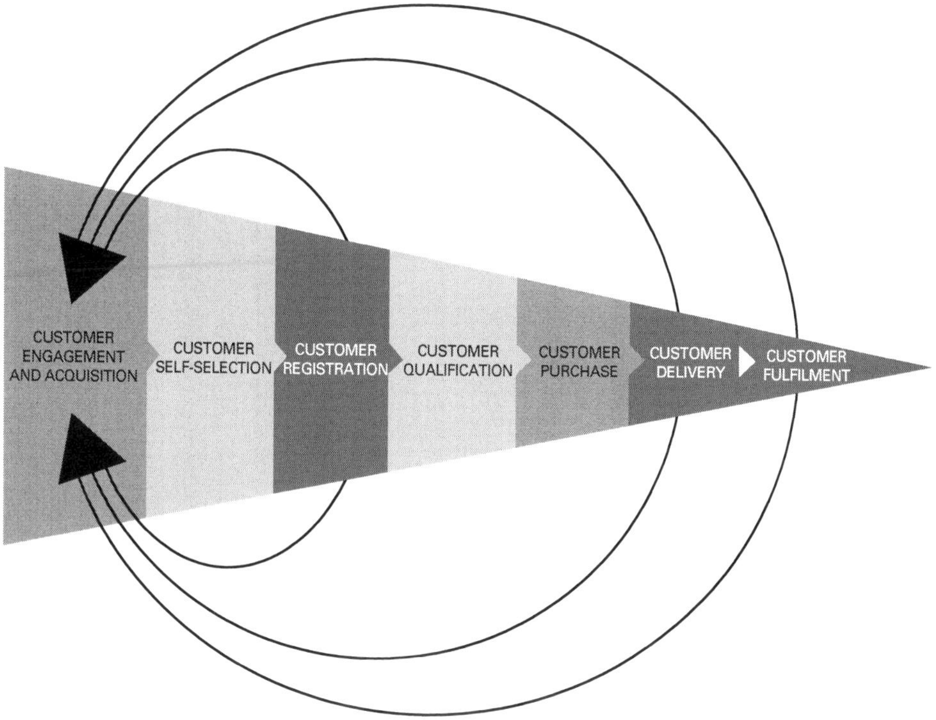

CUSTOMER ENGAGEMENT AND ACQUISITION | CUSTOMER SELF-SELECTION | CUSTOMER REGISTRATION | CUSTOMER QUALIFICATION | CUSTOMER PURCHASE | CUSTOMER DELIVERY | CUSTOMER FULFILMENT

SOURCE: © Good Growth Ltd 2014

structure, an effective sales funnel must capture all activity that attracts, qualifies, manages and 'closes' customers through the lifetime of a relationship. This is also an issue of process.

Figure 3.10 outlines the sales funnel required to deliver superior performance. Both on- and offline, these activities need to be clear, well executed and supported. The online channel can be used to 'test' the effectiveness of each and the best salespeople in the offline channel can be used to inform what is used to 'test': simply put, an online sales engagement should replicate the best offline salesperson.

The stages in an effective sales funnel reflect the following activities.

Customer engagement and acquisition

The effective communication of the proposition to the target customer through key channels that attract the greatest possible traffic into the funnel.

The key to this is ensuring a differentiated proposition that is communicating what customers in the market are looking for in the places where they are most likely to be looking. In the digital channel this is established through a traffic strategy.

Customer self-selection

Customer-driven research and selection of products and how they meet their aspirations in the marketplace. The key to this is presenting clearly the full range of products, service and support for prospective customers consistently and effectively to meet the requirements defined by customers in the market. This requires the development and testing of headlines and copy that work not just on the website but in marketing e-mails, AdWords, online banner adverts and across whatever content marketing you develop. Alongside this is the developing and testing of presentations of the reasons to purchase from your specific proposition rather than from any other in the market.

Customer registration

Customer contact through on- and offline channels as you see fit. The key to this is ensuring ease of access to the organization at times that suit the customer to enable the customer to execute their intention (eg from transactions such as application completion to an enquiry which can be answered live, rapidly after receipt electronically or in a personal follow-up call) and the early capture of accurate basic customer information (name, e-mail, postal address, contact telephone number and intention) to allow for pre-purchase decision engagement. Much if not all of the above can be automated but there are critical commercial decisions to be made here. Unless you are convinced that you are offering the 'must have' proposition for your segment of the market, you cannot ignore access standards that operate in the market. However well your proposition meets a customer need, if you are unavailable to meet it when the customer wants it, and others with a similar proposition are available, then you are likely to lose the sale.

Customer qualification

Customer engagement in the proposition, demonstrating a clear interest in their purchasing. In a classic offline environment this would be a follow-up sales conversation/interaction that moves the customer from an enquiry to a qualified lead. In a digital channel this can be executed in a number of different ways. The most obvious way is using other customer ratings and testimonials at every stage of the online funnel. Increasingly sites present customers with the opportunity to engage through online 'chat' to answer questions and remove concerns. More sophisticated techniques include e-mails that follow up when customers fail to complete a transaction.

Customer purchase

The completion of the required transaction, be that 'buy', 'register', 'call' etc. This will include an easy-to-follow funnel with few distractions and a clear purpose that supports the customer to 'close the sale', available support through the funnel if required and the use of key activities that make the purchase decision 'low risk'. Effective websites often close down the available options in the purchase stage of the funnel to encourage completion.

Customer delivery

Delivery of purchased products and services with feedback loops for customer completion. This would include utilization of products such as microsites, member areas and forums, publications, research papers, satisfaction surveys etc. Key to this is to be able to demonstrate that you don't just take feedback but you also act upon it. In our view, this delivery stage and the fulfilment stage below should also include delivery of services and support to members. Think about what you put in the parcel with the goods or what you include in the confirmation e-mail with the service confirmation. Too often businesses look to reduce their cost of delivery with inserts and paperwork from other businesses – this in our experience nearly always gets recycled immediately, often along with potentially value-adding communications from the original supplier, reducing the impact of the decision to engage with your proposition. Here is a simple question: have you said 'thank you'?

Customer fulfilment

Relationship building to help secure repeat purchase, recommendation and advocacy. Here the business commences relationship building through personalized feedback acknowledgment and reporting back. Successful fulfilment enables any business to create marketing communications that will generate even greater customer acquisition and build a virtuous cycle where current customers want to return and promote the proposition through online reviews, testimonials and recommendations to their friends.

The winners today are those businesses that can aggregate customer segments by value and develop a deep understanding of the requirements of the segment that they want to engage.

The leadership agenda

Part Three: The operating framework

This chapter has focussed on setting the operating framework for an effective digital business and the role that a cross-functional process and a common understanding of an effective sales funnel can play in driving growth in the digital channel. This part of the leadership agenda sets out how you can assess the state of your own operating model and what may need doing to ensure it is fit for purpose.

Killer questions

For this section the killer questions are aimed at understanding how good your customer insight is, how you develop, test and revise your proposition communications online, your process effectiveness and your understanding of your sales funnel.

Insight
- Do you survey customers online and if so how?
- What other online analytics do you do regularly?
- Do you live test (as opposed to user test)?
- How are these insights synthesized to build insight?
- How is that insight used to develop online execution?

Test and learn
- Do you test and if so how often?
- What informs the testing schedule?
- How do you measure success in a test?
- What do you do with a successful test outcome?

Process

- Who drives the decision making for the digital channel?

- Can you map the process used to inform tests, execute them, assess them and then prioritize implementation? How close is it to the Customer to Action® model?

- Are there clear decision rules at key stages in your process? How well understood are they?

- What drives the change list for the digital channel? How is it set and who owns the decision making?

- Who is involved in the process? Is it genuinely cross-functional?

Sales funnel

- Have you got a defined sales funnel? How close is it to the one described?

- At each stage, how do you establish what you expect to happen and who is responsible for setting and monitoring the expected standard?

Leadership action

Your answers to these questions will shape your biggest areas of concern and priority in the context of your business and its goals. Key actions you should consider in your plans are:

- ensuring clarity of ownership of the channel and that the owners of the commercial priority will be able to set the agenda and deliver it;

- building the capabilities that will create deep and powerful customer insight;

- establishing the requirement for a testing hypothesis before new designs and executions are developed;

- ensuring that the process of test and learn is cross-functional and has clear decision rules;

- ensuring that you can conduct several tests a month (though this will depend on traffic as we explain in Chapter 4);

- establishing an agreed sales funnel for on- and offline (if you have it) activity and allocating the accountability for setting and maintaining the required standards for your business.

Notes

1 The articles came from a range of marketing journals, most notably: *International Journal of Internet Marketing and Advertising*; *Journal of Retailing*; *Marketing Science*; *Journal of Interactive Marketing*; *Journal of Business Research*; *Internet Research*; *Journal of Retailing*; *Journal of Business Research*; *Journal of Electronic Commerce Research*; *European Journal of Marketing*; *Journal of Services Marketing* and *International Journal of Research in Marketing*.

2 William Winwood Reade was the author of the highly influential book *The Martyrdom of Man* (1872) which was one of many texts at the time arguing that whilst religion had driven man in the past, it would be science that would drive his future. Reade was a regular correspondent of Darwin and helped shape his theory of evolution. He was seen as a major figure in the promotion of Social Darwinism and political liberalism.

3 Doyle, Sir AC (1894) *The Sign of the Four*

4 http://www.oxforddictionaries.com/definition/english/thesis [accessed 28 June 2014]

5 http://www.oxforddictionaries.com/definition/english/hypothesis [accessed 28 June 2014]

6 http://www.forbes.com/2010/01/11/software-lean-manufacturing-technology-cio-network-agile.html [accessed 28 June 2014]

7 http://www.slideshare.net/sgehlen/2009-internet-strategy-forum-corporate-internet-executive-research-study-4page-sample-brief [accessed 6 July 2014]

The new marketing model

4

EXECUTIVE SUMMARY

In this chapter we explore the transformation of shopping and the customer experience and how marketing is changing as business has gone digital. We look at how multi-channel business models are focussed on driving traffic towards their proposition in the channel preferred by the customer and what that means specifically in the digital channel. We define traffic sources and discuss how they can best be used to attract the segments of the market that you are looking for. We discuss why in a digital world, whilst images play a part, it is design and copy that play the most significant role in persuading the customers you want to engage with your proposition; both in the attraction of potential sales and prospects and the closure to sale or lead. We look at the power of direct e-mail and content marketing and we explore the role, opportunities and pitfalls of social media.

The impact of technology on shopping

As we discussed in Chapter 1 the world in which we live and transact has been changed irreversibly by digital technology. The scale of growth over the last 20 years in internet-based consumer transactions is probably best illustrated by these two data points. In 1995 the global online market was estimated at 16 million users.[1] In 2013 the total was estimated at almost 3 billion.[2] E-commerce, however, has only really taken off in the last 10 years as established 'high street' retailing names and other sector brand leaders moved online and 'transactions' other than classic retailing have moved increasingly online.

Equally, the mass of consumers was initially slow to adopt the new channel, with enthusiasm for online growing quickly only once issues of security and trust had been overcome; then customers quickly began to take advantage of both the significantly lower retail costs that online offered and the availability of products from central locations where local branches may not have them on the shelf. Online brands were able to develop a powerful presence. This was led by lower pricing but was strongly reinforced through outstanding levels of customer service and by successfully building online communities that built loyalty and interaction.

The move online was accelerated even further with the launch of the Apple iPhone in 2007, followed by the Apple iPad and the rush into the market of other providers of increasingly cheaper tablet devices. As of 2014 these devices tend to drive fewer transactions compared to desktop devices[3] but they have had a significant impact on the way we shop and in particular the way we consume entertainment and how we look for information to support shopping, be it for goods or services.

Today, even if consumers do not regularly buy through the digital channel, online is the primary source of information for prices, product specifications and availability. Your customers will engage with you and your proposition way before you meet them face to face or receive their call. We believe there are six things you need to understand about the customer in the marketplace:

- **After price, the most significant driver of consumer behaviour online is distribution.** Research in Australia in 2012 reported 55 per cent of consumers cited price as the main driver of shopping online and 15 per cent distribution, the second largest cited driver.[4] Today's shoppers have the opportunity to shop from their homes and elsewhere, unrestricted by store opening times. Multi-channel operators now offer a range of distribution methods including traditional retail outlets, postal delivery, timed delivery, click-and-collect in-store and even delivery to a locker at a dedicated location.

- **Some recent data to support this comes from a 2013 survey of online shoppers in the US.**[5] This suggests that there are a range of drivers that would encourage them to purchase, the most important being free shipping (80 per cent); this is followed by one-day shipping (66 per cent) and by free returns and exchanges (64 per cent).

Whilst people talk about the impatient shopper, in this survey same-day shipping was rated by just over 40 per cent.

- **Today's customer in the marketplace is extremely knowledgeable.** The internet gives them instant access to everything and they use it: 61 per cent of customers will read reviews online before making a purchase.[4] This shows the importance of this form of third-party endorsement in converting browsers to shoppers or leads. The best online executions realize this and use it to their advantage.

- **Customers today also want to know that they have received value for money.** This means that to compete in this environment, retailers have to engage with – and communicate – the concept of value. They will still pay more for a better customer experience[6] but if you are going to charge a premium you need both a very good reason and the ability to communicate it well.

- **Today's customers are also extremely vocal.** They speak their mind and tell their friends, especially when they have a bad experience. This phenomenon has seen a proliferation of sites offering and promoting reviews as a key part of their functionality.

- **Customers today are not as loyal as previous generations.** They won't stick to one supplier and will have multiple online relationships – even in the same sector. They are happy to see retailers compete for their business and understand the dynamics behind this. Whilst price is a primary driver, customers value service, reliability and stock. The user experience and technical reliability are key elements of the online experience.

- **Enabled by technology, customer behaviours are changing.** One example of this is the technique known as 'showrooming', where physical stores are browsed to select products but purchases are subsequently made online, via a smartphone or on a tablet. This purchase method is greatly helped by apps where a code can be scanned or a product description entered and the user can easily find where the product is available at the best price, with the quickest delivery or a combination of both.

A convergent world

One of the themes linking the changes in today's marketplace is that of convergence. Consumers can now access the internet through their televisions, they can watch television programmes on their phone and, of course, the number and variety of devices that enable out-of-home web access is growing enormously. Therefore, the consumer is far more in control of what they consume and when they consume it.

For marketing, this changes how businesses have to think about targeting and reaching consumers. The challenge is to adapt the way they think from the traditional single-channel approach of paying for media, earning media or owning media to one that has to address these three channels in an integrated way as the channels themselves converge. This convergence is driven by the same technology changes as those impacting customers in the marketplace. Figure 4.1 is a representation of this convergent world. Paid-for media is no longer just television, newspaper and outdoor advertising space: it is also space in search engine results and on websites through paying for content from others that promotes or enhances your proposition. It is developing incredibly quickly with one of the latest trends emerging being paying for teenagers to make six-second videos about your proposition on Vine.com.[7]

FIGURE 4.1   Convergence in advertising media

Owned media now encompasses online content such as blogging, YouTube videos, company or brand Facebook pages and slide sharing sites. Earned media covers all of social media, blogging, customer reviews such as TripAdvisor and product and service reviews that appear on your own or other distributors' websites. As devices become more sophisticated and connectivity inside and outside the home continues to improve, so this convergence will become more established.

Connectivity is undoubtedly a key driver of convergence. In the UK, some 51 per cent of accounts are either on 3G or 4G contracts[8] and worldwide more than 150 carriers in 60 countries are currently committed to 4G deployments and trials.[9] The sophistication of devices – and their uptake at an increasingly young age – is also driving behaviour. Some 72 per cent of UK mobiles are smartphones.[10] As consumers become more connected outside the home, so the need to respond to the opportunity to engage with your proposition anytime and anywhere increases.

The marketing challenge

So, against this background of a constantly evolving world, how do marketing professionals make key decisions about where to invest their resources and plan for the future? Whilst technology may have had a significant impact on how consumers receive and react to messages and how they transact, the core challenges of marketing as a discipline remain unchanged. Whilst there is no single accepted definition of marketing, descriptions tend to congregate around the concept of 'meeting need'. Here are three definitions often employed in professional education and development:

> To create sustainable growth by understanding, anticipating and satisfying customer need.[11]

> The right product, in the right place, at the right time, at the right price.[12]

> Marketing is essentially about marshalling the resources of an organization so that they meet the changing needs of the customer on whom the organization depends.[13]

Marketing communications versus brand marketing

We consider marketing as split between performing two key and discrete functions. *Marketing communications* is focussed on promoting a specific product or service with a prompt to act immediately. The desired outcome is a transaction or response to a specific offer or service. As such, it is often categorized as a 'push' activity. *Brand marketing*, on the other hand, is concerned with expressing the values, characteristics and attributes of a product or organization. The desired consumer response is the development of an affinity with a product or company and therefore a longer-lasting loyalty that is not linked to a specific window of opportunity. The focus for brand marketing is very much on finding a 'buyer for life' and is often categorized as 'pull'.

Choosing a brand-led approach is particularly appropriate when you are introducing either a new product or a new service into an established market. Doing this can often require a business to take on the category leaders in a head-on direct marketing battle where classic 'awareness building' marketing is required. These markets are often characterized as ones where consumers are able to perceive differences between brands and when they choose the brand before they go to the store or book the service they are looking for. The effective establishment of a 'pull' strategy encompasses more elements than the simple look, feel and touch of your products. It also encapsulates the entire product or service life cycle – how reliable it is, the service you receive from the supplier and how it performs against its perceived brand promise.

Whilst in the past this was arguably the preserve of consumer goods and mass market services like holidays and travel, brand has travelled into areas such as professional services where consulting and accountancy firms spend millions on brand promotion and awareness. Brand is equally important for new online products and services. We can see this, for example, with competing insurance and hotel aggregators vying for consumer attention and video-streaming services competing for viewers.

This is the heartland of traditional marketing. Traditionally, brand marketing was directly associated with what marketing professionals described as 'above the line' activity such as direct advertising to the consumer on television, in the cinema, in the press or on outdoor displays. Marketing communications was often referred to as promotional or sales support and was relegated to 'below the line' activity such as in-store communications, direct mail, networking events, the production of research or thought pieces, PR etc. But as consumers become less and less loyal there are now far fewer brands that can claim that their customers aren't just customers but that they are also strong advocates and, even better than that, evangelists. For every Apple, John Lewis Stores and Jaguar Cars, however, there are hundreds of laptops, retailers and cars that have to compete on criteria set by the customer in the market. This in turn means that more and more brand marketing activity has to show a short-term as well as a long-term impact. As a result, we are starting to see the beginning of a convergence between brand marketing and the shorter-term marketing communications' focus on attracting customers in the market. Therefore, 'above the line' is now as much used for 'buy now' as it is for 'buy for ever'; and 'below the line' needs to be as careful about the brand as any high-profile advertising campaigns.

In commercial terms the key difference between the two is measurability. Today, marketing communications is the more important activity of the two because, for the vast majority of brands (certainly those who aren't led by a unique design aesthetic, have a highly distinctive customer base or who don't own a bottomless marketing war chest), and if it is done well, it represents the opportunity to provide greater immediate measurability with the introduction of digital technology. To a considerable degree we can now measure ROI effectively. In other words, it should now be easier to identify more than ever before, the wasted 'half' of marketing spend.

How digital changed spend

When digital transformed marketing it was immediately the traditional marketing executions – TV, radio, print and direct mail – that came under scrutiny. Initially the biggest driver was cost and it is hard to argue against fulfilment measured in pounds, dollars or euros for traditional executions such as direct printed mail through the post, against a matter of a few pence for a mass e-mail campaign, for example. As customers have moved online en masse so the transfer of resources to digital channels has been fuelled by both their cost-effectiveness and wider audience reach. They are also extremely versatile, offering video advertising, advertising on social networks, mobile advertising, e-mail advertising, banner advertising, Google Search advertising and more. For marketing professionals, the key benefits of digital are perceived as:

- **Cost:** it is much more affordable than traditional advertising.
- **Wider geographical reach:** an online campaign can reach a much wider audience and this can be increasingly targeted by geography and demographic.
- **A different payment mechanic:** this is perhaps the unique appeal of online advertising. Whereas in traditional advertising you pay the full amount of money upfront, regardless of response, in online

advertising you have to pay only for the qualified clicks, leads or impressions that it generates. A 'click' however does not necessarily translate into a sale.

- **Measure and learn:** it's easy to measure online advertising results right through to sale, which helps you know what to do and what to avoid in your subsequent campaigns.

Given these widely accepted benefits, it is no surprise to see the continued growth of online marketing spend as a percentage of the total. Data from the Publicis Group[14] published in 2013 looked at reported spend globally in 2012 and forecasts for 2015. Figure 4.2 summarizes their data.

The report suggested that mobile advertising was growing seven times faster than desktop with mobile ads increasing by 77 per cent in 2013, 56 per cent in 2014 and 48 per cent in 2015. However, some care needs to be taken about the definition of mobile as it includes tablets as well as smartphones. In our experience of looking at e-commerce performance, desktops and tablets perform very similarly and whilst it is true that a tablet is 'mobile', so is a laptop. It is a very different experience from a smartphone and their e-commerce functions to date look rather different with browsing being far more associated with smartphones, and transactions still taking place more often on tablets, laptops or desktops.[15]

The data, however, also makes some interesting points about spend on print and other traditional outlets for advertising investment. If the numbers are correct for 2012, the combined spend for newspapers and magazines was greater than that for digital. Television advertising is still by far the largest

FIGURE 4.2 Share of global advertising spend 2012–2015

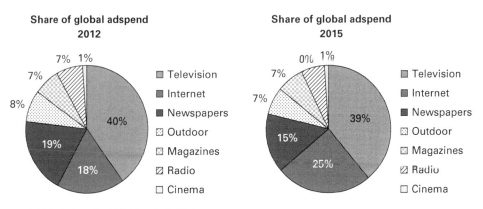

SOURCE: Data from ZenithOptimedia/Publicis

recipient of advertising dollars: 40 per cent in 2012, and declining only by 0.5 percentage points by 2015.

The UK's Advertising Association report for the same period[16] also flags a similar shape of investment but they report slightly differently, looking to attribute to traditional television and print organizations the value of the spend through their digital channels rather than attributing it to 'internet'. As a result they tell a rather different story with a suggestion that traditional channels are reinventing themselves in the face of changes driven by technology and that these are attracting nearly 20 per cent of the reported internet spend.

Whilst advertising agencies are talking about new types of 'relationships' and trying new and interesting digital tactics, the fact remains that the traditional paper-through-letterbox approach is still where over £2 billion is spent: it is the third largest area of spend according to UK statistics.[17] There is a good reason for this: targeted communications, that are well executed with clear content and a clear and compelling call to action, work. So engagement and relevance are two key measures that any marketing professionals must have at the forefront of their minds when they focus their efforts online.

Effective digital marketing businesses have learned that whilst you can produce and transmit significantly more online than via traditional channels, you cannot do so at the expense of quality. Targeting, segmenting and developing a reason to contact are as important as ever and perhaps more so, as competitive propositions that could not afford to compete with established players in the traditional channels can do so online. Persuasive copy and applying the principle of 'test and learn' are essential weapons in creating a compelling online campaign.

The key question that businesses need to ask themselves – whatever channel they are operating in – is this: are you confident that you are doing enough to persuade people to buy from you?

Why Google is the online high street

For the vast majority of products and services, online has created a virtual high street where you can buy what you are looking for from any number of vendors. Today's customer is supremely well equipped to be able to take advantage of this. This has presented businesses with the major challenge of today: how do you stand out in the Google high street?

We have chosen to use the phrase 'Google high street' as we believe from our time working in e-commerce that today and for the foreseeable future,

FIGURE 4.3   UK search engine market share: The dominance of Google (June 2014)

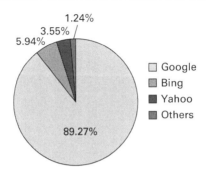

SOURCE: Seomoz.org

because search engines act as the gateway for customer access to the market-place, Google is essentially the internet for customers. Early internet pioneers waxed lyrical about a 'level playing field' and developed the appealing story about retail 'Davids' being able to compete against – and beat – their respective 'Goliaths'. In reality, this internet utopia existed briefly and only for a very few quick, agile and highly responsive companies. Figure 4.3 shows the UK market shares of the respective search engines as at June 2014.[18]

So Google, and the analytics ecosystem that sits around it, is the key to understanding how effectively your website is competing in the marketplace for which it is the only major access point. What follows is a brief guide to the Google Analytics ecosystem and the key terms and definitions you need to know as far as digital marketing is concerned.

Traffic

The traffic on your website is vital in understanding where your audience is being directed from, and knowing what traffic sources work well. Within Google Analytics traffic sources are reported in five areas:

- **All traffic:** this is the summary level and will give you a picture of the type of traffic, the number of sessions in a defined time period, the average length of time each visit took, how many visits were from devices that hadn't visited before (or had cleared all their cookies which according to research is 3 out 10 people[19]). It will also report on the number of visits that arrived on the site and immediately exited (the bounce rate).

- **Direct:** this is usually when someone will type in your URL directly, for example **www.yourcompany.com**. These visits can be analysed in exactly the same way as above but more importantly it can tell you the direct URL that someone has typed or that someone has sent the visitor a link to. This is useful as it will show you the most popular web pages. It will also show you where consumers are bookmarking pages and returning later.

- **Referrals:** these visits come from other websites that have referred the customer to your business. Depending on your business, your top referral sites will differ. For example, in a publisher client it was Twitter whilst in a UK motor retailer it was *Auto Trader,* the leading publisher on- and offline of second-hand car sales advertisements. Referrals can be a good source of business, depending on the quality and relevance of the referring site. Things to look out for here are the most popular sources of referrals to your site and tracking them through to see if these visits end up becoming a lead or a sale.

- **Search:** segments the section of your traffic that searched for you rather than directly typed in your website address into their browser. In search they come in two ways: organically, and when people click through on a paid advertisement (called pay per click). In organic search your interest is whether people are searching for you directly by name or whether certain keywords or phrases are generating a response; and in pay per click you are interested in what words and which campaigns are working and which need further thought.

- **Campaigns:** online campaigns like direct e-mails, advertisements on other websites and paid advertisements can include a tracking code that allows Google Analytics to record the traffic that they generate onto your site. Things to understand here are which campaigns receive the most traffic and – more importantly – converted at the highest rate. This is a useful tool to understand just how effective your investments are as you can track these right the way through to an end goal of sale or lead.

There are many ways to monitor traffic on your website. The most important thing is to pay attention to all sources of traffic and think about what you can be doing better to increase numbers both in terms of visits, users and conversions. Using the acquisitions section in Google Analytics, you can produce a summary report showing acquisition, behaviour and conversion (ABC). These ABC reports were introduced in 2013 as a way to summarize the important data about how users reached the website, how they behave on it and where the conversions to sale or lead came from.

Google Analytics has a range of sophisticated reporting capabilities and your e-commerce team should have an expert analyst who is able to conduct the analysis; but also equally importantly communicate the commercially important information in a way that engages both digital marketing professionals and business leaders and empowers them to take decisions about where to invest and how to grow the business. In Chapters 5 and 6 we share some of the reporting models we think are particularly effective.

The online brand

Consider the online challenges for large retail organizations today with both multiple retail outlets as well as online fulfilment. Professional services firms have multiple teams of differing expertise, all of whom will want their content promoted and linked through to sales. Regardless of sector, if you are of a reasonable size you will have a number of interested stakeholders and as a result the website may have to fulfil several key functions including, but not limited, to:

- selling;
- branch finder;
- corporate social responsibility;
- careers;
- returning customers;
- customer service follow-up;
- company information;
- order tracking;
- statutory information;
- legal information;
- ancillary services (eg insurance/financial services).

In addition to many of these content areas, there is also significant pressure for the online brand to reflect the look and feel of the brand as it exists in physical environments. Thus colours, logos, fonts, imagery and layouts tend to reflect how the brand appears visually in its other manifestations.

Given the twin pressures of both content and brand enforcement, it is perhaps no surprise that websites frequently fail to operate as effectively in commercial terms as they should. Even today, there is often a leadership failure to understand that online is likely to be the single biggest point of engagement with customers in the marketplace and that regardless of any other priority, the customer and their requirements will have to come first.

Over the last few years there have been changes in the e-commerce environment, as brand teams have acted in response to the 'convergence' movement. Increasingly, brand teams are looking to communicate the brand experience through the website. This isn't necessarily a bad thing, so long as it is informed by the customer in the marketplace and not by your latest branding agency. The latter approach has produced a plethora of websites that have been developed, often at huge cost, to reflect the brand aesthetic. In our experience the impact on sales has more often been negative than positive. Indeed measuring how effective the site is in terms of selling, or of converting customers once they have entered sales funnels, seems all too often to be a secondary consideration.

Yet, if improving the commercial performance of a website is an imperative, today's technology offers a range of easy-to-deploy tools to achieve this at low cost. However, it probably also means breaking current brand guidelines to do so. The online world has taught us that you can measure and quickly test different hypotheses against your existing online sales execution to develop more effective propositions both visually and in terms of how effective your sales messaging is.

In pure design terms, testing has demonstrated that just changing the prompt colour of a call-to-action button can significantly impact sales. This also applies to copy, where changing just one or two key words can have a positive sales impact.

This is not a call for the end of branding guidelines, far from it. We agree wholeheartedly that the brand needs to be consistent in its experience and presentation right across every channel through which customers in the market might engage with it. What we suggest is that these guidelines need to be developed with the involvement of and insight from the people who understand how best to engage customers in the market. This will give you brand guidelines that are flexible and have the ability to work for the business in every context.

Content is king

Just as digital engagement demands a different and specific approach to design and web-page presentation, so digital has also created a huge opportunity for professional, well-written and targeted copy. The key opportunity is to be able to develop and test copy quickly for its effectiveness in moving the customer forward in funnels and ultimately sell to them. Effective website content not only attracts users, but also keeps them there longer and persuades them to take action.

One of the fundamental principles of writing good web copy is to ensure that you implement a rigorous test-and-learn process. It is no longer sufficient to view online as simply a digital representation of a brochure. Websites are interactive and highly measurable – which means you can see what customers are responding to and you can gain an in-depth understanding of what makes your products or services stand out in the marketplace.

Thus, research and preparation are intrinsic elements of effective copy writing. The digital arena affords the opportunity to gain insight from customers like no other environment. Moreover, it is important not to make a distinction between consumers who choose to transact with you and those that do not. In today's world, data about why people don't transact with you is just as valuable as data from those that do. In Chapter 5 we will show you how this gets done.

One of the most important sources of input into effective copy is an understanding of why customers do not transact. This is essential knowledge in terms of building a proposition and making it more appropriate and attractive to a wider audience. Armed with the knowledge of what customers in the market actually want, you can begin to construct copy that meets their specific needs. This approach can be taken further by soliciting customer questions and answering them satisfactorily. This is an invaluable opportunity to engage with and spotlight your customers – and to educate them about your offer.

Additional powerful copy tools include third-party endorsement. One such example is validation from an independent external body or authoritative independent source. Consumer magazines such as *Which?* in the UK are recognized for the value their recommendations can bring. Media reviews or articles in business papers such as the *Wall Street Journal* or the *Financial Times* bring credibility in B2B sales environments. Your own customer reviews are also particularly important and greatly influence the purchase decision. Website owners should pay particular attention to building this functionality, including sending out e-mails to request feedback once a product has been delivered or a service consumed. In professional services, case studies endorsed by the client are invaluable sources of reassurance and help encourage prospective leads to reach out and register interest.

In deciding how to construct copy for the web, research and information gathering is the most logical starting point. One resource that companies frequently overlook is their own best sales performers. In developing a pro-position online, it is essential to understand how sales are made – and objections overcome – in face-to-face interactions or by skilled telephone salespeople.

Copy needs to be high quality and useful. It should also be tested extensively amongst the relevant team before being deployed. We would go further and recommend that the transaction is actually completed online – so website owners have a clear understanding of the journey they are asking would-be customers to complete. This process in itself will highlight usability issues and you will be able to determine if the process is as streamlined as you think you designed it to be.

One of the key copy rules you will often hear is 'keep it brief'. As we lead increasingly frenetic lives, the default assumption for customer engagement is that you are now dealing with swathes of the population with limited attention spans who are, as a result, only able to absorb short content.

In the online world, this simply is not true. It is important, however, to break up copy with bullet points, subheads and graphics to help the reader. We know that longer sales pages can be extremely effective in improving conversion, providing the content is signposted and relevant. If you are asking a customer to make a significant commitment to a product or service, the chances are that a large number will want to know about it in some detail – so don't be afraid to be detailed. You also need to think about copy as a dynamic element of the site, changing and evolving as you learn more about your customers. This gives you the insight to update content regularly, which is also a necessity as adding new content on a consistent basis helps your site rank higher in search engines, attracting more users.

Calls to action are key elements of copy. These are the buttons on all sites that invite the customer to transact with you. They should appear on every page of your website – and where you have pages that run long, they should be repeated so that a prompt always exists for the user wherever they are on the page. You should not be afraid to experiment with these either. For the customers in your market, there will be a word or phrase, a timing and a presentation that will be more effective in getting them to transact than any other.

If budget allows, video is a useful addition to your site. Research indicates that shoppers are 64 per cent more likely to buy a product on an online retail site after watching a video.[20] It also helps your site rank higher in search engine results simply because there is currently less competition for video rankings.

We will cover social media later in this chapter, but customers should be encouraged to share both their own and your content on social media as this can drive additional awareness of your website.

Keywords

This is only a short summary of what is available online on effective search engine optimization and the role the right copy plays in getting your product or service noticed by customers who are genuinely interested in transacting. At the heart of successful search outcomes is getting the right keywords or phrases in your copy so that search engine algorithms 'pick these up' as relevant to the customer's enquiry. Figure 4.4 comes from Seomoz.org,[21] one of the industry leaders in search engine optimization. It describes the shape of the keyword market in terms of the number of words used and the number of monthly searches made for those words.

Seomoz.org produces an excellent beginner's guide to search engine optimization which we recommend reading.[22] It offers this set of actions to e-commerce teams:

- **Make a list**: of words that you think are relevant and that will bring value to your business. If you think they reflect what you sell and

FIGURE 4.4   The search demand curve

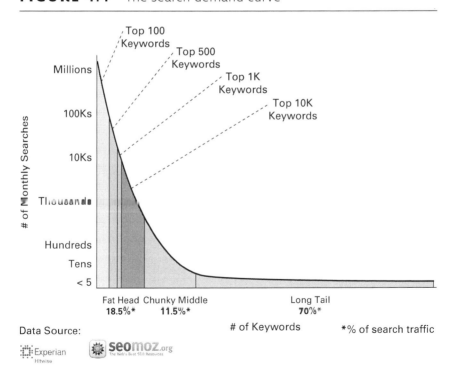

SOURCE: © SEOmoz, Inc. 2009

that people using those words will want what you offer if they arrive on your site then this is the right place to start.

- **Search for the term/phrase in the major engines:** understanding which websites already rank for your keyword gives you valuable insight into the competition, and also how hard it will be to rank for the given term. If there are many search advertisements this means a high-value keyword, and multiple advertisements above the organic results often mean a highly lucrative and effective keyword.

- **Buy a sample campaign for the keyword at Google AdWords:** if your website doesn't appear in a search result for the keyword, you can buy 'test' traffic to see how well it converts. In Google AdWords you can choose 'exact match' (in local monthly searches) and point the traffic to the relevant page on your website. Track impressions and conversion rate over the course of at least 200–300 clicks. This will cost you, but it will show you quickly if it is worth the investment.

- **Using the data you've collected, determine the exact value of each keyword:** Seomoz.org offer this example:

  if your search ad generated 5,000 impressions, of which 100 visitors have come to your site and three have converted for total profit (not revenue!) of $300, then a single visitor for that keyword is worth $3 to your business. Those 5,000 impressions in 24 hours could generate a click-through rate of 18–36 per cent with a no 1 ranking, which would mean 900–1,800 visits per day, at $3 each, or between 1–2 million dollars per year. No wonder businesses love search marketing!

One final point on keywords: do not ignore the value of the terms in the long tail. In reality, the most popular search terms form less than 30 per cent of the searches performed on the web. The remaining 70 per cent form part of what is called the 'long tail' of search. The long tail contains hundreds of millions of unique searches that might be conducted a few times per day, but they still comprise the majority of the words put into search engines. These long-tail keywords often convert better, because they catch people later in their decision to buy. A great example from our own experience was in fine wine retailing where people searching for 'red wine' were more often than not browsing and potentially found a fine wine proposition rather daunting – even if it offered great value quality wine. On the other hand people who searched for 'best offer for a case of Chateau Mouton Rothschild 1982' had their Visa card out and, if presented with the product, bought it.

E-mail marketing

There are an estimated 144 billion e-mails sent each day.[23] Against such a volume, there is a clear challenge to ensure that when you embark on a campaign, you take every care to ensure that you're not lost amongst the significant noise. E-mail marketing can be invaluable, helping you to build and maintain good relationships with prospective customers, existing clients and referrers. For niche products it is particularly effective. Yet, e-mail marketing is not a standalone activity. It should be one element of a joined-up marketing approach.

Successful e-mail campaigns demand extensive research and preparation. This starts with building and maintaining a list, which should be both well targeted and qualified. It is essential that the system you use to send e-mail campaigns provides you with detailed information showing how many e-mails have been sent – and which have been caught in spam filters. You should also be able to determine which parts of the e-mail have been read and which links have been clicked. This is an invaluable source of information to inform future campaign activity, plus you can benchmark your results against known industry standards, particularly with regard to click-through rates. A 2014 report[24] on e-mail marketing effectiveness suggested that, whilst the mean rate was 3–3.5 per cent, the median was more likely to be in the 0.7–1.9 per cent range depending on geography (eg, if Canada were excluded this would narrow to 1.3–1.9 per cent). Sectors varied in customer willingness to respond to a much greater degree, with real estate communications showing a median of 2.8 per cent, beating even non-profit campaigns whilst campaigns from financial services and consumer products languished at the bottom with 1.3 per cent and 0.9 per cent respectively.

Segmentation and purpose are two key requirements in e-mail campaign fulfilment: the more specific an audience, the better its chance of success. If you want to find new customers, get additional business from existing customers or build relationships with clients and prospects, you are unlikely to be able to do so with the same e-mail.

Spam filters are constantly being updated and, as a result, there are many words or phrases that you should avoid. These include 'free', 'opportunity', 'click here', 'call now', 'win prizes' and 'special promotion'. If you think about your own reactions to these words as you read them it should reinforce the importance that content is king and that well-thought-out content, allied to a genuinely good reason to contact, is likely to generate better results.

One of the perceived benefits of e-mail – apart from its extremely low cost – is that it allows personalization. This is undoubtedly true, but personalization is definitely not about putting someone's name in the communication. It goes much deeper than that and successful e-mail campaigns need to be personalized by more than using a recipient's name. Sending an e-mail that acknowledges a subscriber's individuality through their purchase history, demographic or interests is a very powerful technique. It uses personalization in a meaningful way by sending something that is specific to a recipient's needs or their interests.

The theme of test and learn, a thread which runs through this book, is fundamental to e-mail marketing. With a range of data to examine, it is possible to determine what works and what does not, and to feed this back into your planning and execution. Testing will help identify the best subject lines and the best times at which to send your e-mails.

Social media: Role, opportunities and pitfalls

A real phenomenon of the digital age has been the explosion of social media and with it a rush for businesses to get involved. Without doubt, businesses see enormous potential in social media, but it is imperative that these media are used in the correct way to support business objectives, rather than wasting time and resources to no end. There has been an all too common tendency to want to be involved because 'everyone else is', rather than concentrating on planning and developing a strategy that is going to achieve desired results.

Brand building

Big brands have been incredibly successful in establishing a social media presence and the key point about social media is in the title. 'Social' means informal and fun, and is usually geared towards a consumer's entertainment and amusement. As a form of interaction, the leading social media sites such as Twitter, Facebook and YouTube are arguably subversive in their nature. They offer light relief and the most successful 'shares' on these platforms are humorous.

If you are the custodian of a brand and your company has spent years building up a serious and professional image based on a set of core values that have been painstakingly and clearly communicated, you will appreciate that a reputation can quickly be damaged in this environment. It is also important to understand that social media marketing takes dedication, time and resources.

One of the key drivers for big companies to engage on social media was – and still is – reputation management. Undoubtedly, this is an important function and provides a useful mouthpiece, particularly when a company has to manage an issue, such as a product recall or a supply chain crisis. A well-thought-through strategy can show that you are responding immediately to any potential problems and that you are doing something about it. Yet, there are inherent dangers with this.

Here is one example: at the height of a Europe-wide scandal where retailers were caught inadvertently selling horse meat labelled as beef, UK supermarket Tesco was duped into answering a question about where it sold 'Red Rum' (a play on a type of alcoholic drink and the name of a famous racehorse) on its official Twitter feed. This suggests that there has to be careful screening of all responses and emphasizes the fact that the majority of people see Twitter as a medium for fun and entertainment. It is not a primary place to sell insurance or financial services.

The leading social media brands are companies like Samsung (18 million followers across multiple platforms and 86 million views on YouTube), Walt Disney, National Geographic, Nike, Coca-Cola and MTV.[25] These are powerful brands with a strong youth offer.

Relationship building

We have discussed the importance of content elsewhere in this chapter and this is also true of social media. Consumers do not appreciate being constantly bombarded with marketing content in a space they think of as 'theirs'; yet when you look at many businesses' use of these channels, this is exactly what you find.

Think about the kind of people you are trying to reach and what interests them. Will they be more interested in visual content? News articles? Fun facts? Ensure that you get the balance right between content that talks about your proposition and content that engages on a much broader basis. It is the latter that works well in social media. In our view, social media marketing falls into 'brand marketing'. It is not an activity that will yield instant results. It is a slow process of building presence, reputation and relationships. Businesses need to understand both the timescales and resources required to make it work successfully.

Like other forms of communication, there is no one size-fits-all solution, but there are two basic questions that companies need to ask themselves about creating relevant and engaging strategies:

- **Who am I trying to reach?** Whilst this may sound obvious, too many businesses currently launch into social media without thinking about what they want to get out of it. This rarely yields results. Companies need to think about what they are trying to achieve, and work out their strategy from there. A key part of this is understanding the audience. Are you a business-to-business brand trying to reach high-level decision makers, or are you a consumer brand whose main customers will be mothers? Do you have secondary audiences such as regulators, journalists or opinion formers? It is essential to establish who your primary and secondary audiences are.

- **What channel should I use?** Businesses must think carefully about the channels that are most appropriate for their key audiences. If you're a B2B brand, for instance, you may find that you have limited success using Facebook. Equally, if teenagers are your target audience, LinkedIn is not the most appropriate channel. So often when considering social media, marketeers just assume that they need to be on Facebook, LinkedIn and Twitter; even though these are the most common channels, they may not be the most relevant. Working with a global supplier to the hair and beauty trade we discovered the value of Pinterest to this sector. Also, remember that if you have niche audiences, other appropriate platforms may prove more fruitful.

One of the challenges facing businesses is that social media is constantly shifting. Facebook is now seen as mainstream, with around half the UK population having an account.[26] As a result, it doesn't have as much traction with the younger generation. One report in 2014 suggested that Facebook had lost 11 million of its younger users over the previous three years.[27] Another has highlighted the transition many younger people are making towards WhatsApp and other messaging apps and their development into wider social networking platforms.[28] Businesses looking to target very young or fashion-conscious individuals may well be needing to look elsewhere in time – though there is a long way to go until any of these new entrants can rival Facebook's scale or revenues.

Who are the other players?

Facebook and Twitter have been the stand-out commercial channels in social media. The following is a rundown of the other main and emerging players in 2014.

LinkedIn

LinkedIn, which passed the 300 million member mark early in 2014,[29] is much more of a 'business' environment and can play a significant role in recruitment and building a strong company reputation. LinkedIn has reduced the minimum age limit for its accounts to 13, and is providing enhanced functionality, including Alumni search, to woo higher education establishments into spending more time on the site. Presumably the hope is that with an early introduction to LinkedIn, young professionals will accept it as the 'de facto' place for networking and business knowledge online.

Pinterest

Pinterest is a site that describes itself as 'a visual discovery tool'. People use it to collect ideas for projects and interests. They create and share collections (called 'boards') of visual bookmarks (called 'pins') that they then employ to do things like plan trips, develop projects, organize events or save articles and information. A site with a majority of women in its 70 million reported users, it is still heavily focussed on the United States, although it is building a more international base.[30] A 2012 study suggested that it was a far more effective commercial conduit than Facebook for businesses interested in selling to its demographic with 69 per cent of its users saying they had bought something as a result of their engagement on Pinterest compared to only 40 per cent of Facebook users.[31]

Instagram

Instagram is a photo- and video-sharing site that allows people to take and upload instant records of what they are doing and then share them with both fellow users and throughout their other social networks. The tools on Instagram enable smartphone-generated content to be edited and improved. In September 2013 it reached 150 million members and businesses already use it, by asking users to upload and contribute to their pages and get involved with competitions and other brand building activities. A 2013 announcement from the company, owned by Facebook since 2012, held out the prospects of advertising within the next 12 months.[32]

Snapchat

Forbes magazine reports that Snapchat represents the greatest threat yet to Facebook.[33] Created as a result of the mistakes of the first generation to adopt Facebook, it appeals to today's younger generation who have learned the lesson that what you post on social media – the good, the bad, the inappropriate – stays there forever. It is a photo- and video-sharing site, the difference with Facebook being that once a photograph has been seen by recipients it is deleted within a time limit set by the user. It is estimated that 50 million people currently use Snapchat. 'Snapchat Stories' offer 10-second opportunities already exploited by some brands keen to connect with its younger demographic.

WhatsApp

WhatsApp is a cross-platform mobile messenger that works on any smartphone using 3G or wi-fi connectivity. Recently bought by Facebook for $19 billion,[34] it is reported to have 500 million users.[35] It does not offer advertising opportunities.

Social media is another area where time will drive significant change and we will continue to keep this list up to date on the book's website (**www.goodgrowth.co.uk/digitalstrategy**).

What is success?

In order to establish whether your new social media strategy is successful, it is important to define what success looks like. It is often helpful to look beyond statistics such as follower and fan numbers, to more sophisticated metrics like engagement. Many social media channels have in-built methods to help with this evaluation, but also consider online tools such as Bitly (**http://bitly.com**) which can track how many people click on your links, and Google Analytics, which can track where traffic to your website is coming from.

The key point that businesses need to bear in mind in dealing with social media is this: if your proposition is right, people will tell their friends and associate with it. It is therefore of paramount importance that you concentrate on getting the proposition right and then people will affiliate. People are naturally suspicious of centrally generated marketing messages and these will undoubtedly turn potential customers off.

Getting the proposition right, selling it right and fulfilling the customer's expectations will drive far more positive and effective social media traffic than anything any centrally driven strategy can ever do.

The leadership agenda

Part Four: The marketing framework

This chapter has focussed on the constantly evolving challenges facing marketing professionals as businesses have dedicated ever-increasing resources to the digital channel. It underlines the importance of understanding what makes your offer unique and the virtues of articulating these clearly and accurately. It stresses the opportunity afforded by the digital channel in particular to be able to test, learn and develop your marketing activities so that they have the greatest resonance with customers who do and do not buy from you. It stresses the importance, in today's digital world, of understanding the role of copy and content in attracting customers initially and in taking them through to sale. It also reflects on the importance of understanding your sources of traffic, how to ensure your e-mail strategy is effective and how to evaluate and engage in social media.

Killer questions

These are aimed at giving you a clear overview of your marketing spend and ensuring that there are processes in place to ensure campaign measurement and a culture of continuous improvement:

- Is there a clear and shared understanding of your core proposition? If so where is it articulated?

- What are your clearly defined USPs and do you have insight into your strengths and weaknesses both against your key competitors and in terms of how your customers and customers in the market perceive you?

- Is there a clear understanding of the difference between marketing communications and brand marketing?

- Are you able to see, on a monthly basis, expenditure on marketing communications campaigns with specific results and outputs?

- Is there a culture of 'test and learn' associated with marketing communications embedded within your digital channel so that your outputs in this area focus on continuous improvement?

- Do you have an understanding of traffic, such that you know where both customers in the market and your customers (ie those who ultimately transact with you) are coming from?

- How much is your website brand experience informed and developed by the customer in the market?

- If you are engaged in social media, is there a clear strategy underpinning your activities, and what are your measures of success? How do these relate to commercial performance?

Leadership action

Your answers to these questions will highlight your priority areas in terms of marketing and inform your strategy going forward. Key actions you should consider are:

- Ensure that your online execution is led by your customers in the market, not dictated by brand guidelines.

- Review your brand guidelines for flexibility and responsiveness.

- Make sure you have clear and regular visibility in terms of marketing communications spend and ROI.

- Assess whether your proposition is clearly articulated and that it is informed by insight both from customers and from your own best sales resources.

- Ensure that a 'test-and-learn' mindset underpins your marketing communications and that the business has processes in place to drive performance improvement.

Notes

1 http://www.internetworldstats.com/emarketing.htm/ [accessed 19 August 2014]

2 http://www.internetworldstats.com/stats.htm/ [accessed 19 August 2014]

3 http://www.statista.com/statistics/234884/us-online-shopper-conversion-rate-by-device/ [accessed 11 August 2014]

4 https://econsultancy.com/blog/9366-ecommerce-consumer-reviews-why-you-need-them-and-how-to-use-them[#]i.1vo3vppgakcr7s/ [accessed 19 August 2014]

5 http://www.marketingprofs.com/charts/2013/12195/online-shopping-trends-most-popular-categories-top-purchase-drivers [accessed 14 August 2014]

6 http://www.oracle.com/us/products/applications/cust-exp-impact-report-epss-1560493.pdf [accessed 19 August 2014]

7 http://www.bbc.co.uk/news/technology-28692871 [accessed 15 August 2014]

8   http://www.slideshare.net/Posterscope/guide-to-convergent-outofhome/ [accessed 19 August 2014]

9   http://www.slideshare.net/Posterscope/guide-to-convergent-outofhome/ [accessed 19 August 2014]

10   http://mobilemarketingmagazine.com/7-10-people-uk-now-own-smartphone/ [accessed 19 August 2014]

11   The Marketing Society, www.marketingsociety.com [accessed 19 August 2014]

12   Adcock, D, Halborg, A and Ross, C (1993) *Marketing: Principles and practice*, Pearson, UK

13   Meek, R, Meek, HD, Palmer, R and Parkinson, LK (2008) *Managing Marketing Performance*, Butterworth-Heinemann, UK

14   http://techcrunch.com/2013/09/30/digital-ads-will-be-22-of-all-u-s-ad-spend-in-2013-mobile-ads-3-7-total-gobal-ad-spend-in-2013-503b-says-zenithoptimedia/ [accessed 15 August 2014]

15   See for example the US statistics in: http://www.statista.com/statistics/234884/us-online-shopper-conversion-rate-by-device/ [accessed 11 August 2014]

16   http://www.newsworks.org.uk/News-and-Opinion/aa-warc/49897 [accessed 15 August 2014]

17   http://www.dma.org.uk/uploads/putting-price-direct-marketing_53fdbe53b4863.pdf [accessed 15 August 2014]

18   http://theeword.co.uk/info/search_engine_market.html/ [accessed 19 August 2014]

19   http://digiday.com/publishers/13-alarming-stats-about-cookies/ [accessed 15 August 2014]

20   http://www.videobrewery.com/blog/18-video-marketing-statistics/ [accessed 19 August 2014]

21   http://d1avok0lzls2w.cloudfront.net/img_uploads/search-demand-curve per cent281 per cent29.gif [accessed 15 August 2014]

22   http://moz.com/beginners-guide-to-seo/keyword-research [accessed 15 August 2014]

23   http://www.radicati.com/wp/wp-content/uploads/2012/10/Email-Market-2012-2016-Executive-Summary.pdf/ [accessed 19 August 2014]

24   http://www.silverpop.com/Documents/Whitepapers/2014/Email-Marketing-Metrics-Benchmark-Study-2014-Silverpop.pdf?spMailingID=8938339&spUserID=NTIzNzgyNDI1NDIS1&spJobID=340402407&spReportId=MzQwMzU0MDAxS0/ [accessed 19 August 2014]

25   http://mashable.com/2013/12/22/top-10-social-media-brands-2013/ [accessed 19 August 2014]

26   http://www.telegraph.co.uk/technology/facebook/8356755/Facebook-used-by-half-the-UK-population.html/ [accessed 19 August 2014]

27 http://business.time.com/2014/01/15/more-than-11-million-young-people-have-fled-facebook-since-2011/ [accessed 15 August 2014]

28 http://www.theguardian.com/technology/2013/nov/10/teenagers-messenger-apps-facebook-exodus [accessed 15 August 2014]

29 http://blog.linkedin.com/2014/04/18/the-next-three-billion/ [accessed 15 August 2014]

30 http://thenextweb.com/socialmedia/2013/07/10/semiocast-pinterest-now-has-70-million-users-and-is-steadily-gaining-momentum-outside-the-us/ [accessed 15 August 2014]

31 http://www.bizrateinsights.com/blog/2012/10/15/online-consumer-pulse-pinterest-vs-facebook-which-social-sharing-site-wins-at-shopping-engagement/ [accessed 15 August 2014]

32 http://techcrunch.com/2013/09/08/topping-150m-users-instagram-promises-ads-within-the-next-year/ [accessed 15 August 2014]

33 http://www.forbes.com/sites/jjcolao/2014/01/06/the-inside-story-of-snapchat-the-worlds-hottest-app-or-a-3-billion-disappearing-act/ [accessed 15 August 2014]

34 http://online.wsj.com/news/articles/SB10001424052702304914204579393452029288302 [accessed 15 August 2014]

35 http://www.forbes.com/sites/amitchowdhry/2014/04/22/whatsapp-hits-500-million-users/ [accessed 15 August 2014]

The business of e-commerce

5

EXECUTIVE SUMMARY

This chapter looks at what an e-commerce team should be doing and how they can get the best outcome. It explores the three core work streams for which an effective e-commerce team will be responsible: acquisition, conversion and fulfilment. It explains why a relentless and shared focus on customer conversion is critical to commercial performance and how this is achieved through an iterative process of changes to the funnel. These changes are tested through exposing them to customers 'in the market' from where they start to research and engage with your proposition to the point where they ultimately decide whether or not to choose your proposition over those of your competitors.

It argues that a successful e-commerce team should have the power to rapidly execute commercial improvements to the funnel, but only based on tested and proven changes that improve the execution. Whilst its commercial success should be measured in sales, its operational success can be measured by its ability to make changes to its website that are proven to increase revenue.

So what does an e-commerce team do?

The e-commerce team role is to optimize the digital channel such that the maximum number of customers in the market is attracted to your website; and of those, the maximum number complete the transaction that you are offering to them. Optimization requires the team to create and deliver the most effective traffic strategies, online advertising campaigns, product communications, customer engagement, sales execution, service execution and proposition fulfilment. We talk about a team, since any e-commerce operation, unless it is very small, will require a range of resources, technical and commercial, to ensure it is effective. Smaller organizations might create this team from external support rather than internal resources and only have a single e-commerce manager.

Commercial imperative

We will explore the details of measurement in Chapter 6 but from the outset it is critical that your e-commerce team needs to have a central commercial objective for which it is accountable. As with any other channel, it cannot be held to account for things it cannot control, but it also should not be allowed to establish governing measures of success that are technical, or peripheral, as opposed to commercial.

Whilst a digital channel can measure a range of points of engagement for customers such as Facebook 'likes' and Twitter 'followers', the channel should be held accountable to the same profit and loss criteria as any other. To do so, the commercial goals of the channel must be clearly identified and communicated by the e-commerce team to deliver one (or more) of the following objectives:

- leads;
- sales;
- service.

We have two principles on which we base e-commerce measurement procedures, and which we recommend you follow. The first is to ensure as well as you can that you are measuring the commercial outcome. A tweet, like or share is not a commercial outcome – it can lead to one, but it should not be taken or accepted as a proxy for one. A lead, on the other hand, is a commercial outcome because you will have tracking for the conversion of leads to sales that you can apply as a proxy for a commercial impact when measuring e-commerce effectiveness.

The second principle is that, as far as you can, you should try to measure the same commercial outcomes across all channels, so your e-commerce team should be looking at price points, purchase values, margins, cost to serve, displacement savings (eg the cost saved in call handling through a successful online self-service) and profitability after the costs of capital employed. In doing so the e-commerce leadership team can articulate the current performance relative to other channels, and the business as a whole is able to understand relative performance contribution and the value of competing investment requirements.

Whilst every business is different and will want to ensure its e-commerce operation fits into their overall measurement approach, some key measures should be consistent and this is especially important for conversion as this allows you to benchmark. However, we also think there is value to both the e-commerce team and to the business more widely of trying to measure two broad commercial outcomes: revenue per user and customer segmentation.

Revenue per user

Revenue per user (RPU – also called revenue per visitor) is increasingly being proposed as the key commercial measure that e-commerce teams should refer to in judging the optimization effectiveness of the channel, especially in retail sites where there is a relationship between the value of the products put into a basket and the likelihood that a customer will complete the purchase.[1]

As a general point, in our experience business leaders do not pay attention to the vast majority of marketing measures. They focus more on the areas of primary concern that reflect the company's ability to generate more profit and faster growth than its competitors. This focus in e-commerce is potentially best addressed through adoption of RPU as a key measure where it could become one of the financial performance metrics of your site, and one of the primary objectives in any revenue performance optimization strategy as it measures the money a website makes every time a customer enters an online store. Increasing RPU is as important a commercial goal as increasing the number of customers who purchase.

We have argued for the supremacy of conversion as the primary measure and believe that it is such because it can act as a simple measure of effectiveness and it is translatable across businesses. But conversion doesn't measure value and this is where RPU comes in. One of the main goals will be to generate more revenue on your e-commerce site and it is very logical to think that increasing the number of conversions (ie visitors who buy product on your site) will result in revenue growth.

In e-commerce, the conversion rate is the proportion of users that converted (ie made a purchase on the site, became a lead or completed any other central transaction). The commercial problem is that where the conversion is a completed sale the measures taken to increase the conversion rate can generate more transactions yet still produce lower overall revenues. This is for the reason that whilst transactions could increase, the individual value of those transactions could reduce to such an extent that overall revenues remain static or reduce. This can happen for a number of reasons but the main two are attracting customers who buy less of the product or service or who buy lower-priced products or services.

Some companies think that the key for their revenue growth is to take measures to increase the average order value. For example, that is why product recommendation solutions that suggest to customers a particular product or service are so widely used. Average order value (AOV – sometimes referred to as an average ticket) is a measure representing the value of an average order within a period of time. It is simply calculated by dividing revenue by the number of conversions in a specific period of time. However, it can also be true that there are no guarantees that an increase in AOV will translate into a proportional increase in revenue. This approach may encourage sales of higher-priced items, but the number of people who will make a purchase might go down, resulting in a decrease in overall sales.

RPU is a composite measure that combines conversion rate and AOV into a single number that represents the value of revenue per user within a period of time. It is calculated by dividing revenue by the number of users in a specific time period (normally, to smooth out anomalies, this should be at least a month):

RPU = (revenue for time period) / (users for time period)

It also represents an interaction between conversion rate and AOV and it is one of the most reliable predictors of e-commerce revenue, as you can also calculate it by multiplying the AOV in a time period by the conversion rate for the same time period:

RPU = (conversion rate for the time period expressed as a percentage of users who completed a transaction) × (AOV for the same time period)

It is therefore an early indicator of optimization impact. If the RPU trend remains consistent or increases then the activities you are undertaking on the website are having a positive impact; if it starts to decline then it's a good early warning that you will need to adjust what you are doing. The baseline calculation in online retailing sites is therefore to understand the current value of the calculation:

R (revenue) = number of conversions × AOV

We generally calculate this and other key measures on a moving monthly average basis to try and smooth out seasonal and other variables such as promotions or new product/service launches.

Customer segmentation

Once the e-commerce platform has the basics performing effectively, given the importance of securing consistent or even better RPU performance, more sophisticated e-commerce teams will work closely with finance to build a commercial model to capture the lifetime value of users who transact on the website.

Whilst important as a measure of overall trends on items such as basket value, the average customer is less interesting than the segments that make up the average. This is very different from consumer segmentation. Consumer segmentation should help you understand the market and in particular what part(s) of the market your e-commerce operation is targeting. This helps set a tone of voice, a retail engagement and shapes the copy and calls to action.

Customer segmentation looks at the part of the market that transacts with you and separates it out by size and/or frequency of purchase. Knowing what the better-than-average customer looks like (ie the customer who spends more per transaction or who repeat-purchases more often) enables better decision making on future sales and marketing strategies. As you understand this better, so you can either encourage more customers to behave like this through better proposition execution or understand where they come from so that you can find more customers like this who currently do not buy from you.

Particularly in online business models, profitable growth comes from securing as many better-than-average customers as possible. Whilst the cost of acquisition may be higher, their collective profitability is far higher. We have developed a simple model for this (Figure 5.1) that can help you think through the overall customer mix and where the greatest value is to be had in an online market.

Table 5.1 presents a worked example that will help you think through this issue for yourself. Taking all your customers and delving below the average data, look to identify clear value segments and to differentiate and discount those customers who are the least profitable.

Once segmented in this way you need to identify the costs associated with the acquisition and retention of customers in each segment. At a simple level these costs will include overheads and activities associated with all commercial activities. Over time, and with a sophisticated cost allocation method, a business could allocate all costs associated with the product or service. This, however, is complex and potentially non-value-adding. Start at least with a simple model: it should tell you much if not all of what you need to know (Table 5.2).

FIGURE 5.1   Customer segmentation model

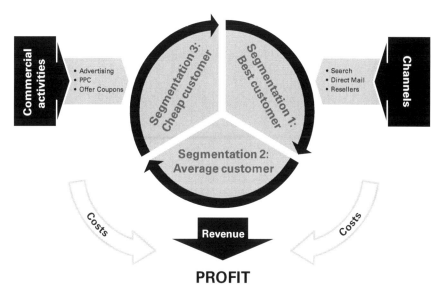

TABLE 5.1   Customer segment performance

	Best Customers	Average Customers
Purchases per year	9	6
Average order value	£45	£30
Total revenue	£405	£180
Gross profit margin	10%	10%
Gross profit	£41	£18

The key to the process, however, is that full data is not necessarily required. Work with the data available and build as comprehensive a data set as is thought sensible over time. The beauty of the model is that so long as the assumptions are applied consistently across the segments then this is sufficient.

TABLE 5.2 Customer segment costs of acquisition

	Best Customers	Average Customers
Gross profit	£41	£18
Acquisition cost	£8	£4
Net profit	£33	£14

The reason why businesses can utilize this decision-making tool effectively is not just that it provides supporting information rather than an answer, but that it presents this information in a way that can help commercial leaders see the relative profitability of each segment. Management expertise and insight combined with this support information create a dynamic discussion at the executive level and drive better-quality decision making to build profitable growth.

Ultimately, the outcome desired by the organization is that it makes resource allocation decisions that optimize profitability and cash generation. For example, if one segment is particularly significant, even if it is relatively less profitable, working to increase profitability of each transaction, even modestly, will make a significant impact on commercial performance.

Critical to subscription models or to sectors where repeat purchases drive business models (eg insurance, mobile phone operators) is the importance of factoring in the value of a repeat purchase over time versus the value of multiple single purchases. The tool offers businesses the ability to add in a 'lifetime' value. For online subscription businesses the average customer lifetime is currently estimated to be six months.[2] This value can be offset by a straightforward net present value (NPV) calculation, although for periods (such as at the time of writing) with very low rates of inflation this may not be considered necessary.

In the following example (Table 5.3) using an online subscription model the cheap customers are those taking the introductory discount offer for three months and then falling off, the average customers are those taking the full value model for six months and the best customers are not just lasting for longer than average (nine months) but are also happy to buy an additional premium service via the platform.

TABLE 5.3 Customer segment lifetime value

	Best Customers	Average Customers	Cheap Customers
Life Expectancy (Month)	9	6	3
Revenue Month 1	£45	£30	£10
Revenue Month 2	£45	£30	£10
Revenue Month 3	£45	£30	£10
Revenue Month 4	£45	£30	
Revenue Month 5	£45	£30	
Revenue Month 6	£45	£30	
Revenue Month 7	£45		
Revenue Month 8	£45		
Revenue Month 9	£45		
Lifetime Revenue	£405	£180	£30
Gross Profit Margin	10%	10%	10%
Lifetime Gross Profit Margin	£41	£18	£3
Acquisition Cost	£8	£4	£4
Lifetime Net Profit	£33	£14	−£1

There are considerable advantages of understanding the relative profitability of different customer segments. These include the ability to:

- drive more profitable customer acquisition;
- direct investment at the segments and channels where the returns are greatest;
- disproportionally reward those channel partners who provide you with your most profitable customers.

All of these benefits help build a strong advantage for the early adopters and will enable them to resist the competitive challenge of later entrants or adopters of this approach.

There are, of course, issues with any such decision support tool. They require the same granularity of data for each customer segment identified. They will require data to be sourced from web analytical tools and from ERP/financial reporting systems. There will be some spreadsheet manipulation and the business will have to allocate analytical resources to establish a credible database. The key is to focus on the collective segmentation rather than individual data. In our experience, the best way of starting out is to start small and work up when the model has sufficient validity. Your objective is to apply an 80/20 rule and we believe that for the majority of businesses this will provide better data than they have currently sourced.

Managing the sales funnel

The sales funnel online can be divided into three sections: customer attraction, customer transaction and customer satisfaction. Each part is serviced and supported by an e-commerce team through the following set of activities.

Customer attraction

As we have seen in Chapter 4, customers in the marketplace are encouraged to visit an online store by the use of advertisements across a range of outlets on- and offline. Online advertising effectiveness should be the responsibility of the e-commerce team as they are aimed at getting the customer to 'click' and visit your online store. The role of the e-commerce team is to identify the best performing advertisements. This is the first stage of optimization. For most e-commerce operations advertisements appear as a result of a specific search term being entered into a search engine (eg Google, Bing) and are presented to the customer in one of two ways: naturally, in order of attractiveness as defined by algorithms applied by each search engine; or bought, in order of the price paid and the effectiveness of the page, also defined by search engine algorithms.

Natural search performance can be maximized through search engine optimization (SEO) and paid search effectiveness can be assessed in looking at the performance of pay-per-click (PPC) advertisements in terms of their position, the click-through rate and eventual conversion effectiveness. Both of these activities are core to e-commerce effectiveness and whilst there are specialist agencies available to support your advertising strategy, setting the right framework and managing the development of the most effective approach is a task which we believe should not be outsourced unless really necessary.

The roles of traffic generation and sales effectiveness are interlinked. An e-commerce team will use the proposition as set by marketing and any commercial imperatives associated with, say, supplier-led promotions or new product launches, to define what search terms the most attractive customer segments in the market are most likely to use when they look to buy. These terms need then to populate the copy, headlines and proposition so that when the search engines present the most relevant options to customers in the marketplace using these terms, your proposition comes towards the top in natural search and, if you are paying for placement on the first page, that it is placed in the best position for the money you are prepared to invest.

The reason this is so important is because a top spot in search rankings gives you a disproportionate benefit. A summary report from 2011 suggests that if you took an average of the studies undertaken up until then the first-placed spot on Google attracts 36.4 per cent of all customers in the market.[3] These results also mirror work done by our own research and analytics team which shows that even second or third place is substantially disadvantaged in attracting customers in your particular marketplace compared to being first. In our analysis a business that comes second would get two and a half times fewer customers than the business that comes first and the business that comes third about five times fewer customers.[4]

Identifying the best keywords

Given the competitive advantage at stake, an essential component of an e-commerce team is the generation, support and maintenance of a registry detailing the keywords for which the organization wants to compete to attract attention when customers are searching online in their market. Chapter 4 has suggested one approach to establishing a keyword list and this should be done as part of the strategy development for your e-commerce operation. This is, however, not a one-off action. Keywords and keyword performance need regular review in markets that change quickly. Keep key competitors and new entrants under review and be willing to keep evolving your strategy.

Once the keywords are agreed e-commerce teams should reflect them throughout the copy on the site. Finding the best combination of keywords and phrases around which to build site copy is by definition a test-and-learn process. It requires a constant review, monitor and improve approach and regular assessment of competitors as well as your own performance. In terms of organic search, your site will only become relevant for the target audience once search engines decide that your copy is more relevant than other competing propositions. Copy is therefore one of the critical success factors in search engine optimization (SEO) for any e-commerce site; however, it is important even before this in presenting the most attractive headline and supporting copy on the advertisement itself.

Even if you are paying for traffic there is a penalty for poor copy. Google will place your ad even if it's completely irrelevant. It will cost you more because your 'quality score' will be low, for which Google then penalizes you financially. (This is informally known as the 'stupidity' tax.) Of course, if your advertisement is irrelevant to the keyword a user searches, your click-through rate and conversion rate will be poor.

It is worth remembering that there are such things as negative keywords. These are keywords you don't want your advertisements to appear for. You see this all the time when you search for something and an advertisement appears for something that is not relevant because of a semantic problem. For example, if you own a stationery business, you might want to create an advertisement group to sell notebooks. Wordstream offers a free negative keyword tool (**http://www.wordstream.com/negative-keywords**) that suggests clusters of terms that may trigger your 'notebook' ads. If you try putting 'notebook' into this tool most of the terms that appear are related to notebook computers, not spiral notebooks! You wouldn't want to bid on these computer-related terms as it would be a total waste of your advertising budget.

Developing the most effective snippets

Snippets are the advertisements that are placed in front of the customer as a result of a search enquiry. They consist of a headline (or meta-title) and a description. The art of producing a successful snippet is to communicate so complete a message that they attract more clicks than competing alternatives and so drive and then maintain themselves at the highest possible level in a search outcome. They have to do this in a very limited number of characters for a title and 140 characters for a description. This is one of the biggest copywriting challenges in online marketing communications: using these limits to create a compelling message that attracts more clicks than those of competitors.

Since Google changed their font and style of presenting search outcomes the industry standard has reduced from 70 characters for a title to more like 55.[5] The rationale for this is primarily that as other characters are rarely presented to the customer, it is a waste of effort and more than likely it will mean that what the customer is really looking for may not be on your title and therefore fail to attract their interest.

This is equally true for the descriptor that can help customers decide where to click when they are searching for a product or service rather than for a brand or business name. Often e-commerce businesses fail to meet the limit requirements and their snippets end up finishing in ellipses. Snippets that do this are said to attract fewer clicks despite their positioning as the really relevant text is hidden from view.

Presenting the most engaging site links

'Sitelinks' or 'rich snippets' are six additional pages that are presented to the customer by the business that gains top place for an organic search result. We believe that good e-commerce practice should be to select these pages for their attractiveness to customers in the market: one approach to doing this is to present the 'most landed upon in the site', another would be to present 'the most searched for propositions in the market' and a third is to present the six best landing pages in terms of sales conversion. Whatever the strategy is, the team needs to make an active decision as to the pages presented, otherwise the search engine will make the decision for you on the basis of the most visited pages.

Using Google Plus

Relatively new at the time of publishing, Google Plus is an enhanced search offer that has particular value in the SME sector. Google argues that when you create a Google Plus page, you can create new business opportunities across all of their products: from bringing you closer to the top in searches, to having a map with directions to your offices/retail sites appear when someone searches on your name.

Ensuring good site health

The e-commerce team must also take responsibility for the page performance of a website. Page performance is driven by having what we describe as a 'healthy site', which means that it is error free, accessible and has little 'technical debt' (ie few if any HTML or CSS errors), by attaching effective descriptors and 'snippets' which sell the proposition in a way that encourages click-through and by having a site well linked to other effective sites.

Maximizing the return on paid advertising

As well as determining the SEO performance of the company website(s), the team will also be responsible for executing all online advertising campaigns. Paid advertising comes in two forms: advertising that appears as a result of a customer search, normally called 'pay-per-click' (PPC) and banner adverts placed on other sites (for example, online media sites and sites with similar customers to your own target segments) which are either paid for in advance regardless of the number of transactions they generate or paid for in relation to the number of clicks they generate.

Much is made of PPC and a great deal of myth has built up around it; however, PPC execution strategies are best built around a simple model that divides investment choices into three key buckets:

- **Brand:** investing in terms that use the brand. This is normally done in markets where competition is high and as market leader other competitors are buying your brand or where aggregators are active and are using your brand to attract customers to their site as opposed to yours. In less competitive markets buying the brand is often used to highlight a promotion or special offer taking customers to a dedicated landing page. In niche markets this isn't normally an effective investment as a business can end up paying for visitors who would have clicked through on the organic search link at no cost.

- **Fat head:** investing in terms that are the most searched for in a particular product segment or proposition. This is a classic strategy, often best employed in markets that are very competitive and where similar or same products are widely available to the customer. Here the strategy is to identify a list of c 20 terms and to be able to outbid the majority of the competition sufficiently to gain a 'top three' advert placing. The better the landing pages for these adverts at converting visitors to a 'sale', the higher the bid that can be placed on the term. This strategy requires a disciplined 'test-and-learn' approach to term selection and both the advert and the conversion performance of the landing page.

- **Long tail:** investing in discrete terms that are not subject to significant search volumes but where the value in the transaction is

FIGURE 5.2   An analysis of PPC strategy effectiveness

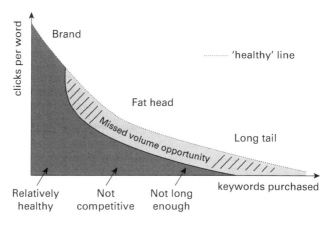

SOURCE: © Good Growth Ltd 2014

substantial as the searcher is looking for a specific product with an assumed higher propensity to buy. This strategy can be used powerfully by niche businesses that are serving a smaller, well-informed, and normally higher-value customer base. Here the approach is to buy as many terms as possible as the cost per click tends to be very small, and although the click-through rate is very low, the value created by a sale gives a powerful return.

Figure 5.2 uses the model introduced in Chapter 4 to think about the effectiveness of a campaign strategy. This is a retailer in a highly competitive market where there are a few volume products and a very long tail of niche products. Here the model would be to buy brand, buy a limited number of fat-head terms closely aligned to the key volume products and then buy a very large number of long-tail terms where specialist buyers are much more likely to choose the supplier who has the specific product they are looking for. In this example, the e-commerce team was not buying sufficient keywords to support its commercial objective.

Such a decision might reflect a lack of confidence to convert potential paying customers into sales and if there is a low conversion rate on fat-head terms in particular then consideration should be given to separate landing pages which reinforce the desirability of buying the product from you over any other competitor.

An effective e-commerce team will know the cost it is willing to pay for an advertisement to 'buy' customer interest. This should be established through demonstration of the ability of the landing page to convert the interest into cash. Once they know a page converts effectively, they can raise their bid for the keywords associated with the brand and test for the headline and descriptor that optimizes the number of customers in the market who are willing to click through to the page. They will also know over time the days and the times of day when their advertisements are most likely to be effective for the customer segments they are trying to attract. The most effective e-commerce teams are able to consistently outbid competitors and appear in the top three advertisement slots in search when they want to do so.

Testing and learning about what works in terms of attraction and conversion in your market is important and it is unlikely to be the same across sectors. In another example, with a retailer of family cars, we learned that customers are far more likely to engage with advertising that communicated a financial saving as opposed to a percentage saving. Testing is critical in this area just as much as in sales execution. Recent research published following a study by eBay in 2013[6] suggested that for big brands in particular there was little value in buying advertisements when they were confident that they would appear at or near the top in organic search rankings. The results suggested that paid advertisements were much more likely to work for people who have never thought of engaging with a proposition before. The major lesson from this and other studies is the importance of being prepared to test for impact as opposed to running complex data manipulations to try and link performance to activity. This is more than likely to end up with you conflating correlation with causation.

Finally, at some point you are likely to come across the debate about the value of first or last click in the conversion of a customer in the market into a sale or lead. First, to help understand this, here are some definitions. When analysts talk about 'first-click' and 'last-click' attribution, they are referring to which click of a keyword or text advertisement is credited for a conversion event in a search engine marketing campaign. First-click attribution means that the first click in the process should get the credit, even if a user performs additional searches and responds to adverts before they convert. Last-click attribution means that the last click or advertisement should get the credit, no matter how many other searches came before.

Early models of PPC effectiveness were only able to report against the last-clicked advertisement and credit this with a 'sale' or 'lead' even if the customer's initial interest was triggered by an earlier response to a different execution. However, with advances in web analytics software, first-click attribution is no longer out of reach. This allows us to ask the question of whether the first click or the last click is more important in a pay-per-click transaction.

Search behaviour seems to suggest that people will search for one thing, click on a few ads, refine their search using information they found on the first attempt, and continue this process until they find what they are looking for. Users may even click on several of your advertisements before they come to a decision. Each one of these clicks is important in pushing the user towards the conversion.

This is the digital marketing version of Swift's great Lilliputian debate on which end of the egg to eat from.[7] Just as in Lilliput, there's no real right answer: if you ignore first clicks, you're ignoring the broader terms that make users aware of your offerings; if you ignore the last clicks, you're omitting the valuable elements of your campaigns that close the deal.

It is much better to look at this issue in a different way, by making sure that you are using keywords that target users at every step of the buying process. Both types of click are important, so if you leave one or the other out of campaigns, you could be affecting the entire conversion process.

Maximizing the effectiveness of other traffic

Having determined its customer acquisition strategy, the team will focus on the quality and quantity of customers visiting a site. This is referred to as site traffic and ultimately it will come from a range of different sources, not solely organic search or paid advertising. Whilst organic search remains in most studies the most effective source of traffic that will convert to a sale, many e-commerce marketing teams believe that direct mail is still a powerful source of potential sales or leads. A 2012 survey of digital marketing professionals suggested that whilst 29 per cent thought their best generator of converting traffic was organic search, 25 per cent cited e-mail direct marketing.[8] Less effective were referring sites and even less so social media. Despite this, they are all part of the mix and their volume trends and conversion effectiveness over time should be reviewed and responded to.

E-mail direct marketing is something every e-commerce marketing or acquisition team should be expert in. This is another area where, whilst there are agency offers out there, building an internal capability could be a real competitive advantage. After all, who knows your products and your customers better than you – or at least who should know them better? The approach to e-mail marketing optimization is exactly the same in principle as that of overall website optimization: test and learn. It is perfectly possible to split test e-mail marketing communications and work out which ones are more effective. One thing we have learned about e-mail direct marketing is that it is nearly always more effective to have a separate landing page associated with the campaign, reinforcing the campaign messages that have triggered interest. If you just send them to your standard sales page then you may lose the sale.

Customer transaction and satisfaction

Once you have attracted customers to your site you have to engage them with your proposition such that they stay with you and complete the purpose of their visit. Regardless of whether your proposition is for a single time period or whether it covers a longer-term transaction such as a membership or monthly subscription, you will also want to retain a customer once they have engaged with you. This is where the next stage of the optimization activity lies – getting the greatest number of customers who land on your site to 'convert' into a completed transaction and then to retain them. The key activities associated with this are set out below.

Mapping the customer journey

Having established the commercial ambition for the channel and acquired traffic to the site, the first activity is to map and record the main customer journeys. This is normally done through the establishment of funnels that represent the journey or journeys taken by the majority of customers. Even in the simplest of e-commerce sites there will be many variations that customers could choose to adopt to engage with the proposition and it is unprofitable to record and monitor every one. Any analytics software package will enable the team to identify the main customer flows. Looking to optimize these will have the most significant commercial impact and will most likely help improve the effectiveness of every possible journey. The purpose of mapping the main journey(s) is to achieve two things:

- To be able to assess and then look to improve the overall sales effectiveness of the channel for a specific product or objective ...

- ...and to do this through identifying the areas in the funnel where customers 'leave' before completing the objective – this will be where you want the team to spend most of their time working on changes.

Measuring sales and service effectiveness

The flow through the customer journey will allow you to record the completed 'transactions' as a percentage of customers who start the process. This will produce the conversion rate of the channel.

FIGURE 5.3 Example online sales conversions rates

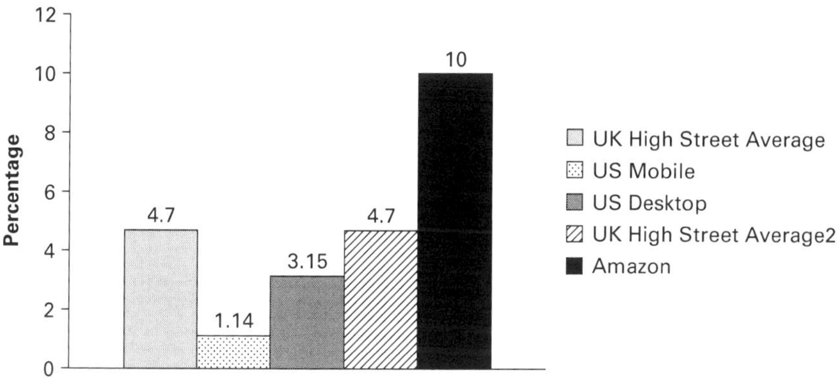

SOURCE: © Good Growth Ltd 2014

There is no all-industry benchmark and in highly competitive markets with multiple ways for the customer to buy your products you may well be regarded as successful even if you only convert as little as 25 per cent of the current online average. That should not stop you from working as hard as possible to improve and to retain your effectiveness in the face of competitors who will be trying to steal customers from you.

As an indication of average and best-in-class performance Figure 5.3 shows four key data points: average online conversion for US (desktop), average online conversion for US (mobile smartphones),[9] average UK high-street retailer conversion (all devices),[10] and a figure for Amazon[11] considered by many to be the highest converting online retailer. We separate out an example of mobile conversion rates as in our experience they are lower and potentially reflect a rather different behaviour on smartphones from other devices where so far at least, although they provide increasing levels of traffic, they still tend to be used more for browsing than transacting.

A key factor in determining the overall sales conversion rate is the starting point for measurement. Good e-commerce teams will start the measurement from the point where the majority of customers enter the site. This is typically a home or shop page. Whilst a business may well have a range of products and services for customers to buy, the team must establish the ability of the channel to engage customers as soon as they enter their 'ecosystem'. A common mistake is for businesses to measure from further down the funnel such as a product page. Instead, it is more important to measure and understand the flow of the whole customer journey. The unit of measurement is of equal importance. Even if, as some business choose to do, the organic brand search sends every search regardless of intention to the key sales landing page, moving away from this as the core measure risks ignoring potential customer interest.

Although definitions change over time, the unit measured throughout the customer journey should be the individual user, irrespective of how many times they revisit. Senior commercial leaders need to insist on their e-commerce teams reporting on this basis as it is the only one that they can use to be able to judge performance and use as an industry benchmark.

The same approach and standards should be applied to customer service journeys, such as account management, self-service transactions and interactions. They are key goals for any e-commerce team and particularly so where you are looking for the customer to self-manage and reduce the traffic flowing through call centres.

A final note of caution: due to the range of external factors such as quality of traffic, sales cycles etc, it is hard to compare sales conversion rates across companies, industries and time. However, whilst taking this into consideration, the measure *should* be used to provide a sense of the scale of growth possible.

Reporting performance in an engaging way

The risk for e-commerce teams is that they drown in data, and that, not content with this, they will then report to the rest of the organization in a way that ensures they drown in it too. The perceived complexity of data and the time required to manage and process it can often mask the real commercial story. Rather than lines of data in a spreadsheet or endless PowerPoint presentation slides we recommend that teams produce a simple graphical representation of the customer journey.

This enables all parties to assess the situation easily and grasp the scale of any problems. It also facilitates a conversation that explores the drivers behind what people can see. In Figure 5.4 is an example from one of our clients. Whilst the data presented about the customer journey had existed within the business for over two years, the e-commerce team had not presented it in such a way before. Each of the bars represents a page in the main customer journey and they are scaled in width to reflect the number of customers in the funnel at that stage. The black arrows show exits from the funnel. This report can be further developed by adding funnel entrances at each stage and by showing site exits from the funnel as well as funnel exits.

The impact was dramatic as it engaged senior leaders from all over the organization who were encouraged to ask critical commercial questions of

FIGURE 5.4   Example of a sales funnel report

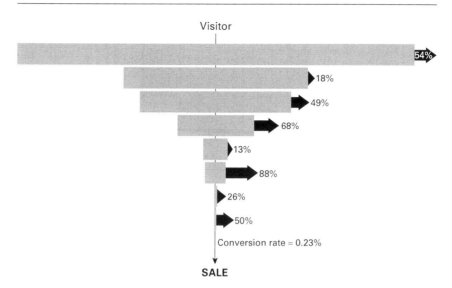

the data and what reasons might be behind it. The use of colours, scale and arrows is key. For reasons of confidentiality we have removed any specific data points but it is still clear from this visualization that for this business the primary area of concern is at the beginning of the customer journey with 54 per cent of potential customers simply leaving the site. This naturally begs the question why – and whether this is good or bad.

Focussing on the greatest commercial opportunity for improvement

The analytics will highlight where customers leave the funnel through reporting and highlighting the problem areas. The challenge is to identify where the biggest opportunity lies for revenue improvement and make this the priority.

The analysis will often identify one critical issue where improvement will make a real commercial impact, assuming the effectiveness of the rest of the funnel remains the same. Sometimes this may be the home page or an early stage in the funnel. If there is no stand-out issue but overall performance is poor, then the simple principle we use is that work should start as near to the point of transaction completion as possible. By working at improving the performance of the funnel from completion backwards, you are ensuring that, as you push more people through the sales funnel, so the impact will

FIGURE 5.5   A valuation model for conversion improvement

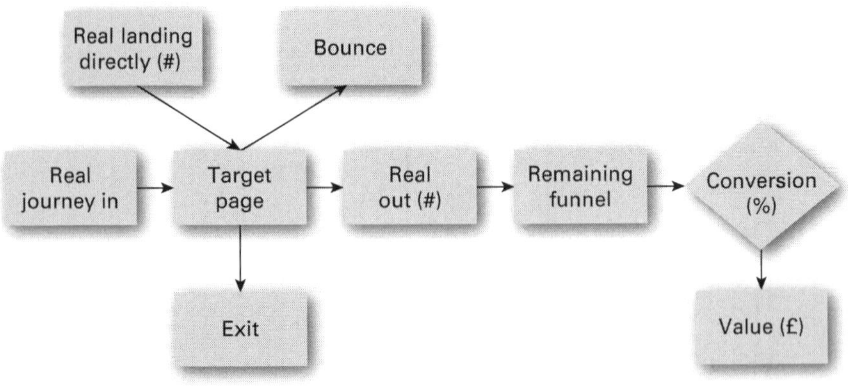

SOURCE: © Good Growth Ltd 2014

be maximized and the 'end' of the funnel is working as well as you think it can work, given the proposition.

Establishing a potential value for change

It is also important to establish a commercial value goal for the area you are working on. Working with the team at O2 we developed a simple model that helped establish a potential value for change to the performance of a product page. Figure 5.5 shows this model and the relationship of changes to the levels of page effectiveness to value created for the business. In this model, value can be defined as gross revenue or margin, depending on how the business reports e-commerce performance. If the e-commerce site converts to leads and there is then an offline activity that converts leads to sales (eg a call centre) the model could include an additional step by putting in the current conversion percentage performance levels to create a monetary value.

Again, detailed definitions are in the glossary, but briefly, to help explain how the model works a 'bounce' is when a customer lands on your website and immediately leaves and an exit is when they remain on the site through at least one stage of the funnel in question and then leave. What is important is to build this as a dynamic spreadsheet so you can see the variation impact of both improving exit rates and bounce rates by specific amounts. The judgement challenge comes in setting what you believe are reasonable improvement goals for both measures. This will come from a combination of experience and trial and error. As in so much of this, there is no standard benchmark; however, levels of both of 40 per cent should be looked at carefully, particularly as you go further down the funnel.

The following example demonstrates how to use the model in calculating the commercial impact of the change. We are looking at a product page on which customers can land directly whilst searching for a product as well as arrive from elsewhere on the website.

Establishing a value at stake

To identify the value of any conversion improvement on a page, two things are assumed: first, that the exit rate reduction is a combination of any improvement in the bounce rate and the conversion performance of the page (ie any improvement in the number of users who enter the page and click though to the next page in the sales funnel); and second, that the conversion performance of the rest of the funnel remains unchanged.

To value the performance of this product, we have used the following values for the required data points:

- average revenue £50;

- baseline conversion performance of 0.50 per cent;

- product page bounce rate of 50 per cent;

- exit rate of 45 per cent;

- 150,000 visitors a month to the product landing page ...

- ... of whom 15,000 arrive directly.

Evidence from other organizations in similar direct product retailing suggests that it could be possible to achieve a bounce rate of 30 per cent and an exit rate of 25 per cent on a product page.

The calculation (which would normally be run through a spreadsheet model that plugs in the target bounce and exit rates that the e-commerce team believes should be achievable over time) would therefore look as follows:

1. Users moving through to next stage = current number of users moving through to next stage + additional users (bounce rate reduction + exit rate reduction)

Using the values above this would be:

135,000 users from website flowing through @ 55%	*= 74,250*
15,000 direct users flowing through @ 50%	*= 7,500*
Current users moving to next stage	*81,750*
Additional users from 20% improvement in bounce rate	*= 3,000*
Additional users from 20% improvement in exit rate	*= 27,000*
Users moving through to next stage (new user value)	*111,750*

2. New monthly value = (new user value × baseline conversion performance) × average revenue

Based on the new user value just calculated, this now gives:

(111,750 × 0.005) × £50 = £27,938 new monthly value

3. Annual value at stake = new monthly value − old monthly value × 12

(£27,938 − £20,438) × 12 = £90,000 annual value at stake

This should help set a target for testing responses to hypotheses – if a page currently converts to the next stage in the funnel at x per cent delivering £y at the end of the transaction, and if you think it is reasonable that the page converts to the next stage in the funnel by 2x per cent so that the whole funnel contributes £2y, then you can set the team the task of finding an alternative sales execution to deliver 2x per cent. This starts to create a commercial imperative at every stage of the team's work.

Setting an appropriate frequency in reporting

When a team has established the target customer journeys, they should maintain a regular review for any change due to unknown factors. Whilst the day-to-day conversion rates may move on a daily or weekly basis for all sorts of reasons, longer-term trends are what require attention. We recommend assessing the commercial performance on a monthly basis for the main customer journeys. For a high-frequency transaction site, the commercial sales numbers should be viewed with the regularity the business requires – often daily. We would also advocate maintaining a regular watch of the RPU for the site. This will ensure this key commercial driver for the site is reported and investigated if there is any significant variation in performance.

Finally, it is worth referring briefly to website analytics software tools in this section. Whilst Google Analytics is still the most commonly used tool, over recent years we have seen the introduction of a number of enterprise solutions such as IBM's Coremetrics and Adobe's Omniture which offer a far greater breadth of analytics and ways of reporting performance.

Larger businesses in particular have been persuaded of the value of such additional analytical power that, it has to be said, comes at a considerable implementation cost and quite often with associated licence fees and ongoing support costs due to the complexity of their operation. One of the key reasons given for supporting these suites of analytical and testing tools is their granularity of reporting and the ability to undertake complex data manipulation.

In any channel, complexity is the enemy of growth. In the digital channel this is a particular danger as the availability of data and the ability this offers analysts for manipulation is far greater than in offline activity. Complex reporting rarely if ever illuminates commercial decision making. What good decisions require is the right information presented in ways that are easy to understand and clearly understood as widely as possible.

Whilst both approaches have their supporters, external assessments[12] of these enterprise tools such as those offered by Adobe are critical for the reasons that they are expensive, complex to set up and use, and this complexity makes them cumbersome and costly to run. In any business, commercial leaders need tools that are simple, accurate and agile. Our conclusions from working with large organizations who use them is that these tools often act as an amplifier of complexity rather than a provider of powerful insight that drives commercial activity.

And a last point on one piece of analytic software you need to get right: telephone numbers and call recording. If your website encourages people to call as well as or instead of transacting online you need to make sure that you have two things in place so you can measure the impact of activity online. First, make sure your website number is a different one from the one used elsewhere – that way you can track calls and therefore leads generated online and then track them through to conversion so you can measure conversion effectiveness of the online engagement against any other type. Make sure your sales systems can place a tag on sales through the web number so you can analyse these easily. Second, you need to make sure your telephone system software can record the number of calls made, calls answered, calls unanswered and the time of day the calls came in.

Developing the inputs that generate customer insight

Having assessed the website and identified a problem page or area, the e-commerce team should seek to understand the poor performance from the perspective of the customer. Irrespective of market, customer, channel or category, there are some good practices that enable a team to blend a series of data points to create a hypothesis for the poor performance. Following the process we have described in Chapter 3, what follows is a description of how the team can go about building the various inputs required.

All of what is described can be undertaken using easy-to-install and simple-to-use, off-the-shelf software tools. We have used all of these with clients and generally they take an IT team considerably less than an hour to install. They are ubiquitous so have already been tested and proven by e-commerce operations in every sector and of every size. Typically they cost between £50 and £200 per month.

One characteristic of the analytical tool market is that it is developing as fast as all the other aspects of digital business and by the time you read this there will be new entrants into the market. The following sections therefore talk about tool type and direct you to the leading providers as of the end of 2014. We will keep this assessment updated on the web page associated with the book so it will always be worth checking this for any updated views (**www.goodgrowth.co.uk/digital leadership/**).

Assessing page engagement

Page engagement analytics assess how effective a specific page is at engaging customers to complete the desired call to action. The key questions an e-commerce team will want to know from customers are:

- Is it clear what you want me to do? Is the call to action visible and stands out from the rest of the body of the site?

- Are the copy, headlines and proposition supportive of a customer seeking to make a decision? Is the information communicated on the page suitable at the stage of the customer journey?

- Is the 'retail space' on the page used effectively to communicate the core proposition? Do customers engage with the whole page or just specific parts?

Page engagement analysis is normally undertaken through tools that record activity, interest and attention. They are generally grouped together under the heading of 'heat mapping'. The leading providers are Crazy Egg (**www.crazyegg.com**) and ClickTale (**www.clicktale.com**).

Heat mapping tools record and aggregate all visits to a website from the initial landing page to their exit. They use mouse activity to create a series of 'pictures', of which three are of real interest:

- click counts that show where visitors interact on a site (confetti map);
- click counts that shows the most and least engaging parts of a site (heat map);
- mouse scroll activity that shows how far down a page each visit got (scroll map).

In a confetti map you are looking for the location of the bulk of interaction on the page. For example, outcomes that indicate very little interaction with anything other than links and calls to action suggest that the page is failing to engage customers and outcomes that show people interacting with images and headlines suggest that customers are looking for these to be links to more information that they cannot find on the page.

In a heat map you are looking for areas of interest and engagement. For example, on a product page if customers are engaging only with those specific parts of the page focussed on the product and the action to put it in the basket and they are hardly engaging at all with the recommendations for additional products, this suggests that a large part of retail space is not compelling. One alternative with a result like this would be to consider presenting additional products after the main product has been put in the basket.

Finally in a scroll map you are looking for the degree to which the whole page retains attention. For example, if you have a page where all the interest was at the top and where key information and 'sales' points about the proposition are presented further down the page, this suggests that customers are missing key elements of the sales engagement and as a result may not be buying.

Assessing page performance

There are two simple analyses of page performance that many e-commerce teams miss, that can help identify potential areas for improvement very quickly: a fold test and a Gaussian blur test.

A fold test assesses what can be seen on a standard screen and what will fall 'below the fold', ie what cannot be seen by a customer unless they choose to scroll down. In any e-commerce operation, the goal is to present sufficiently attractive information 'above the fold' plus key calls to action that will either encourage the customer to move onwards down the funnel or scroll down to find out more. Figure 5.6 shows an example that presents a home page as the majority of customers will see it as their browsers open. This page is our own website and as it is a long home page we have ensured that some key sales elements such as clients and products and the calls to action are clearly visible to all.

FIGURE 5.6   A fold test

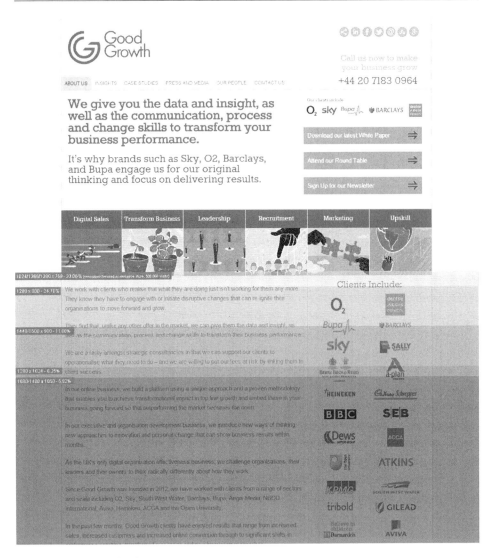

SOURCE: © Good Growth Ltd 2014

A Gaussian blur test assesses the impact of what you want to stand out to the customer on a page by putting an opaque transparency over the page such that you see what will attract the eye and therefore the attention of customers. Here you are checking for clarity of your signposting to the customer – does the design and layout reinforce the next step you want them to take, or does it distract or confuse? Figure 5.7 shows a basket page, which

FIGURE 5.7 A Gaussian blur test

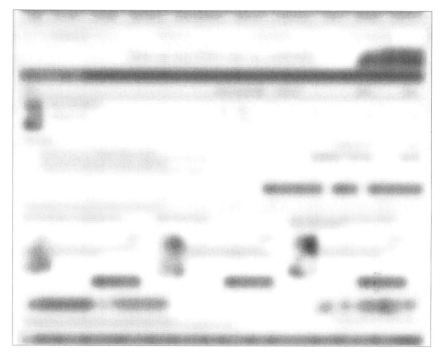

SOURCE: © Good Growth Ltd 2014

generally speaking you will want to be clear, simple and with no distractions, to encourage customers to move through to payment and 'close' the sale. This page is busy with a great deal that can catch the eye and could distract from a sale closure, suggesting that de-cluttering should be considered, ensuring that the 'buy now' call to action is the clear stand-out invitation.

The tools we have used in these examples come from Whereisthefold.com (**www.whereisthefold.com**) and Seashore, which is a picture editing tool for Apple Mac OS X.

Listening to the customer

Most e-commerce teams would claim they survey on their website. A good one recognizes the difference between survey data and valuable information and will look to secure as much of the latter as they can.

Most online surveys are no more than a poll of customer reactions to the opinions of the e-commerce team. Polling surveys are the ones that ask you a range of questions and ask you to rate or tick or put a cross against one (or more) of a list of pre-set alternative answers. At their worst they provide customers with no room to add any feedback, at best they may ask you for comments at the end. Whilst easy to run and analyse these provide information that can only ever be of limited value and are as much an assessment about the quality of the e-commerce team's opinions about the issues on a website as anything else.

A good initial survey will enable the customer to outline in their own words their experience of the website and what did and did not work for them. What you are after specifically is understanding two things: why those customers who completed the call to action did so – in other words what they valued; and why customers in the market who failed to complete the call to action did so – in other words what has to change to generate more conversions. A good practice approach would be to structure the survey into three open questions:

- Q. What was the purpose of your visit? A. Free-form reply.
- Q. Did you get what you wanted today? A. Yes/No
- If yes: What did you value most about the website?
- If No: What stopped you from completing the purpose of your visit?

In an e-commerce proposition that offers online transaction, these questions have been tried with good results:

- What were you looking for on the website today?
- Did you make a purchase?
- If no: what stopped you?
- If yes: what persuaded you to buy?
- Is there anything else you'd like to tell us?

Some tools will allow full customization, others will have additional required questions or limit you slightly in free-form construction. The best two we have found are Qualaroo (**www.qualaroo.com**) and Fluid Surveys (**www.fluidsurveys.com**). If you are required to give some choice around 'purpose of visit' we tend to give three: send an e-mail, change my account, other. The vast majority of people will say other and will then complete this field in free-form text.

The wording of questions should be as engaging and as open as possible. It may well be worth considering incentivizing responses through a prize draw or something similar, but more often than not you will find customers in the market will be willing to give you their opinions as long as you ask them for their views and not constrain what they might want to tell you.

This sort of survey will often be triggered via a 'pop up' window as customers are leaving the site: the trigger generally being a mouse move away from the site towards the browser navigation. It might pop up early on and ask customers if they would participate at the end of their visit and if they say yes will then present at the end.

As teams drive towards specific issues they should then consider utilizing a single-page survey, often using just one question. So, for example, trying to find out what would have made the journey even easier, you would use a pop-up question that appears on the 'thank you' or 'confirmation' page along the lines of: 'Thank you for buying from us/registering with us/etc. We are really keen to improve this process for customers so could you answer one question? What nearly stopped you from completing your purchase/ registration/etc today?' Again, notice the wording. It is deliberately engaging and asking for criticism. It shows a team relentlessly looking to improve.

You do not need to have thousands of responses. A good practice standard is to try and gather c 200 negative responses. In a general survey you can be pretty confident that this will pick up the major issues with the site generally and combined with the other key insight inputs will help build a credible hypothesis for testing. For a page with over 10,000 visitors a month this would normally take between two and three weeks.

Once the feedback has been collected, the e-commerce team will complete a rich-text analysis of the responses where they are looking to create 'buckets' of similar issues that can illustrate the key themes for both failure and success. Typically, the feedback will have 4–6 key themes around which many responses can be grouped and then a long tail of near individual concerns. The key to these themes is that they should be described using the words that come directly from the customers themselves. It is their agenda, not the agenda of the business, presented in some form of priority order by customers.

Almost always, the negative responses are challenging both to the e-commerce team and the wider business. Figure 5.8 is an example from a retail business where the really significant issues, accounting for over 50 per cent of failures to complete according to customers, were delivery terms and problems completing the checkout process.

This issue was not being prioritized by the e-commerce team: not because they had not seen the large number of customers exiting at this stage, but because it was not their responsibility. Their solution to the exit problem was to focus on something within their control: search and navigation. There was very little feedback from customers that search and/or navigation were significant problems. Presenting this data back into the business enabled the team to get changes made which have significantly increased

FIGURE 5.8 Example online survey outcome: Reasons for non-completion

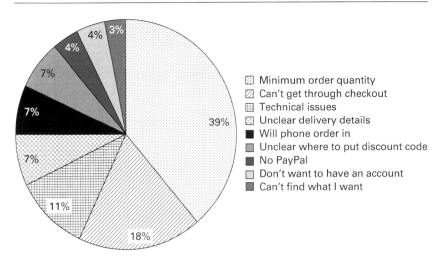

Legend:
- Minimum order quantity
- Can't get through checkout
- Technical issues
- Unclear delivery details
- Will phone order in
- Unclear where to put discount code
- No PayPal
- Don't want to have an account
- Can't find what I want

SOURCE: © Good Growth Ltd 2014

their sales performance and avoided them working on changes that might have been time-consuming and costly and may well not have generated any significant improvement in sales.

Live customer testing

Whilst user testing has its benefits in the development process, nothing beats the richness and quality of the insight you can get from conducting live customer testing. This is the process of watching and listening as real customers in the market seek to buy your product or register to be a lead through the current engagement.

The first stage of successful testing is recruitment. It is critical to record those customers who are really seeking to complete the customer journey through the current execution and to ensure that where you have a portfolio of products and services you get a representative sample across the different customer segments. Per segment, however, you really only need between 5 and 10 people. This is enough to highlight where the real challenges are in the online journey.

A simple-to-use tool to recruit customers online as they seek to purchase is called Ethnio (**www.ethn.io**). It is cheap and easy to install. Once installed, it can be commissioned to target the recruitment of particular customer segments, ie iPhone customers, B2B customers as opposed to B2C customers. Equally you could use one of the survey tools to recruit.

We recommend that participation is incentivized with a significant value per interview: on this basis, on a high-volume site, recruitment will only take a few days. The team should try and complete the interview as soon after a positive acceptance as possible. This is because having captured a willing customer you don't want the process to lose the business a potential sale.

The interview is conducted remotely, with the interviewer in a quiet room without distraction or background noise. Through the use of VOIP tools such as Skype and screen-sharing tools such as Join.me, the interviewer will record the commentary of the interviewee and the activity on their computer screen through the whole customer journey. This interview normally takes 45 minutes.

The script used during effective live customer testing is as important as the recruitment process. The interview must not 'lead' the customer in any way. It is seeking to explore and record the observations as the customer navigates the site to complete the objective. By getting the customer to 'think aloud' the business can hear from the customer what information is unclear or lacking throughout the engagement. The interviewer should follow the customer's interest so, for example, when a customer says that they cannot see the information they require, the interviewer should ask for the specific information they are trying to find and where they would have expected to find it.

This 'live' data can present businesses with significant challenges to their perceptions of customers in the market. Figure 5.9 records two quotations from live customer testing completed for a motor retailing client.

FIGURE 5.9   Example of live customer feedback

'those bloody phone
numbers (0845) drive me
mad....I call from a mobile
and it costs me more'

3 out of 5 User Tests

'I can't find what I am
looking for on the New Car
Information'

2 out of 5 User Tests

SOURCE: © Good Growth Ltd 2014

In this example the live testing threw up two specifics that explained outcomes that were puzzling senior management. The first explained why, having adopted a national code phone number, calls to the showrooms had fallen off. Customer reaction to these numbers was nearly universally negative as they were perceived to be more expensive than the local number code and if you dialled from a mobile were treated as a premium-rate number. The second explained why customers in the survey kept responding that they couldn't find the information they needed: the comments referred to occasions when test customers left the new car site and looked for similar cars in the used car site where details such as mpg, tax etc were much more readily available. Both of these pieces of insight drove significant changes to customer engagement and drove up leads generated for the business.

Creating hypotheses

As we discussed in Chapter 3, with this depth and range of customer insight, it is possible to build a *hypothesis* for why the page is not performing. At any time, an e-commerce team should be able to share the hypotheses they are currently working on, explain something of the value opportunity of solving the problem and demonstrate how the hypothesis and the insight have formed a testing strategy that is looking to improve conversion.

Building a response

A testing response should be based on customer insight and whilst clearly there is a role for expert opinion and experience in designing the response, the issues under review have to be customer-led.

A testing response should be developed with the sole aim of improving performance in one or both of two ways: the conversion impact of the page under review and the conversion impact of the site as a whole. In early stages of optimization, there should be quite a lot of opportunity to make these improvements without significantly altering website fundamentals such as templates, functionality or branding. Your website template and current design treatment may not be the most up to date but it probably is not the biggest cause of lost revenue. A good response will accept constraints and work around them in the first instance to look for maximum improvement with minimum cost and time.

In three years of working across many sizes and sectors the obvious areas for early change tend to be the same:

- lack of (or poor) sales copy;
- wasting prime retail space;

- clutter on the page;
- unclear calls to action;
- information important to the customer hidden from the customer;
- unclear critical terms and conditions;
- irrelevant or unnecessary information.

If your website is both 'the place' and 'the person' it has to be as least as good as your best 'place' and your best 'person'. The person is a copy challenge and the place is a design challenge. In our list above the person challenges are all about getting the right copy. This is not as hard as you may think and may not require the services of an expensive marketing agency. It is possible to identify the most effective person in the business at overcoming the objections highlighted in the hypothesis.

Typically, this is the best salesperson either in a call centre or face to face. Day in and out, they will be hearing the objections that customers in the market bring and have practised and perfected responses that enable them to 'close' the sale more times than their peers. These people are your richest source of great sales copy. When researching and listening to the most effective sales messaging, the team must capture the specific words used to convey the message. If there are several approaches then the testing strategy can be set up to test the effectiveness of each, identifying the one that works best. This information should then be shared back with the offline sales teams as it will help them build their effectiveness in turn.

The place challenges in the list are about design, specifically presentation. When it is clear what the customer wants to know, then the design response must put this first – however much the designer disagrees. There are many beautifully designed websites that don't deliver revenue and some great examples of sites where function has triumphed over form to great commercial effect: Amazon for example. The key thing about design is to make sure the team has established the focus and the function of the page under review and been clear about the allocation of space and whether specific images or copy (say for legal reasons) has to be on the page.

We are firm believers that a wireframe designed by the e-commerce team with its commercial partners and the designer together is far more likely to form the basis of a successful test than a written brief on its own. A wireframe design can range in detail and complexity, but in essence, it will detail the broad layout of the specific page. It can be completed as a simple 'pen and paper' exercise or in PowerPoint, Visio or specialist software. Figure 5.10 is one we developed for a retailer for a search results page:

FIGURE 5.10   An example wireframe

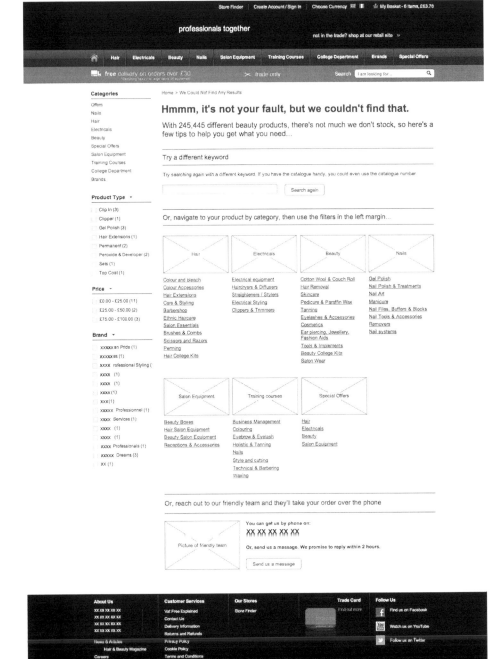

Testing alternatives

A successful testing strategy is based on three principles:

- test insight not opinion;
- establish success criteria before the test starts;
- any outcome is a good outcome – a test that fails can tell you as much as a test that succeeds.

Our job here is not to turn you into a technical expert, rather to understand the principles and assess whether your e-commerce team are as effective as they could be. Most testing that will happen on a website is called split testing or A/B testing. This is where a proportion of traffic is directed to an alternative execution (a new page or through a different funnel for example) and the results of both the 'normal'(or 'control') execution and the 'challenger' are then compared. In larger organizations or sites with significant traffic you may also come across multivariate testing. This testing tends to happen when an e-commerce team is confident that they have the right content on a page (eg they have had some optimization success already) but then want to explore whether presenting it differently (copy, headlines, placement of calls to action etc) could improve performance even further. If your team is using multivariate testing as a standard approach and there is a general belief that online sales could improve significantly, then it is probably not the most effective strategy they could follow.

Figure 5.11 is an example of how we designed the A/B testing approach for education provider The Open University that generated the page described in Chapter 3.

In our approach there are always three pages in a test such as this: the original page in the site and then two pages in the testing software that measures the comparative impact. You always keep the original page and site running as some customers may not have the device or bandwidth to be put through the test and you still want them to be able to engage with your proposition. The bulk of the traffic goes through the test environment, often split 50/50 between the two options, but this is not necessary. You just need enough customers to see the test to get a statistically valid result within a sensible period of time. The test then runs until there is a statistically significant 'winner' (although occasionally you do get statistical 'dead heats').

Effective e-commerce teams will focus not only on the page performance, but also on the overall sales funnel effectiveness. As we have already stated, this test was successful: 100 per cent more leads were generated, creating 33 per cent more sales.

FIGURE 5.11   A split testing strategy

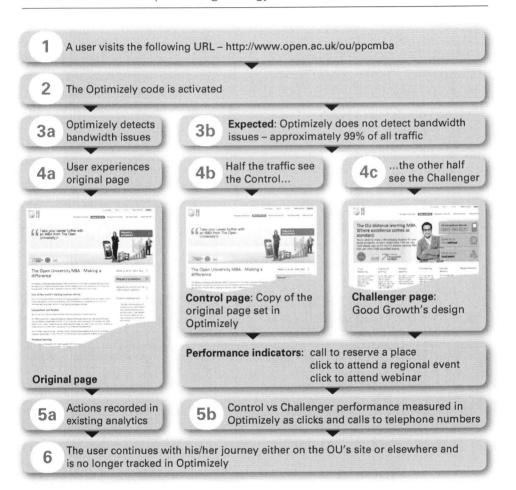

In most tests it should be possible to maintain the customer insight tools above on the test page. This enables the team to collate customer insight data that will inform both the assessment of the test, but will also start to build new hypotheses to keep driving improvement in performance.

As with the analytics and customer insight tools, there are a range to choose from. Once again, the emphasis should be on speed of implementation and ease of use. The latest generation of tools enable you to design alternatives in the tool itself rather than rely on having to build pages every time you need to test them. The market leader in this type of offer at the time of writing is Optimizely (**www.optimizely.com**). It is easy to install, relatively cost-effective and, most importantly, it is quick and easy to create new sales pages for testing. Rather than consuming considerable developer time, it is possible to create new sales pages using its own editor. This enables the team to focus on creating hypotheses that can quickly be created and tested. Whilst complex pages will still need development, the editor approach will enable many simple copy and design changes to be tested quickly and cheaply.

There are solutions linked to some of the enterprise models out there such as Adobe Target. Just as with the analytics tools these solutions tend to be expensive and complex. There is a similar debate about the merits of Adobe Target compared to Optimizely and, as we write, for many of the same reasons that Google Analytics still outranks Omniture and Coremetrics, so Optimizely seems to out-perform Adobe Target in external assessments.[13]

Iterative changes that build value

The continuing focus of a world-class e-commerce team is both on improving the existing sales execution through test and learn and growing revenue per user. This combination will help drive a key strategic business goal that sits at the heart of long-term growth: growing the lifetime value of a customer.

The leadership agenda

Part Five: The capability framework

Effective e-commerce is like any other commercial activity: a combination of disciplined processes and sound capabilities supported by technology that is fit for purpose. It should be driven by a clear commercial purpose and be able to justify its priorities and resource allocation through a clear link to financial gain. This section has looked specifically at the capabilities of an e-commerce team – what it should be doing and how it should do it.

Killer questions

These should be focussed on the specifics behind the activities and plans of the team:

- What do the team use to measure and judge their own performance internally?
- Is there a target conversion rate in place?
- Is there a 'revenue per user' ambition?

- What has been the RPU trend over the last 12–24 months?
- Do they have a customer segmentation model?
- What is their advertising strategy and how effective is it?
- What is SEO performance today and what is the strategy to maintain and/or improve it?
- What drives decision making on priorities?
- How comprehensible is their reporting to non-team members?
- What analytics software is employed and if there is a cost, how is this justified?
- What do the team do to assess page engagement and performance?
- What customer insight can they share with you?
- What software are they using to test and why have they chosen it?
- How do they source alternative sales copy?
- How do they develop alternatives to test?
- What testing are they doing and why?
- How do they measure testing success and how quickly are successful tests implemented across the site?

Leadership action

In this area there are five things you can do immediately if you are in any doubt about whether or not you have the right capabilities in place:

- make sure RPU and conversion are regularly reported and discussed;
- take the complexity and cost out of analytics and testing;
- agree how the team will build customer insight going forward and how they will share it with key stakeholders so that testing options have wide support;
- make sure that there is interaction across channels to source the most effective sales engagements;
- ensure there are clear success measures in place for every test.

In the longer term get the team and how it works audited against these or similar standards and work out where the largest gaps are and how to close them.

Notes

1 There is quite a lot on RPU, or as it is more generally referred to, RPV. We term it RPU to be consistent with the nomenclature used in the book and with the new Google standard terms adopted in 2014. For more detail see http://blog.realmatch.com/trade-publishers/revenue-per-visitor-the-metric-that-can-transform-your-website/. It is used in a number of ways outside internal business performance monitoring, particularly by analysts looking at subscription and advertising models online. Two good examples are: http://research.scoutanalytics.com/arpu/revenue-per-visitor-vs-unique-visitors-at-thestreet-com/ [accessed 11 August 2014] and this comparison of social media site performance: http://www.marketingcharts.com/online/social-revenue-per-visit-tumblr-overtakes-twitter-pinterest-39441/ [accessed 11 August 2014]

2 Median value sourced from a survey of 550 paid subscription sites globally, source: Subscription and Membership Site Benchmark Report, November 2009

3 http://searchenginewatch.com/article/2049695/Top-Google-Result-Gets-36.4-of-Clicks-Study [accessed 11 August 2014]

4 Proprietary research by Good Growth Ltd completed in 2012 suggested that the top three places attracted 69 per cent of all customers in the market. This is towards the top end of other publicly available studies but shows the same distribution advantage that is displayed in all the results in the previous reference.

5 http://moz.com/blog/new-title-tag-guidelines-preview-tool [accessed 11 August 2014]. Also take a look at an earlier piece which goes into the limits and why sticking to them is generally a good thing: http://moz.com/blog/title-tags-is-70-characters-the-best-practice-whiteboard-friday [accessed 11 August 2014]

6 http://www.slate.com/articles/technology/technology/2014/06/online_advertising_effectiveness_for_large_brands_online_ads_may_be_worthless.single.html

7 Swift, J (1726) *Gulliver's Travels* – Gulliver encounters the Lilliputians who have great arguments over whether to break eggs at the big or little end.

8 http://www.marketingsherpa.com/article/chart/effective-website-traffic-sources [accessed 11 August 2014]

9 http://www.statista.com/statistics/231884/us-online-shopper-conversion-rate-by-device/ [accessed 11 August 2014]

10 http://evigo.com/8296-uk-online-retail-market-15-building-growth-august-september/ [accessed 30 June 2014]

11 http://www.conversionblogger.com/is-amazons-96-conversion-rate-low-heres-why-i-think-so/ [accessed 30 June 2014]

12   There is extensive research supporting the use of both tools. The following references support a view that whilst Adobe is of value, Google Analytics (compared against it in its premium form as used by large businesses) is the most effective tool considered against the criteria of: How robust is the data? Can the data be manipulated easily for analysis? Is the tool easy to use and install?

See: http://www.neboagency.com/blog/google-analytics-vs-site-catalyst-2/, http://blog.datalicious.com/google-analytics-premium-vs-adobe-site-catalyst/, http://www.businessbee.com/resources/news/operations-buzz/google-analytics-vs-adobe-sitecatalyst-data-analysis-platform-better-business/, http://www.blastam.com/google-analytics-comparison.aspx

13   Optimizely became the no1 split-testing solution in the world, beating Adobe Target (then called Test and Target) despite it being much older (9 October 2012). See: http://blog.optimizely.com/2012/10/09/optimizely-surpasses-omniture-testtarget-to-become-1-website-optimization-platform/, http://techcrunch.com/2012/10/09/optimizely-vs-omniture/

Website Experiments says Adobe Target has a lot to learn, including the flexibility allowed through manipulation using jQuery. See: http://website-experiments.com/test-and-target-learn-from-optimizely/

Trustradius rates Optimizely higher, although the sample size is very small. See: http://www.trustradius.com/compare-products/adobe-test-and-target/optimizely

In terms of number of features, Optimizely seems to out-perform Adobe Target. See: http://socialcompare.com/en/comparison/website-optimizer-split-testing-optimization-software-tools-list. http://vschart.com/compare/optimizely/vs/adobe-test-target

The growth organization

6

EXECUTIVE SUMMARY

At the heart of building an effective digital business is the development of an effective organization. It does not matter how good your technical capabilities are if they are applied to the wrong goals and operate in conflict with other activities in the business. In this chapter we explore the component parts of a growth organization by setting out an organization model, identifying the core capabilities required to make it work and the culture that it requires to operate successfully. We cover some key issues for leaders' digital organizations, in particular how to think through the expertise required for an e-commerce operation and how it could be organized. We propose a ratio for resource allocation between technical and non-technical staff in an e-commerce structure and describe what needs to be seen and understood at board level through introducing a model for e-commerce performance reporting.

The organization model

In our experience the single biggest thing that prevents businesses from growing is the organization they have constructed to manage themselves; and, in our experience, businesses of any size rarely think strategically about how they organize. Whilst for smaller businesses organization is much more likely to be driven by meeting customer needs, as businesses get larger so the drivers of choice in this area are more likely to be things like cost saving, financial metrics, geography and the balance of power both between brands and sales and the centre and the markets. The voice of the customer can get lost in larger businesses amongst the competing agendas and the concerns of functions whose job is to enable the company to deliver its proposition.

What replaces this voice are a series of proxies, delivered though expert interpretation that can drive businesses to act in ways that only depress their performance further. At one of our clients the 'customer' story as described by the e-commerce team was all about price. We were told that they would sell more if they could only match the pricing of the leading 'discounter' proposition. Once we had worked to isolate and amplify the voice of the customer, what became clear was that plenty of customers wanted to buy from our client, but what they also wanted was price clarity. Our research discovered that as customers in the market searched for a product, they had already established what they wanted to pay. In their interaction with our client's website what they told us was that they could not find out what our client offered them for this sum.

This example shows just how important it is to make sure that what customers are really saying is properly heard and reported. Without this it is very difficult for leaders to understand exactly what will drive performance improvement and this in turn drives frustration.

Working with senior leadership teams on improving their digital performance, we have been presented with a series of organizational issues that time and again confound all attempts to improve the commercial situation.

These fall into seven core themes, each of which is explored in detail below:

- a lack of alignment around a common purpose and core set of goals;
- a lack of leadership understanding of the mechanics and metrics of a digital channel;
- ways of working that fail to connect and leverage the customer insight from different channels;
- using data to evaluate performance rather than make decisions that add value;
- processes that support structures not customers;
- control of customer engagement set through the process of technology change not through commercial objectives;
- cultures that reward the technical expertise rather than customer focus.

Common purpose and core goals

For many quite understandable reasons digital teams in many multi-channel businesses have grown up and been developed in a slightly disconnected fashion from the rest of the business. Often originally seen as an innovation or a technology project, they were rarely placed at the heart of the organization. They were an experiment and the ways in which they were managed and performance assessed were often differentiated from the rest of the organization. Over time, particularly as digital channels offered transactional and interactive opportunities, few organizations have ever gone back and thought about the alignment of people and processes across the business. What happened instead was the addition of new processes and measures that in many cases have had the result of adding complexity and resources.

The result of this rather haphazard development is that e-commerce teams often face competing objectives and conflicting measures of performance. As a result the task of driving both commercial performance and what can be a significant change programme for the channel becomes a near impossibility. What can make the task even more challenging is that quite often both commercial and technology agendas can be established by functions with little or no understanding of the processes and activities required to execute the changes they want.

In our view e-commerce organizations are commercial units. They need to be driven through a business' standard commercial financial management process. They need their own profit and loss framework and, in the same way as any other part of the business, should be held responsible for driving a positive return on capital employed. Whilst this may be a technical point we argue that the capital employed should not be the total cost of the website or the linked back-office systems but certainly those parts of both which support its operations.

To be able to do this, businesses need to give this channel the same importance and standing as any other. They need to ensure that everyone within it understands their role in delivering the overall purpose of the organization and how they fit into the whole. They need commercial goals for revenue and margin and they need to be held to account for performance.

This has implications for other functions, especially IT, marketing and those with responsibilities for commercial/buying activity in the retail sector. They will need to accept a partnership role very similar to the one they hold with the traditional established channels in the business.

Finally, there has been much talk of the rise of a combined marketing and technology leader unsurprisingly christened 'chief digital officer' (CDO). McKinsey promotes the concept as the answer to many of the problems we have explored in previous chapters:

Find the right digital leaders. Leadership is the most decisive factor for a digital program's success or failure. Increasing C-level involvement is a positive sign, and the creation of a CDO role seems to be a leading indicator for increasing the speed of advancement. These developments must continue if companies are to meet their high aspirations for digital.[1]

We are not supporters of the trend to appoint chief digital officers. This potentially undermines the single most critical lever in commercial organizations – direct commercial accountability for the performance in specific channels. A CDO produces the potential for serious confusions in the ownership of technology, marketing, sales and logistics/distribution whilst having the potential to act as a brake or barrier to customer responsiveness and market developments. A staffing trends report in May 2014[2] suggested that, despite the hype, only 1 per cent of businesses were expecting to hire a CDO. Criticisms abound, especially from the technology and marketing functions and they have some validity. An opinion piece in the UK's *Marketing Week* is representative of the criticism:

> Isolating 'digital' to one individual risks wandering into a dangerous territory of categorization. Is the ad you placed on 4oD 'digital'? Was the content partnership you negotiated with Guardian Labs a 'digital' media buy? Where does the attribution apply on the customer who went into your store, asked your customer service staff's recommendation on a sofa, tried it out, but then went back to her desktop PC at work to order a different colour to be delivered to her home address – was that a 'digital' conversion?[3]

The answer, however, is not to give digital to marketing. That is where we and the opinion writer in the UK's *Marketing Week* magazine part company. In a traditional channel, businesses rarely allocate full P&L responsibility to the marketing function (even if they create brand P&Ls to understand better returns on total brand investment as opposed to just advertising spend). They usually allocate it to a general manager responsible for all aspects of activity within that channel. That is the model businesses should adopt for e-commerce going forward.

The answer to the technology choices associated with digital and non-digital activities should be the responsibility of the chief information officer/chief technology officer. That's what they exist to do and more importantly what they have the capabilities to do well. The challenge for CIOs/CTOs, for their marketing equivalents and for all other senior leaders, is to ensure they are as familiar with the digital world as they are with the non-digital and that they understand where to source the best advice in the market when they feel their own in-house experience is insufficient.

The mechanics and metrics of digital business

We have explained why the digital channel has two powerful roles in modern businesses: to generate business, be it completed transactions or through identifying leads; and to listen and understand customers looking to purchase in their market. This is equally true for organizations in other sectors. Charities can generate income as well as engage supporters in a wide range of activities and government at every level can enable service delivery; both could use the channel to listen to all sorts of audiences (donors/taxpayers and service users for example). These two roles have to be understood in every part of the organization, as have the metrics through which the organization monitors and evaluates their performance.

Simply put, the leaders in an organization have to understand how digital transactions flow. They need to understand this just as well as they understand how transactions flow in their non-digital operations. They also need to know what key activities and processes are required to ensure that the business is sustained and grown. In addition they need to understand the role digital can play in understanding the customer in the market and how that happens, in particular the importance of insight, hypotheses and the process of test and learn.

In our experience, this understanding improves substantially through the identification of a small number of key performance indicators and their regular reporting at the most senior operating levels. Table 6.1 sets out what we think leaders need to track carefully and understand, identifies the best measure and defines them.

Using data to add value

Modern organizations do not suffer from a shortage of data: most will tell you that they have too much and that little of it provides any meaningful information, let alone insight. Measurement is the bedrock of performance achievement, but an excess of measurement data can often distract from performance improvement. Unless there is strategic clarity, the ability of the analytics systems to produce seemingly endless data can produce reports that overwhelm e-commerce teams and commercial leaders.

In our experience such data without purpose drives more questions and in response to these questions will produce still more data, much of which may not address what could be done. In several of the organizations we have worked with e-commerce teams were reporting up to 100 data points on a weekly basis to leaders who openly admitted not paying a great deal of attention to any of them.

TABLE 6.1 Key measures, their purpose and definitions

Role	Requirement	Measure	Definition
Commercial Performance	Understand the commercial performance of the channel	Conversion	The percentage of users to the home page, or the first main sales landing page in the funnel who complete the transaction(s). If the channel drives people to a voice centre then the website number needs to be different so calls generated by online activity and their ultimate conversion can also be measured. The time period is your choice and should reflect whatever time period is standard elsewhere.
		Revenue per user	The average value of each transaction measured over the standard time period for conversion reporting.
Business Performance	Understand the impact of the proposition in the marketplace	Traffic sources	The number of users who land in your channel reported by source and compared to the same period in the previous year as well as measured on a rolling 12-month moving average trend.
	Understand the effectiveness of digital marketing investments	Cost per sale	The ultimate cost of digital marketing investments be they PPC, direct e-mail, banner advertising etc.

TABLE 6.1 *continued*

Role	Requirement	Measure	Definition
Customer Insight	Understanding where the sales funnel isn't working	Funnel effectiveness	Key product funnel performance showing exits/entrances at each stage and ultimate conversion effectiveness. Select these carefully – choose your best sellers, they tend to be very representative. Try not to have more than 3 or 4.
	Understanding why customers do and do not buy	Customer surveying	How many surveys have been carried out in a month (number). Key findings (qualitative).
	Exploring customer behaviour	Hypothesis creation	How many hypotheses have been created this month.
	Testing and learning about customer behaviour	Testing	How many tests have been completed or are under way (number and results).
	Implementing lessons learned	Process effectiveness	How many successful tests have been mainstreamed.

Organizations get depressed with analysis and cultures arise where massive and interminable PowerPoint presentations layer data set on data set: absorbing hours of management time and driving little action of real value. The question business leaders need to ask themselves is: what are they using the data for? In digital channels in particular the availability of data in itself presents a problem that can then be exacerbated by analytics packages that enable digital teams to go further and further into data mining.

The best data can show businesses where to go next for growth, what opportunities lie ahead and provide tested responses with proven revenue and margin outcomes. The combination of performance evaluation criteria, these 'tested' solutions and more decision-enabling data allows adjustment and response to developments in the market.

Understanding what data makes a difference and why – and, even more importantly, how to get it from your online channel – can help transform growth. It can also help cut costs: fewer people, less reporting and fewer meetings and presentations are some of the many benefits associated with taking this approach.

This really means making some clear choices about what data your business requires that will help you make decisions that add real value. The core dashboard in Figure 6.1 presents one way of reporting the key value-creating data points from a commercial leadership perspective. There are some others that specific businesses will want to consider in addition. For example, lead generators may want to measure additional goals around the collection of contact details associated with a newsletter or piece of marketing collateral.

Figure 6.1 is a board-level example focussed on channel performance, based on a model we built for a channel with two key goals: online sales and telephone sales.

Much of what currently gets reported in e-commerce activities outside of these core KPIs is of little or no commercial value but it creates a great deal of noise and, even more concerning, creates an opacity around digital operations that makes them difficult to understand easily.

In our view there are six questions for identifying key performance data in a digital channel:

- Does it tell me about revenue and/or margin performance?
- Does it tell me about the success or otherwise of sales and marketing investments?
- Does it show me where there are opportunities for growth?

continues on page 158

FIGURE 6.1   A model e-commerce board report

E-Commerce Board Report
August 2014

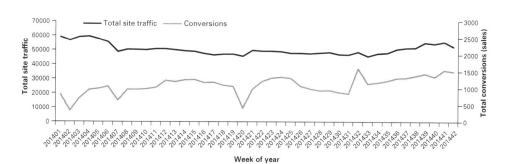

Overall Commentary:
- Site traffic has remained level year to date
- Traffic from CPC has increased noticeably as has revenue generated from CPC traffic
- Site conversion rate has increased

Key Issues:
- The number of calls received has fallen compared to July 2014
- Although the number of new accounts created during August 2014 is greater than for July 2014 and August 2013, site conversion rate to new accounts has not significantly increased

Key Actions:
- Continue optimization of the account creation process using Test and Learn
- Build and run a split test of the site banner with improved presentation of a centralized contact telephone number
- Continue to refine design for basket page split test
- Complete build of and activate product page split test

Monthly indicator

Traffic	→
Revenue	↑
Conversion	↑
RPU	↑

Year-to-date fluctuation in site traffic and number of conversions to sale
4-week moving average of users to the site and users who complete an online purchase.

Revenue Reporting
Total product revenue, average revenue per transaction and revenue per user have all increased compared to previous month and the same period last year.

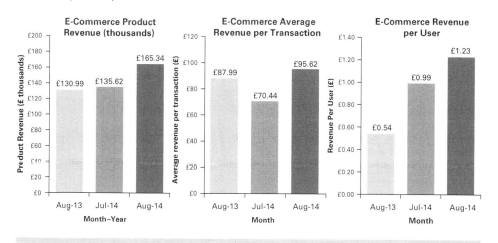

SOURCE: © Good Growth Ltd 2014

FIGURE 6.1 *continued*

E-Commerce Board Report
August 2014

Traffic to site by medium and overall conversion to leads compared to same period 2013

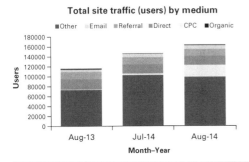

Total site traffic (users) by medium

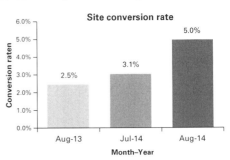

Site conversion rate

Fluctuation in CPC traffic to site
Year to date

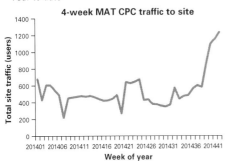

4-week moving average of unique visitors to site by the CPC (paid) medium

Sales from CPC traffic
(Last non-direct click attribution)

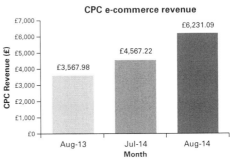

Unique visitors from CPC who completed a purchase

Top performing products
Ranked by quantity sold

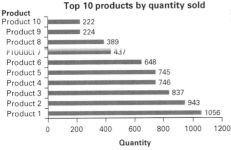

Top performing products
Ranked by revenue (£)

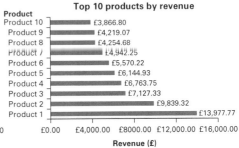

FIGURE 6.1 *continued*

E-Commerce Board Report
August 2014

Volume of calls received and purpose of calls compared to July 2014
Overall call volume is down however the breakdown of purpose of call is largely unchanged

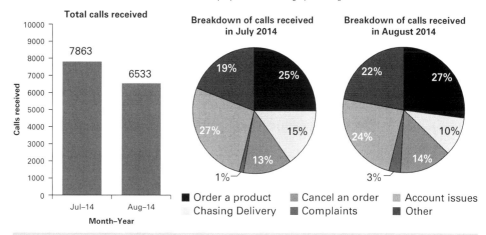

Year to date fluctuation in total site traffic and new account registrations

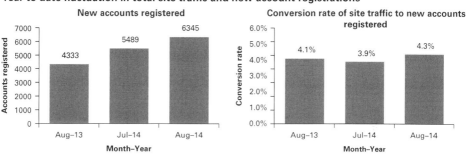

Website optimization
Summary of current optimization activity

Hypothesis creation	Tests in design	Tests in build	Test live	Test validated and in build	Main-streamed
Poor account creation process	Basket page	Product page	Account registration page	Product page	Home page
Basket page	Basket page	Product page	Purchase completion		Home page
Presentation of telephone number		Site wide banner			

- Does it help me understand customers in my market better?
- Does it help me evaluate the effectiveness of proposed sales and marketing responses?
- Does it help me understand the potential of an innovation?

If what your e-commerce team is reporting does not do this then stop them reporting it. They will have their own technical performance indicators that might help better inform hypotheses and test responses (things such as bounce rates, time spent on page, click-through rates and exits) but you don't need to know them and they should not be making them the focus of their interest or performance evaluation.

Connecting and leveraging the experience in all channels

One of our biggest discoveries quite early on in our work in organizations is that there is real in-depth understanding of customers in the traditional channels that never seems to be appreciated by those working in digital. The creation of a wall around digital operations and activities and, quite often, the physical separation of those who work in the digital channel from the rest of the business can create a vacuum into which the voice of the customer never penetrates. Worse still, the value of those who interact with customers day in and day out is never recognized or even in some cases understood.

One of the keys to successful digital business is in the understanding that the website has to be as effective in its communication of the proposition as the most effective salesperson. In a purely digital operation this is challenging as there is no other channel in which to listen: this is why the most successful drive their teams to test and learn online continuously. In a multi-channel business there is a real opportunity to leverage what is learned in both the traditional and the digital channels to develop and refine the communication of the proposition such that it resonates with the largest number of customers in the market.

This requires an organization to operate in a much more fluid fashion, particularly around the building of customer insight and in the test-and-learn stages of the processes. Customer to Action® is a cross-functional process and for it to deliver growth it needs to have participation from a number of functions: marketing, e-commerce and other channels, IT and finance. The participation of the other channels is particularly important to growth. This is because, as the different sources of insight data are blended into a hypothesis, having the perspective of the 'live' channels acts as both a source of further data and as a safeguard from misunderstanding. It adds richness. For example, in one global membership client the perspective of their voice channel enabled us to develop a far sharper and much more challenging hypothesis as they provided data and insight about exactly what it was that drove dissatisfied customers onto the phones.

Alternative copy is often the most important element in building a test page. Here the traditional channels are a potential goldmine of alternative approaches. As we identified in Chapter 5, our strategy when faced with copy re-writes is to ask to talk to the top three or four best performing salespeople, both in voice centres and in face-to-face interactions. By salespeople we mean anyone responsible for converting a customer in the marketplace to a sale. We share with them the issues that online customers raise as reasons for failing to complete the target transaction and ask them how they deal with these objections. From these conversations we can identify possible alternative sales executions and use them in a test-and-learn strategy.

To make this a way of working requires ownership of the process and the decisions within it from key players in the other channels. They have to understand and commit to the outcomes and to their role in ensuring that key inputs from their areas are delivered when required. There is also one other significant opportunity: for digital to add real value to execution more widely. Given that customers choose the channel through which they want to engage with your (and others') proposition and that they can shift channel at will it is a fair assumption that what works well online (on the website, in PPC advertising or in e-mail marketing) is more than likely to work offline.

The digital channel therefore can be central to building insight into customers in the market and in managing the process of 'test and learn'. In our experience, the best performing e-commerce teams can carry out several tests every month.[4] The advantage of building this capacity and capability is not only in optimizing online sales but also in presenting all marketing communications to customers in the market before these are approved and launched. This approach would reduce the risks associated with major advertising investments which Viscount Leverhulme so pithily described.[5]

Processes that support customers

Many organizations are designed to suit the people within them rather than the commercial outcomes required. They organize (and re-organize) around responsibilities – take your pick from geography, product, function etc – and, as structures emerge, processes are then developed in order to make them work. Designing processes this way creates a disconnection between roles, often blurs accountabilities and can produce workflows that are costly and inefficient. Energies are expended in constant boundary management, dispute resolution, bridge building, negotiation and positioning.

These are the organizations with cultures that accept perpetual meetings, veto rights for many decision-making participants and have a lack of clarity on criteria for decision making (or enforcing them). They often have significant headcount allocated to 'change', 'project' or 'planning' activities and yet still face regular requests from commercial teams for more resources. Even where organizations are designed around the process, the processes themselves are usually created around the organization as a producer of goods or services and not around the customers they aim to serve. Most enterprise resource planning (ERP) offers are aimed primarily at improving internal efficiencies not external effectiveness. Not that they are hugely successful in this regard, a recent survey reporting less than one-third of these types of programmes delivered their promised benefits.[6]

The challenge for business leaders today is to develop simple core processes of commercial decision making driven by the voice of the customer. These, in turn, should have clear accountabilities and their own decision-making criteria around which structure decisions can be made. The opportunity in thinking this way is the potential to fundamentally improve responsiveness as well as significant reductions in overhead costs. To do this well requires an organization to subject its current customer-facing processes to a review against the following criteria: a) What does this process ask the customer to do that benefits them? and b) What does this process ask the customer to do that benefits the business?

The bigger the gap, the more likely it is that the organization will need to rethink the process to restore the balance in favour of the customer. In a world where competing propositions are available at the press of a button, the more you make it difficult for the customer to transact with you, the less likely that they will buy or that they will remain with you when they have the chance to move on.

Control through commercial objectives

All businesses are now digital to a greater or lesser extent: increasing numbers of customer journeys start online, whether lead generation or transaction, business-to-business (B2B) or business-to-consumer (B2C), or simple information provision.

For many businesses this is a difficult shift. Product and service models developed for one or more 'offline' channels have then been transferred into the digital channel without the integrated thinking and 'clean sheet' advantage that is available to the digital-only business models that have emerged since the late 1990s. These 'evolved' business models bring with them the multiple challenge of offline thinking about product or service delivery and the mindset with which they approach the issue of technology development.

One of the increasingly challenging issues – especially in larger organizations – is the role and approach adopted by IT functions to the commercial imperatives of quick change, experimentation, flexibility and responsiveness needed to be successful in the online environment. We have seen reactions to a request to run a tried and tested customer survey product vary from a test and sign-off within 15 minutes to one where change and testing processes could take up to six weeks (ironically within a business with low online transaction volumes).

IT functional cultures are a challenge in themselves, but there is no doubt that there is a part of the IT world that prefers internal build rather than third-party solutions (often at a significant cost disadvantage for the business, although based ostensibly on 'security' and 'robustness'), that thinks 'big system' rather than 'small solution'. These are cultures that are so obsessed with the purity of their product and change management that they impose routines for small changes that ensure that opportunity hurdles are high and revenue is lost for months after it need be.

Recent moves to adopt LEAN and Agile techniques haven't always helped commercial teams in the way they thought. Whilst product owners, 'scrums' and constant priority adjustment are terms that suggest flexibility and a primacy for commercial judgement, if badly implemented or over-engineered these approaches can rapidly drive out the important merely to satisfy the urgent – regardless of its long-term commercial impact.

We are not promoting speed over quality, far from it. We believe that commercial gain should be promoted over adherence to 'best practice' change processes. Business leaders have to ensure that those responsible for prioritizing and delivering change to improve the performance of their online channel are commercially literate. They have to be focussed on the commercial objective and be measured against performance standards that link through to increased revenue and margin and not to those built to reflect a 'quality' process.

To be effective, e-commerce functions need to have a range of capabilities that enable them to operate reasonably free from controls imposed by over-anxious IT and marketing teams. We outline a structure model further on, but given the pace at which markets change we know that to enable a fast response that is effectively controlled and de-risked, an e-commerce operation should manage its route to market through a content management system (CMS) which should give it the autonomy to change all content, employing a simple template strategy.

Small-scale changes requiring development should also be handled within the team, enabling a rapid response capability to mainstream successful tests. It is critical that there exists between the e-commerce team and the IT function a clear understanding of how change will be handled: what will get treated as a small change and what has to be put through the more structured and managed processes in IT given the degree of risk associated with site stability or interfaces with other key systems. This can often be best identified through a definition of change approval levels.

In Figure 6.2 we offer a delegated authority framework where an e-commerce team could implement everything in the first two levels (but needed external to the team approval, their business board being the cross-functional team responsible for their Customer to Action® process) but technology changes in the third level are managed through the IT change process.

FIGURE 6.2   A change control delegation schedule

Type of change	Example	Sign off
A within page change	Changing a headline, changing a button colour, changing copy, moving a call to action	Project owner
A site change	Changing a landing page, changing navigation across a section of the site, adding a new page, adding an interstitial, removing a page	Business Leader
A business change	A change to the core offer and/or core purpose, a change of marketing message, a major revamp of the site imagery or of branding	Business Board/Key stakeholders

SOURCE: © Good Growth Ltd 2014

This freedom to act balances the risk of commercial failure with that of technology failure.

Cultures that reward the 'champion of the customer'

The tell-tale signs that growth imperatives will founder can be seen in the way people in the organization choose to behave and the behaviour norms that are accepted around decision making, communications (especially e-mail) and cross-boundary collaboration. One client famously cited as one of the reasons behind wanting to extend our engagement the fact that we had engendered more effective collaborative working between two key functions in three months than had happened in the previous year.

This did not surprise us. When the processes in an organization are primarily about making the organization work internally this can trigger behaviours that focus firmly on internal positioning and politics. The control frameworks imposed on technology, marketing communications and product development in these systems are often cumbersome and disempowering. As a result, the behaviours adopted, and encouraged, will be those that either find ways around the system or use position and power to force the system to respond in a particular way.

Whether passive–aggressive, or just aggressive, behaviours that make it more and more difficult for rational, evidence-based decision making to be effective increasingly develop. In this environment, there is a tendency to look for 'technical experts' and to rely on their judgement to break deadlocks, cut through disputes and be the sole arbiters of 'what is right'. Expert cultures are extremely dangerous in emerging environments where, at best, this expertise is based on only a slightly more advanced understanding than anyone else of a world which changes so often that any expertise is likely to be out of date relatively quickly.

This is absolutely the case with e-commerce and the world of digital marketing and design. We have heard the phrase '...as an expert in...' so many times, only for it to become quite obvious that there were as many alternatives on offer from other 'experts', some of whom put forward the completely opposite view. In the many organizations we have worked with or interviewed, senior leaders often classify themselves as 'digital immigrants' and, like immigrants everywhere, can intuitively judge if something is not right, but are unsure of just how wrong it is.

Business leaders need to challenge actively the expert cultures that often dominate in their digital channels and they should look to reward and incentivize behaviour that focusses on getting the voice of the customer right in the centre of debates on online performance. They should require their digital teams to stop cloaking themselves in jargon and suspect expertise

FIGURE 6.3   The values and behaviours model: How values
drive culture

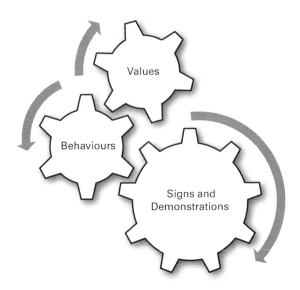

SOURCE: C Bones, *The Self-Reliant Manager*

and create business-oriented processes and measures that reflect what the business is really for.

Culture is a tough nut to crack. In *The Self-Reliant Manager*[7] Christopher Bones shared a model (Figure 6.3) that he built with colleagues when working in United Distillers on a major global project to build a shared operating culture that shows how working practices in organizations reflect real, as opposed to espoused, values.

A value is a belief that is so important that you put it into action – in other words it influences how you behave and the choices you make. Whatever values an organization espouses, what drives the behaviour of those who work for it are their own values. Whilst some of these will have been formed through home and school, others, particularly those that shape their interactions with other people, can be influenced and aligned with those the organization believes will drive its business best.

Our definition of culture is this: 'it's the way we do things around here'. Think about when you joined your current organization. As part of your induction you no doubt asked a great number of questions and in the way these got answered you built an understanding of how your work colleagues chose to behave. To succeed, you probably adopted many if not most of these behaviours: what you did when judgement was involved in deciding a reasonable expense; how you challenged people from other teams; what you decided to accept without challenge from others; how you used e-mail and when text or phone or face to face was preferred and so on.

Changing cultures is a process whereby you have to change individual behaviours. To do this requires strength of purpose from leaders not just to define clearly what the new standards are but also to challenge continuously when they are not upheld and recognize constantly those who display them. The culture you need in any e-commerce operation is one that is customer-centric and that prioritizes commercial goals over technical development. So what can you do as a leader to drive this culture? Here are five possible actions:

1 **Link everyone's objectives to ultimate conversion improvement.** If there is a commercial incentive scheme, tie everyone's rewards to improving this one figure.

2 **Encourage learning from the customer** by setting up monthly informal lunches for all the team where the latest hypotheses are shared and tests reported back on.

3 **Get all the team working one week a year in a store or in the voice centre** and when they've done it get them to share the experience and any insight gained with everyone else.

4 **Build a working practice where everyone always asks 'what is the insight that underpins this proposal?'** when faced with suggestions for change from the team or from colleagues in marketing and commercial functions. Get people to assume that they should always test their ideas first through your test-and-learn process before asking the team to make a change.

5 **Challenge assertions based on expertise** (we've heard some corkers over the last few years) and challenge anything that sounds as though it's wrapped in jargon. If you do not understand it, the chances are the person who just said it does not really either!

Structures

Over the last three years, we have built a structure model[0] for e-commerce organizations that is deliberately challenging of what has emerged to date. Until now there has been an assumption in resource planning for digital development that this required considerable headcount. We have come across businesses who only sell a few products online where between development resources, product owners, acquisition specialists, analytics experts, user-testing experts and designers they were employing well over 50 and sometimes nearer 80 people. In addition they were also likely to be retaining agency expertise in SEO, PPC and website design as well as services associated with e-mail marketing and social media management. Digital has become an industry and given the shortages of people with significant experience it has also become an increasingly expensive one.

You need to think about an e-commerce structure in the same way as you do any other sales channel. You will need the following capabilities:

- **development:** design and build of the infrastructure through which you will trade;
- **design and copy:** design of the sales funnel through which customers will pass;
- **product/category management:** merchandising and engagement at key stages to reinforce the likelihood of purchase;
- **analytics:** channel performance reporting;
- **optimization:** continuous performance improvement of the channel;
- **traffic:** marketing in the channel;
- **retention:** in businesses with customer relationships that extend past one transaction, online customer service and interaction.

These are not all necessarily different people, but they are different capabilities and some can be found grouped together, for example, good optimization specialists can cover analytics, traffic, copy and page design.

In multi-channel businesses customer fulfilment (eg delivery logistics, service follow-up etc) tend to sit outside the channel structure, as do most functional activities. In a larger channel there may be an argument for a separate financial analyst role. Depending on the degree of autonomy or integration applied within the business as a whole you will need to decide where any category or product leadership will sit and where decisions will be made on promotions and offers, product portfolio and range and pricing.

In smaller businesses, as in any other channel, the commercial leadership and decision making will come from the head of e-commerce working with key peers. As digital channels get larger and start to transact in significant volume there will be a need for more of a leadership team within the channel organization. However, the manner of their interaction with the customer and the single point of transaction should mean that headcount can still be very tightly controlled.

The biggest bottleneck in e-commerce structures is the rate at which changes can be made to the website. There is never any shortage of ideas (especially if people are allowed to have ideas admitted into the change process without it being built on insight and then tested) but there is always a finite limit on developer time. This can be worked around to some extent through using a suitable content management system (CMS) to enable product or category owners to adjust commercial information and optimization teams to make smaller changes after successful testing. However, the defining decision in resource allocation is how many developer hours (yours or a third party's) you are willing or able to afford.

A simple site with few products, transaction or lead generating, will not need significant development time. If your approach is along the lines outlined in Chapter 5 and you are using a simple software tool rather than an over-engineered solution you should be thinking of between two and four developers (or the equivalent in developer hours if you are buying this in). This should suffice even if you are running 10–12 tests a month. As the site builds in complexity and size the number will need to be increased accordingly.

The key ratio in an e-commerce structure is that between development resource and product or category owners. These roles, often called digital marketers, are the people who should own the commercial agenda. Like their compatriots in an offline channel they need to own the schedule for commercial activity such as promotions and product launches and be the bridge between brand and product champions in marketing when coordination has to happen over all channels for business-wide products and services. They are also key players in the Customer to Action® process working closely with the optimization teams to help build new executions that can go through the test-and-learn process. In our experience, you can only have one product owner for every two developers. Any more and you will end up with long lists of changes that never get done.

We put the structure in Figure 6.4 together for an e-commerce channel with a turnover in the £10–25 million pa range and offer it as an example of how these capabilities come together and how the ratio between development and 'ideas' resources works in practice.

This client had a distinct B2B as well as B2C operation on separate websites for different portfolios. Fulfilment was to be handled outside the channel along with all functional support. The segment commercial managers set the portfolio strategy, and the offer and promotional programme. The traffic

FIGURE 6.4   Model e-commerce structure for £10m pa turnover channel

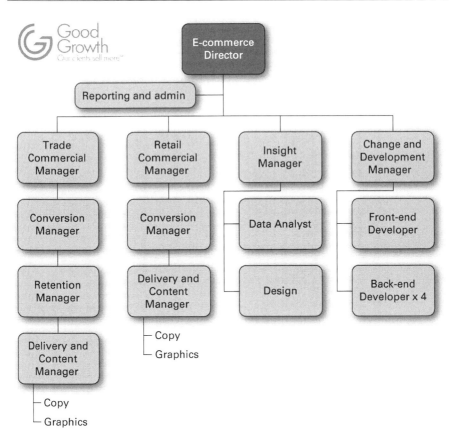

and conversion managers take accountability for the effectiveness of the funnels. The retention manager supports trade customers in self-service account management, as well as sales value improvement and the delivery.

The content managers execute all the changes able to be handled through the CMS. This client had a significant content management activity with several thousand separate product lines and what could be well over 100 additions every month; less complex product portfolios could be managed with even fewer resources. Optimization and the change process are run for both segments jointly as are the insight platform development and analytics. The key ratio here is three 'ideas' leads (including the optimization leader) to five development ones: just under our 1:2 ratio standard.

In Figure 6.4 design, copywriting and content development for blogs etc was externally sourced and the team was supported by a traffic agency and by other specialist teams who worked across all channels such as PR. Whilst for many businesses there is value in buying in specialist support in traffic and in design, we believe that copywriting in particular is a key capability for effective e-commerce operations and serious consideration should be given to building this internally, especially where there are many competing propositions in the marketplace. We reached this conclusion in working with teams who needed to be able to make quick changes and develop alternative executions in sales copy, headlines, PPC wording and landing pages.

To succeed, a website has to be as effective as the very best salesperson you have. The best salespeople really understand the customer and the proposition and how to bring these together to close the sale. The secret of effective e-commerce copy therefore is to have it written by someone with a deep understanding of the customer and of the proposition and how the best salespeople use this to close the sale. The best way of establishing this is to have that person working close to the customer every day.

The leadership agenda

Part Six: The organization framework

This chapter has focussed on the drivers of a high-performance organization and the framework that senior leaders need to establish to ensure that their e-commerce operations have a good chance of success. Every business is different and whilst we have described what we consider to be sound principles and demonstrated these in action with examples, your own context as defined by portfolio and transaction complexity, investment levels, contribution value and market competitiveness, will all combine to define the eventual shape of your organization framework.

Killer questions
Alignment

- When you ask current e-commerce team members about their goals, what do they tell you and how close is this to your commercial imperatives?

- Look at recorded objectives in the team – what links are there to strategic priorities of the business as a whole?

Metrics

- What are the KPIs of the e-commerce team today?
- How does e-commerce performance get reported to the leadership team?
- How effective is the team in ensuring leadership understanding and engagement with the challenges it faces?

Connectivity

- How well does the e-commerce team leverage insight and expertise from other channels?
- Are the most successful sales units a source of information and insight into effective customer engagement?
- Is the digital channel used by marketing as a test bed for new campaign executions?

Data

- How does your business use data that is reported to you today?
- What do you want to know that would help you make better decisions?
- What don't you need that is being generated by your e-commerce team?

Process

- What is the process in your business that prioritizes investments in and changes to the digital channel?
- Who makes the decisions in this process and on what basis are decisions made?
- What role is there in this for customer insight?
- How many ideas in test today are based on developing a response to customer insight?
- How many tests or changes in line to be made have been generated outside any recognizable process of challenge and review against customer insight?

Control

- What sets the pace of activity in your digital channel, IT processes or commercial goals?
- What are the biggest bottlenecks in responding to changes in the market?

Culture

- What drives rewards in the e-commerce team?
- How collaborative is the e-commerce team with other functions?
- What drives the debate in the digital channel – customer insight or opinions on customer behaviour?
- Listening to the language used in e-commerce team interactions and presentations, what is the ratio of jargon to straightforward and easy-to-understand words?

Structure

- How many content/marketing people work in your e-commerce team and how many products do you sell/generate leads for?
- What is the current ratio of 'ideas' roles to 'development' ones?
- How many people are working on generating customer insight?
- How many agencies are retained by your e-commerce team, what costs are associated with them and how well integrated are they into any processes or standards set internally?

Leadership action

Your own gap analysis should give you a sense of priority and urgency, but organizations are complex things and if you start in the wrong place, however big the gap, you are unlikely to make rapid progress or even generate the outcome that you want. As a rule of thumb, these key actions should be considered in this order:

- Be clear on what you want the digital channel to deliver and be ruthless on this. Don't let the tail wag the dog – yes, media and investors are important stakeholders and recruitment is critical too, but if this is an e-commerce channel then this is what should drive the team and the focus for performance reporting.
- Decide where it sits for reporting and what activities should sit within its direct control.
- Establish the key performance indicators and how you want them reported to the leadership team. Don't accept KPIs that aren't directly about goal achievement and do not accept any that measure effectiveness from part-way down the sales funnel, regardless of what you may be told.
- Next, work out the process by which the channel should be managed and how decisions regarding investment and changes will be made

and prioritized. Agree where other functions have a role to play in these functions and at what levels key decisions will be made – delegating authority is very important here to allow agile business as usual but at the same time to ensure there is rigorous challenge and review for more significant change.

● Then establish some behaviour standards – link these to your business-wide frameworks or values if you have them. Don't accept any exceptions to these and be clear to the channel leadership that they will be held accountable for ensuring these are maintained.

● Get the reward linkages right. Think 'team' not 'individual' and put the vast majority of any incentive-type rewards on the overall commercial success of the channel.

● Finally, when this is clear, you can work out what you should have in-house and what should be sourced from external agencies and then what structure you need to deliver your goals. Keep using the key ratio as a check.

Notes

1 http://www.mckinsey.com/insights/business_technology/bullish_on_digital_mckinsey_global_survey_results [accessed 10 July 2014]

2 http://www.forrester.com/Trends+2014+Staffing+And+Hiring+For+eBusiness/fulltext/-/E-res115945 [accessed 10 July 2014]

3 http://www.marketingweek.co.uk/sectors/technology-and-telecoms/opinion/the-chief-digital-officer-role-is-dead-good-riddance/4010645.article [accessed 10 July 2014]

4 This does depend on traffic volume. The larger the traffic to a site, the quicker it is to complete tests and therefore to learn and move on to the next one.

5 William Lever, 1st Viscount Leverhulme, Wikipedia, the free encyclopaedia [accessed 11 July 2014]

6 eg http://panorama-consulting.com/Documents/2013-ERP-Report.pdf [accessed 11 July 2014]

7 Bones, C (1994) *The Self-Reliant Manager*, Routledge, London

8 We would like to acknowledge the work here of Good Growth associate Rupert Angel who has been pivotal in developing our thinking in this area.

Leadership in change

EXECUTIVE SUMMARY

In this chapter we explore what it takes to be an effective leader in digital business, in particular we look at the challenges of staff engagement in a fast-changing environment where staff churn is a significant problem. Creating a high-performance culture is critical to achieving business goals and building this, requiring as it does new processes, measures and ways of working, is a change leadership challenge. We share the latest thinking on change, some key tools that can help lead transformation and insights from a range of disciplines including systems thinking and behavioural economics. We introduce some leadership principles that we believe will differentiate effective leaders from the rest and lay out a personal development agenda that can support the building of the capabilities needed to succeed.

Engagement in a world of change

In Chapter 1 we described a world that is changing faster than we can learn. This is a radical shift in the pace of change in the environment in which we try to create wealth. The consequences are far reaching for all organizations and will demand of all of us significant changes in what we do and how we do it. What it does for leaders is fundamentally alter the job description: they will no longer be able to rely on past experience as so much will have changed around them that past solutions may no longer work. They move therefore from the old-world model of being the person who can solve a problem to a new-world model where they have to be the person who knows how to get the problem solved.

Many of the issues discussed in this book are as challenging in non-digital channels as they are in digital. Alignment, understanding, commercial focus and establishing processes and cultures that enable growth are not solely digital concerns. However, in digital business they are more challenging because the channel is still relatively new, the technology we employ changes rapidly, and the rate of staff churn is much higher than in many other sectors; indeed digital industry leaders have some of the highest rates of churn of any major organizations, with the average member of staff in Amazon and Google staying around 12 months.[1] Media and agency businesses regularly cite staff 'churn' rates of over 50 per cent and in a recent guide for procurement professionals in the issues they face in purchasing digital services, digital marketing agency churn rates were said to be as high as 70 per cent.[2]

What strikes us is that competitive advantage will, therefore, come to those businesses that work out how best to build a culture of real engagement in their digital channel that will underpin successful achievement of business goals.

In an article for the *Ivey Business Journal*[3] Christopher Bones explored the linkages between commitment, engagement and success and argued that they were well evidenced. Without engagement no organization can hope to align the efforts of its people with the goals it has set. Without alignment there is far less hope of successful execution of strategy. Ultimately it is the successful execution of strategy on which leaders must be judged.

Work published by Gallup,[4] Sirota *et al*[5] and other studies have shown that there is a correlation between engagement and superior performance. They also pinpoint an important distinction between commitment and engagement. Commitment is the emotional attachment one has to the organization within which one works and the pride one has in its achievements. It is driven by a personal association with positive values that are clear and adhered to, by an active engagement by the organization with the community and by a positive culture.

Engagement, on the other hand, is more than commitment in that it is the demonstration of discretionary effort to ensure the organization achieves its goals. Discretionary effort not in terms of working long hours, but rather in terms of thinking more carefully about the organization as a whole before drawing up plans and acting upon them. It is driven not by the organization but by the experience of being managed within it on a day-to-day basis. The differentiation is important to understanding the role of leadership in an organization as opposed to that of management.

Many organizations run employee surveys. Many of these identify and measure employee engagement. In today's digital business, the biggest people challenge is to maximize the potential of your human resources through building the highest levels of engagement.

In our experience in working with a large number of businesses, there are two repeating insights that seem to be central to an understanding of the role of leaders in delivering superior performance. First, there is always a gap between the level of commitment in any organization and the level of engagement[6] – and the superior performing organizations are those with smaller gaps. Second, whilst commitment can be influenced significantly, though not exclusively, by the leadership of an organization, engagement is primarily, though not exclusively, the outcome of the interaction between an individual employee and their line manager.

At Cadbury Schweppes, this was expressed in the following way: 'My line manager is the lens through which I look at the company, and through which the company looks at me.'[7]

The leadership agenda in organizations is therefore far less about what leaders can do directly (apart from when they are acting as line managers themselves) and much more about what they have to get others to do. So as a leader, they need to be a role model of excellence in managing people and a champion of investing in the development of world-class people-management skills.

This explains why so many organizations find it difficult to convert commitment into engagement. To do so requires that every line manager has the capability to have a positive impact on everyone who works for them. However, it is also true that you cannot have engagement without commitment. So, what do leaders have to ensure their line managers have to do effectively to maximize the talent available to them? David Sirota *et al*[8] posit that engagement is driven through three key factors: equity, achievement and camaraderie. They defined equity as being treated justly in relation to the basic conditions of employment. The basic conditions are:

- physiological – such as having a safe working environment;
- a balanced workload and reasonably comfortable working conditions;
- economic – such as a reasonable degree of job security, satisfactory compensation and benefits;
- psychological – such as being treated with respect, credible and consistent management, and being able to get a fair hearing for complaints.

These are interesting as they are basic requirements, yet despite that, they can be affected radically by an individual line manager. Whether or not there is a respect for safety, whether one is treated as an adult rather than a child or an untrustworthy adolescent and whether issues are dealt with fairly are all down to the individual. Even reward is ultimately an individual issue for many despite the fact that organizations have pay and benefits structures. Other research would add one further driver here with which we would concur: the proper handling of poor performance.

For an individual, there is nothing more discouraging than working hard and watching others get away with far less. For McKinsey, this was something they too stressed in their model for building a 'talent' organization. However, their focus was much more about not tolerating 'underperforming' leaders than addressing and resolving performance problems. In the excessive way underperformance was addressed in some organizations this was rapidly translated into a policy of 'firing the bottom 10 per cent'.[9]

Camaraderie is defined as having warm, interesting and cooperative relations with others in the workplace. Gallup[10] asks one single question in its survey to get at this: 'Do you have a best friend at work?' This may be for some a rather simplistic measure, but in our view, one of the largest differentiators in the UK's *Sunday Times* 100 Top Companies survey is the pride and comfort employees have in the community that is the workplace. It is, after all, a basic human requirement to want to belong and to be accepted as belonging. Again, as in the other areas, so much of this can be determined by the behaviours and attitudes of the individual line manager.

There is one very important point to be made here: there is a very big difference between an integrated positive high-performing team and a group of people bound together in the collective belief that everything would be fine if it wasn't for the other people that work within the organization. The latter will still rate working together highly: they just won't be rated highly by anyone else in the organization!

Being relevant to the workforce of the future

The trends first identified in the mid-2000s make this challenging for today's leaders. These started to show the beginnings of some major changes in the nature and management of work.[11] First, in the next 20 years there are demographic changes in the structure of the workforce in many developed and some developing economies. For example, there will be 10 per cent more people in the UK workforce by 2025,[12] yet the economy is likely to grow roughly at the same pace over the next 20 years as it did in the previous

20, when 48 per cent more people entered the UK workforce.[13] This can only exacerbate key skills shortages and continue to drive tensions about the nature and purpose of immigration.

Second, the nature of the work itself will change with a growth in demand for 'social capital' skills – the ability to work collaboratively. As we have been pointing out, this lies at the heart of successful digital channel exploitation. Skills such as 'listening carefully to colleagues' (and to customers) will become central to work.[14]

Third, the dramatic changes in how people work today will accelerate even more quickly. Today, over 5 million people in the UK, almost one-fifth of employees, spend some time working from home or on the move. Mobile workers are likely to become one of the fastest-growing groups of employees and the way they are managed will have to change dramatically.[15]

Fourth, if we are right in our view that the best chances for growth will come from being close to the customer then the nature of organizations could well change, with innovation being led from the most customer-facing of employees. Digital business leaders will develop into the role of designing and coordinating networks which allow others to lead where they have expertise. Being a leader will be more about designing, managing and repairing such networks.[16]

Ultimately, if the futurists are even half-right, success in every channel will be fundamentally about the importance of building engagement for successful performance. This is not the job of one leader, but of many leaders and all managers. Their roles are described in the rest of this section.

Be clear about the organization's core purpose

People work best in organizations where there is a clear and commonly understood reason for that organization to exist and with which they can easily identify in their daily routine. In *Built to Last*, Jim Collins and Jerry Porras[17] explain through examples across a number of sectors the importance of what they have defined as 'a core ideology' to the consistently effective performance of some of the world's leading firms. This provides an organization with a common purpose to which, they argue, every employee can commit and which helps guide decisions about priorities, resource allocation and people development.

Importantly, it is not a vision nor is it a mission statement: it explains why the organization exists. It reminds employees why they come to work and what collectively they are all trying to achieve. It is absolutely not a goal or a measurable outcome or something to do with creating shareowner value: it is a motivating reason to stay and to ensure you try your best to ensure your work is done well. It is a core requirement we believe to build commitment and a prerequisite for creating an engaged workforce. It is also a powerful attractor of people. Interestingly, interviewed about the leadership lessons from his research for his book *Good to Great*, Collins made this observation:

> There is a direct relationship between the absence of celebrity and the presence of good-to-great results. Why? First, when you have a celebrity, the company turns into 'the one genius with 1,000 helpers'. It creates a sense that the whole thing is really about the CEO. At a deeper level, we found that for leaders to make something great, their ambition has to be for the greatness of the work and the company, rather than for themselves.[18]

It is this sense of the 'whole team' that is so important for success in the way organizations are constructed and their priorities communicated.

Recruit for attitude: You can build many of the 'digital skills'

This sounds counter-intuitive and certainly challenges much of the thinking that supports the drive to buying in 'digital expertise'.[19] However, it seems clear that commitment and engagement come as much from the attitudes of people in the organization in that they are willing to work collaboratively and suborn their own ambitions to those of the group as it does from having leaders and managers with the right interpersonal skills. The right attitude will deliver far more than the perfect experience or what look like the right set of technical skills.

We have built our business on this principle, bringing in able, well-qualified people and investing in their acquisition of conversion optimization tools and techniques rather than employing ready-trained, or university-educated specialists. We are not the only business in our field that has done this successfully. After all, as we have argued throughout the book, successful e-commerce performance is not the product of a specialist team but of commercially-minded smart people working together to drive sales. Yes, we need people who can code and people with an eye for design, but most of all we need people with good listening skills, excellent data analysis skills and a pre-disposition to judge on the basis of evidence rather than expert opinion.

Ours is not the only industry to benefit from this trend, particularly where immigration in Western Europe and North America has brought in new entrants to the labour pool with a strong work ethic. Those motivated to succeed in their new environment display an ability to transform their language skills rapidly to be able to progress through to more rewarding roles.[20] Research conducted in the United States reinforces this from the opposite angle, showing that the contagion spread across a work group by one person expressing negative emotions was significant. A negative and uncommitted employee can impact group attitudes, structures and behaviours. Leaders looking to have a positive impact on the emotional environment, and to use it to their advantage to drive change, should be aware that regardless of their efforts a corrosive employee can have a far greater impact:

> ... a situation in which emotions that may seem trivial to an outsider can greatly influence insiders due to a build-up of continuously dealing with the other group members' emotion.[21]

In other words, small but continuously undermining behaviours that reflect a negative attitude to work, to workmates and to the purpose of the organization itself can over time have a significant impact on the performance of the organization as a whole.

Develop your own resources so they stay with you

In a previous book[22] Christopher Bones highlighted that the problem with internal candidates, especially for promotion, is that we know their faults. The problem with external candidates is that we don't know theirs. The consequences are that, more often than we think, the candidate we know least about is the one we appoint. What is particularly interesting about selections in these circumstances is the impact they seem to have on the organization itself. Research conducted in Australia suggests that where an internal candidate is appointed this is seen as being a better and fairer outcome as far as others already in the organization are concerned.[23] Other research suggests that far from there being the positive outcome often associated with justifications for going outside for senior roles there is evidence that demonstrates a negative relationship.[24]

It often seems like a much easier option to recruit an experienced person or someone with the right set of skills on their CV. Given the staff turnover that faces leaders in digital businesses perhaps there is more benefit to be gained by investing time upfront in training and development of someone with the right attitude than there is in investing significant periods of time in regularly re-recruiting for the same job.

Retention comes from development

Keeping able people in a tight employment market has always been a challenge and in our view money isn't the answer. When someone leaves you they will almost always talk about the offer they got as being worth more to them financially than their current package. But that's not why they left. People leave because they are not satisfied in their current employment relationship. What we know about satisfaction in employment was developed by Herzberg in 1959 in a study that has never been contradicted. He identified two factors, dissatisfiers and job satisfiers or motivators – things associated with successful performance in the job. In Herzberg's own words: 'The job satisfiers deal with the factors involved in doing the job, whereas the job dissatisfiers deal with the factors which define the job context'.[25]

Money is just one part of the architecture within which the employment relationship will be conducted. It can never be a motivation, but it can become a source of dissatisfaction, particularly if one party feels that their employer is not meeting their requirements for being satisfied in the job. It is important to understand that the motivators identified in the Herzberg model reflect many of the elements of 'engagement' described earlier:

- **achievement:** the ability and the resources to achieve within the job;
- **recognition**: regular and positive recognition from your line manager for achievement;
- **work itself:** a satisfying role that provides sufficient variation and opportunity;
- **responsibility**: the ability to take decisions required to do the job and to be given responsibility for goal delivery;
- **advancement:** the opportunity to advance within the organization.

One of Herzberg's conclusions was that salary rarely if ever acts as a motivator. It is required to attract staff but does not often play a key role in retaining them. He called it a 'hygiene factor': something required for people to turn up to work. This perception of salary as something other than a motivator continues to be borne out by research.[26] In 2013 a UK survey found that more than half of people quit their jobs because they were unhappy at work – not because they wanted more money. The survey found that rather than quitting over low pay, the majority of people resigned because they had no faith in their boss, felt unappreciated and were disengaged in their work. Twenty-two per cent left their last job due to lack of faith in the leadership team, 19 per cent quit because they felt 'unappreciated' whilst another 19 per cent left because they felt 'disengaged and unmotivated.' Significantly down the list of reasons to leave was lack of financial rewards at just under 13 per cent.

In challenging and competitive markets, leaders need to become as conscious of motivators as they are of hygiene factors such as salary. We are supporters of the use of 'development contracts'. For obvious reasons an employment contract is inevitably a document that is static rather than dynamic and rightly so as it forms the foundation for what is hopefully a long-term relationship. A development contract has the opportunity to be a living document, updated annually where the organization and the individual focus on longer-term goals they both share and recording personal progress and the activities that support it.

These contracts should be framed to identify changes to the job and the levels of responsibility, resources and time allocated that will be made by the organization to enable the individual to deliver their goals. Like a development review, it should identify the things the employee does well and how these will be developed and used over the next year and it would be the ideal place to identify the employee's aspirations. Doing this would allow for a shared understanding of how these will be supported by the organization in activities such as coaching, mentoring and more formal training and, when appropriate, the identification of a new opportunity. Discussing this regularly would create a far more positive environment and relationship than the annual performance review and we believe this is far more likely to drive a more engaged employee and therefore better performance.

Leading change in a digital channel

Change is now referred to as a constant. We are obliged to make adjustments every day to the way we live our lives. This comes from the need to react to information that requires us to respond such as assimilating the research on foods to eat and foods to avoid or adjusting to the impact on the weather of a changing climate in our part of the world. It also comes from our engagement with the digital age, whether it's getting to grips with the latest technology, trying to understand how our children are being taught at school or working out how to use the latest version of a piece of software or a website.

Therefore, just as we individually learn to adjust and absorb and regulate the pace of change where we can, so businesses and other organizations must do the same. Their markets change, their customers develop, their competitors innovate and at times governments impose new requirements or change their priorities or ways of working. As a result all organizations have to learn how to manage change. Successful organizations are those who generally have learned to change with the least possible disruption and the greatest possible level of willingness to adapt amongst their staff. Given that an organization's capability is the sum of all individual capabilities this means that it depends on the capability of every individual leader to work with their teams to navigate through an ever-changing environment.

In the digital channel we face additional changes associated with a fast-moving and constantly developing function. Along with changes in the market and to competitor propositions and traffic strategies we have to factor in changes to technology, software tools, browser mechanics, social media sites and online marketing practices. This is a world where even the tools of the trade can change within months, let alone the context within which those tools are being applied. It requires therefore an adaptive, learning culture that is externally focussed with a belief that there is always likely to be a better way of doing things than the way we are doing them today. For us this sits at the heart of successful leadership of change in the digital channel and it is where many e-commerce teams go wrong today. Here are our strategies for success.

Always explore and understand the potential of the new

One of our observations of e-commerce teams is they can very quickly lock-in on a set of tools and a way of working that reduce their flexibility to find alternatives when performance is not meeting aspirations. As a consequence their solutions tend to be expensive – new platforms, new websites, new functionality, the purchase of new traffic for example. Yet as we discussed in Chapter 5 there is a need for an effective e-commerce team to keep abreast of the changes to tools and techniques. In reality they not only have to do this but also select tools and techniques that are cost-effective and enable them to make quick shifts in their practices as the technology advances and new tools come onto the market.

To support this we suggest that the one of the roles in the team also be given a specific brief to keep up to date with the very latest tools and techniques that can drive performance. The optimization role is normally well placed for this given that their purpose is to improve performance. Have alternatives to current tools on test on your own website – the business model employed by new tools is a cost-free trial period and you should use this to test, understand and evaluate potential. This should support the ability to adopt new ways of working and new tools and approaches as soon as they are shown to be more effective – either in terms of better impact on performance or of reducing the cost of activities already undertaken. Try and avoid locking your e-commerce operation into lengthy and expensive solutions – nearly all 'enterprise solutions' we have come across fit into this category and few seem to add the significant additional value required to justify the costs incurred.

Collaboration as a way of working

Change is best handled when those involved come to a shared conclusion that things need to be different. We are creatures of habit and as soon as we find a way of working that we understand and becomes routine we quickly find any suggestion from others that we make changes to it rather challenging. We also develop the habit of listing all the things others should change that would make our job easier and regret their unwillingness to adopt our ideas with enthusiasm. The problem here is that we all have a partial view of the problem as a whole.

This problem is faced by many e-commerce teams. First, they are probably not the only digital organization, there will be competing teams in IT and possibly in areas such as product development and recruitment who will be pushing their own priorities and working to achieve their own objectives. Second, they are not the product owners: these will be in marketing. In some sectors they will not be driving the commercial agenda but having to respond to agendas created for other, more dominant, channels. Third, they will not own the process of prioritization of change and investment. Even if they can run the day-to-day changes on the site, anything that requires 'heavy lifting' will also require input from IT, finance and possibly other functions.

However these organizations manage their line-reporting structures, this is working in a matrix and doing that successfully in a rapidly changing environment is hard work. Work done originally by Richard Stacey[27] suggested that as the environment around us became more ambiguous so our response to the resultant increase in complexity could be seen in two ways: a growing sense of uncertainty and greater evidence of disagreement as to how best to move forward. His suggested prescription was that organizations needed to embrace different ways to engage their employees in change. In Figure 7.1 Stacey suggests that the 'old-world' approaches of tell, sell and consult are being replaced by the collaborative approaches that

FIGURE 7.1   The Stacey matrix

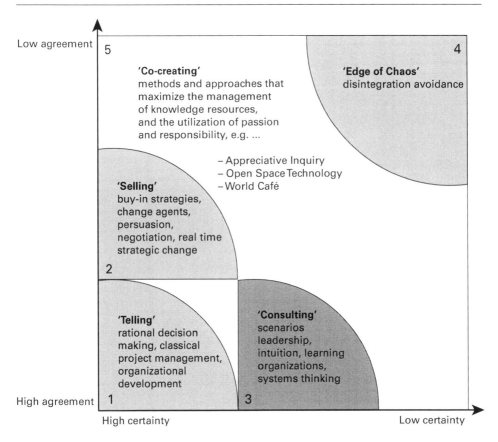

SOURCE: Good Growth Ltd, based on work of R Stacey

enable co-creation of the next steps in the way the organization needs to develop.

In a digital business expertise is unlikely to be at the top of any structure and customer insight and understanding may well be held in pockets across the organization. In this context, especially if the control of process and resources lies elsewhere, approaches to change that maximize the management of knowledge, resources and the utilization of individual passion and responsibility are likely to have far greater impact.

One effective method we employ is to create process groups that engage every key stakeholder, develop hypotheses in ways that include product owners and customer champions in other channels and ensure that your e-commerce team does not become an insular and self-reinforcing working group. It's easy to run a team where it's you against the rest of the organization – it won't be a team that succeeds.

Building a shared understanding of the real issue

In fast-moving environments, one of the biggest leadership challenges is ensuring that any team has a clear and shared understanding of the issues it faces. This is one of the most significant organization issues businesses face with their digital channels: there is often a very wide gap in perceptions between senior commercial leadership and their e-commerce team. What causes this seems to be three things:

- **Failure to communicate clearly and without jargon.** This tends to be a fault of e-commerce teams but leaders have their responsibility too. Digital has its own jargon which unless used carefully and with wide acceptance of the need to use it just sounds like meaningless jargon. Jamie Whyte[28] in his book *Bad Thoughts* argues that this is a foundation for success in consulting: selling the simple and straightforward as complex and insightful and being able to command significantly inflated fees for so doing. He argues that, if you want to do this well, you should employ as much jargon as possible. He reminds us that there is a significant difference between jargon and terminology:

  Jargon in management consulting involves the substitution of bizarre, large and opaque words for ordinary, small and well understood words. The substitution is no more than that. Consultese brings with it no extra rigour, no measurement precision lacking in the ordinary language it replaces. Where terminology in science aids clarity and testability, consulting jargon shrouds quite plain statements in chaotic verbiage.

  In the world of digital, jargon dominates and this builds doubt and uncertainty amongst leaders who for their part feel like immigrants. Many senior leaders we meet just dismiss all of this, useful or not, as 'bullshit'. In his seminal paper *On Bullshit*[29] Harry G Frankfurt points out that the essence of bullshit is not that it is false, but that it is phoney. It is unavoidable, he argues, whenever circumstances require someone to talk without knowing what they are talking about.

- **Failure to work towards a shared commercial goal.** This is also a very common issue. Commercial leaders focus on the top and bottom line; however, unless carefully managed e-commerce teams can become distracted by the range of possible measures available and focus on the technically interesting without any reference to whether this is commercially important. We have laid out the key measures elsewhere but the responsibility for setting these lies with the leadership of a business. In our view too many teams have been left to define their own success.

- **Failure to understand the implications of major decisions on e-commerce performance.** This is a classic organization disconnect and one that often arises due to the fact that e-commerce teams often get positioned to the side of organizations rather than in the centre where both commercial and technology leaders will inevitably sit. This creates significant risks and hidden impacts. In one client we discovered that an ERP[30] implementation project had determined that their new system would be controlling systems for all digitally-held data including that on the website. The implications of this decision for the e-commerce team were significant and unappreciated. As a result they went from managing a retail website through a content management system that allowed for bulk uploading, changes and general updating of a complex product portfolio with roughly 500 product additions or changes a month to having to handle all changes through an ERP interface that only allowed a product-by-product approach. The result was a team whose role changed from performance managers to content up-loaders with a consequent knock-on for the improvement agenda which just got longer and longer.

Leadership approaches to change

So, what can leaders do to make sure that there is a clear and shared understanding of the issues faced in the channel? Adopting some of the organizational approaches described in Chapter 6 will undoubtedly help as understanding will increase across the key parts of the organization that need to work together to ensure success. There are also some leadership approaches to shaping the issues and building shared understanding that can improve the chances of a successful outcome in change.

Establish a common lexicon

Regardless of how much you understand about the mechanics of your digital operations you have to understand performance and how this is measured and what this might mean for the business. As a leader you do not, however, have to accept that it needs to be presented in digital hieroglyphics. Sit down and agree with the team what works for you and for the business as a whole.

Here is an example we created to help a leadership team of digital immigrants understand what was going to come to them out of a gap analysis of an e-commerce operation, technical and operational. This was a well-educated leadership group with traditional business backgrounds. We thought about the team and how best to engage them and introduced the concept of a 'Micawberometer'.

We built this around the famous saying of Mr Micawber from Charles Dickens' story, *David Copperfield*:

> Annual income twenty pounds, annual expenditure nineteen pounds nineteen and six, result happiness. Annual income twenty pounds, annual expenditure twenty pounds ought and six, result misery.[31]

To help the team calibrate we put together an approach that rated key digital measures in terms of happiness and misery. These measures were important for a specific audit and the values relevant to them so we are not suggesting these as any form of industry benchmark, rather as a way of thinking creatively about helping commercial leaders engage with digital performance. First, we provided some simply defined performance ambitions and the measures we were using to help determine performance (see Figure 7.2).

Next we created a visual representation of the continuum of performance (Figure 7.3) that we gave to each member of the leadership team. We asked

FIGURE 7.2   Definitions of performance: The measures of digital happiness and misery

Happiness

- The right quality traffic landing on the site
  - SEO RANKING FOR KEYWORDS
  - CONVERSION FOR KEYWORDS
- No significant blocked arteries as the traffic moves through the site
  - EXIT RATE
- Significant numbers of people at the checkout queue handing over cash
  - CONVERSION
- Simple, clear and obvious sign-posting demonstrated by clear customer journeys
  - CLEAR CUSTOMER FLOW

Misery

- No new traffic from non-branded sources
  - SEO RANKING FOR KEYWORDS
  - CONVERSION FOR KEYWORDS
- Traffic getting lost and giving up
  - EXIT RATE
- Visitors landing and leaving without acting (if paid for – even greater misery)
  - BOUNCE RATE
- Abandoned baskets at the checkout
  - CONVERSION

SOURCE: © Good Growth Ltd 2014

FIGURE 7.3   The Micawberometer

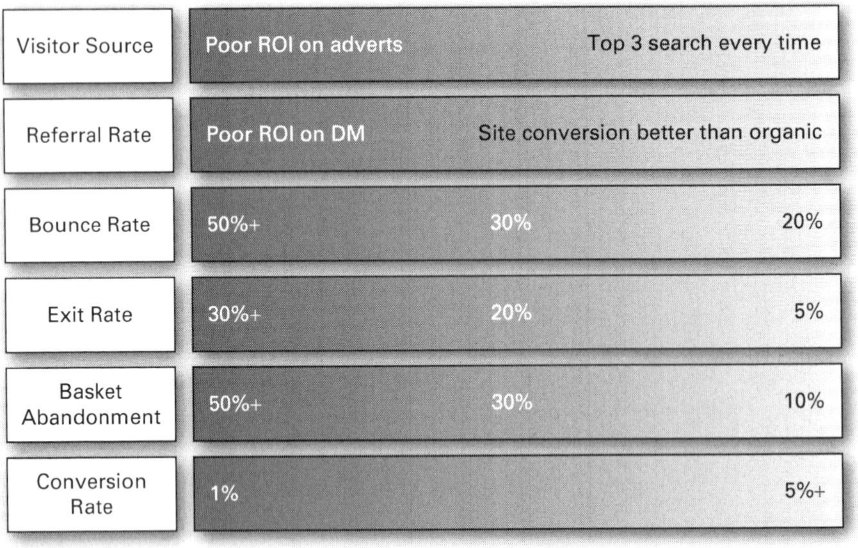

Visitor Source	Poor ROI on adverts		Top 3 search every time
Referral Rate	Poor ROI on DM	Site conversion better than organic	
Bounce Rate	50%+	30%	20%
Exit Rate	30%+	20%	5%
Basket Abandonment	50%+	30%	10%
Conversion Rate	1%		5%+

SOURCE: © Good Growth Ltd 2014

them to use this during the presentation of the report to help them assess for themselves where they thought performance was. We got them to 'score' performance individually and at the end created a collective assessment. This helped create both a better understanding of how to measure performance and a shared perception of what performance they were currently getting.

Establish a shared understanding of the facts

One of a leader's biggest headaches is trying to get to the bottom of a problem. Hold a meeting and often you can find yourself called upon to adjudicate between competing versions of the truth. Inevitably, faced with this, many leaders just reach for the automatic response – that is for someone to go away and produce even more data. Whilst sometimes this may be a good call, quite often all it will do is allow all versions of the truth to build their cases further.

What you are probably experiencing is a failure to establish a shared understanding of the facts and the consequence is that in any meeting many of the participants are trying to solve different issues. This explains why so many meetings take so much longer than planned, that people get frustrated, that you see aggressive or passive–aggressive behaviour, disengagement and ultimately departures from the team or even the business.

FIGURE 7.4 Building engagement with change

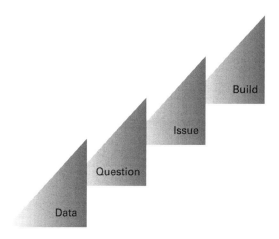

Build

Issue

Question

Data

Building a shared understanding takes more time upfront, but saves considerable time, energy and resources as you move from problem identification to problem solution. In a digital channel, this process is facilitated by the availability of data and through applying the front end of Customer to Action®: building a hypothesis. The way we recommend this is done reflects the principles you should adopt in any engagement where you know that things have to change and you want to engage people in the best way forward. Figure 7.4 sets this out as a simple model.[32]

- **Setting out the required data:** for a hypothesis this is raw data extracted from analytics tools and customer survey and testing. For other problems you agree upfront as a group what data you want and the sources from which you will extract it.

- **Ask questions of the data:** we have described the sorts of questions we would use to build rich customer insight. As a general rule these need to be open questions not closed ones. So discourage people from asking 'do you agree with me that...?' or 'isn't this saying...?' and try to get people to build their understanding through asking questions that explore alternatives: 'what is this saying about...?', 'how does this compare with...?' 'would this be implying...?' are great starting points.

- **Generate issues:** as the data gets explored so good facilitation will enable a shared agreement to emerge on key issues. Once these are confirmed as the issues then a business is in a much stronger position to move forward quickly and with energy and commitment. In our thinking about how to do this in a digital channel, this is the role of a hypothesis. It is a shared understanding of the issue(s). It may not be right (that's why we use the term hypothesis) but it's our best understanding given the data and we can quickly move forward to test it; in proving or disproving it we learn and create a better understanding of the issue. The important thing about describing an issue is that the description should not suggest a solution. What generates heat in change (but often little light) is an analysis of the problem that is linked to one particular solution. The focus rapidly becomes a debate on the solution and you lose the important objective of ensuring that everyone agrees on the problem.

- **Build solutions:** test and learn is one approach to how to build solutions in a world that is changing fast. Hence our attachment to it as a core part of Customer to Action®. Your degree of confidence in the description of the issues will set the best approach for finding the best solution. In issues associated with cost, efficiency and productivity it is often easier to set out in a particular direction. Where you are unsure of how to get there, however, then you might be better setting several paths to explore in parallel – a physical version of 'test and learn'. You choose the solution approach that shows greatest promise using key metrics set in advance – just as you would in a digital test-and-learn approach.

The key to successful leadership at this stage, however, is to learn how to empower others to build successful solutions rather than continue to rely on you to drive these from the top. For many reasons leaders are not best placed in a world of constant change to make content decisions. By content decision we mean deciding the best sales execution, the best process or way of working, the best marketing communications.

As a leader you bring with you a great deal of experience – some of which is no longer relevant. This is as likely to get in the way as it is to support the generation of a great solution. As a leader you are unlikely to be as knowledgeable or as up to date about the market and current customer trends. You are also less likely to have real insight into the generation from which you are sourcing your future talent. For all these reasons it doesn't make you the best-placed person to make the decision.

You are the right person, however, to decide how best the decision can be made. Your job is to set criteria against which a successful solution will be judged – financial, human and commercial. You should define the length of time for it to be finalized and implemented. You can ensure that those you ask to create solutions have the resources they need and the support they need to do the best possible job they can. Most importantly of all you can ensure that if they fail, they are not punished, but they share the learning and help others avoid the pitfalls that befell them. Working this way is the most powerful way of generating real employee engagement where your team give you their best as they have a shared stake in solving a problem they all agree is important.

Establish what would happen if you went and acted as planned

This is a technique that comes from our work in coaching for high performance in business. Often change proposals are met with reactions that suggest that what is being asked cannot be done. This is often expressed as an imperative: 'we have to do (whatever it is) the way we do it today', 'we can't change (whatever it is) as it has to be done this way'. Faced with change, many people just can't see past what they do today and, feeling threatened by the new, will resist it by any means possible; others may believe that any change may undermine their position or authority will do the same, and some may know more than you do and might just have a point.

So how can you separate out the noise from the useful insight and just as importantly help those who are struggling with change to engage in a more constructive way? Quite simply by asking a carefully worded question: 'What would happen if (we did what is being proposed)?' This question is far more helpful to you as a leader than asking people why they are objecting. Asking why someone holds this or that opinion in moments of stress makes people defensive and encourages justification.

Getting people to engage with the impact of your proposed change will generate one of two responses: either they will help you (and themselves) get over the perceived problem by identifying real issues that can be resolved, or, critically, they will share a potentially value-destroying impact which no one else has seen or understood. Either answer helps you – the latter to avoid serious failure and all that this implies.

Mitigate the risks of the wrong outcome

One of the great moments in Douglas Adams's *Hitch Hiker's Guide to the Galaxy* is when after 7.5 million years of processing, the computer Deep Thought, built to answer the great question of life, the universe and everything, offers its answer:

'All right,' said Deep Thought. 'The Answer to the Great Question...'

'Yes..!'

'Of Life, the Universe and Everything...' said Deep Thought.

'Yes...!'

'Is...' said Deep Thought, and paused.

'Yes...!'

'Is...'

'Yes...!!!...?'

'Forty-two,' said Deep Thought, with infinite majesty and calm.[33]

Acting on the business equivalent of '42' is an increasing risk as in more and more circumstances we don't know what to expect and if we act on what we get we can go very wrong. In the old world there was less chance of 42 not being spotted. Experience and greater knowledge in more senior people or around a board table tended (though not always) to filter out or challenge data that didn't seem to fit with an established pattern.

Working in a world of uncertainty where there are fewer established patterns significantly increases the risk of getting the wrong outcome. E-commerce is one of those areas of business where unfamiliarity is rife and where non-technical expertise is in short supply. This combination offers considerable risk to both e-commerce team leaders and those responsible for the overall commercial performance of the channel. How can you avoid acting on 42? How do you know if someone is giving you insight or inanity? There is no failsafe way, but spending just a little more time upfront checking that there is real clarity on three things can reduce the risk:

- **Being clear on what you want done or what someone wants you to do.** Let's take a simple example: we all know what a report is, do we not? Well, from our experience the answer is we don't. We all have a view, we all think we know, but the problem is that we all know what we think. Being clear upfront, especially in a digital environment where terms can be unfamiliar, measures unclear and conclusions always directional, can make a significant difference to what comes out from analyses and requests for answers to questions around customer behaviour. Not only are terms confusing – sessions (visits), users (unique visitors), impressions, clicks etc are all very different starting points – but also digital numbers are more than not likely to be directional rather than precise. Google Analytics standard tools work on a sampling basis; most testing software also operates on a sampling basis and makes assumptions about statistical probability: both of these will drive imprecision.

We ask the question of our clients, ourselves and our team: 'What exactly do you mean by (the request)?'. That way we ensure that we are both talking about the same thing.

- **Being clear on how you want it done or how someone wants you to do it.** Again experience tells us that there is a plethora of ways of going about a task – the problem is choosing the way that is most likely to generate a successful outcome. Mapping out how you want someone to go about solving a problem or establishing a data set will ensure both of you understand the assumptions and the process through which answers will be generated. This will help you understand the degree of probable variation for any figures presented and if and where proxy measures are to be used.

  We ask the question of our clients, ourselves and our team: 'How do you/we do (the requested action)?' That way we ensure that we both understand how a task will be approached and agree that this is the best way to approach it.

- **Being clear on the point of measurement.** For all we think digital is a data-based discipline it has surprised us considerably how little consistency there is across e-commerce teams and even within them about the point of measurement and the evaluation of the significance of any movement. Measurement in itself tells you nothing; it is the direction, the point of comparison and the value of that difference to your business that is critical. Our general rule of thumb is that unless you can put a financial value on it, it doesn't tell you a great deal. Bounce rates and exit rates are great examples. They sound important, they can give you information about page and funnel performance but they can also be misleading. A high bounce rate from a page where people are finding a telephone number and calling it is a good thing. A moderate-sounding exit rate at point of payment may well be a bad thing. Knowing why people are leaving cannot be separated from this type of data. A 50 per cent increase in the rate of conversion might be impressive, although if it's taking you from 0.5 per cent to 1.0 per cent and you are a mainstream retail site it sounds far less impressive when, at least at the time of writing, we understand the average UK high street retailer's e-commerce conversion rate is 4.7 per cent.[34]

So why won't people just accept it and move on?

Here are our final thoughts on change. After all we are not asking people to do anything more than make a simple change to how they work. To achieve this simple goal, however, is just about the single most difficult thing an organization can be asked to do. This can be put down to the fact that whenever anyone is asked to make a change – from a small adjustment to a radical transformation – their reaction will be driven by emotion, not by logic and this comes from their brain (Figure 7.5).

Essentially, humans have an 'emotional' brain. The large prefrontal cortex in the human brain does give us a huge capacity for logical thought and this makes humans unique within the animal kingdom. However, we still have the more 'animal', prehistoric part of our brain. This means that there is no such thing as a purely logical thought.

The brain's workings have their origins in prehistory, where it was critical to perceive threat quickly in order to move into a 'fight or flight' response. If you saw a snake there was not enough time to stand there rationally considering

FIGURE 7.5   The human brain

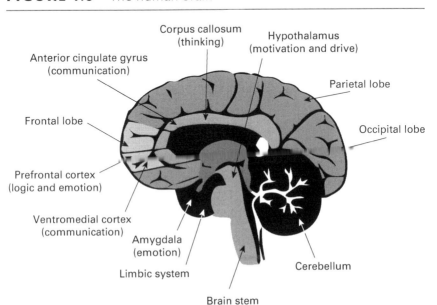

SOURCE: © Good Growth Ltd 2014

what to do. You fought it if you were brave or you ran away if you had seen other brave people fight and lose! So why is this relevant?

The brain is clearly 'wired' to pick up on threat before we can think rationally about what is going on. For prehistoric humans, threats were to physical safety; for 21st-century humans, threats relate to potential damage to livelihoods, income, future careers as well as higher-level needs such as values and aspirations.

For most people many change situations will be perceived as threats. Indeed, even when change is positive, it involves threatening aspects such as elements of fear, disruption and sadness. Only where someone has been through repeated change situations, and the unconscious emotional memory recognizes the situation as a non-threatening one, is there no emotional reaction to change.

What happens with the 'fight or flight' response is that the body is instructed to release hormones, adrenaline and noradrenaline, into the bloodstream. Heart rate goes up and fats are released to create energy for the heart and muscles. (This is why repeated stress can lead to heart disease.) In this state, research has indicated that people lose concentration, don't remember things they are told and find it more difficult to make decisions. Similarly, the first reaction people have to loss is denial, quickly followed by anger. And much the same effect applies.

So once an emotional response is triggered, it is very difficult for the pre-frontal cortex to regain control. Trying to get people to focus on being rational about change, or seeing the positive aspects, is very difficult if they are still dealing with the aftermath of an emotional reaction. In this context, whilst there are many models that try and define the 'change journey' for human beings, the one that we believe best encapsulates the emotional challenges in change is that developed by William Bridges.[35]

As illustrated in Figure 7.6 Bridges argues that people have three, some-times simultaneous, reactions to change: a willingness to engage in the new, an emotional commitment to what is finishing and the process of 'letting go' and the consequent sense of loss this creates and an emotional disengagement with both the past and the future – an ambivalence to the present which he believes is potentially the most important part of any transition

Figure 7.6 also illustrates the process of transition over time for an or-ganization. If the *vertical (y) axis* represents the levels of staff in an organization with the most senior at the top and the *horizontal (x) axis* represents progress over time after the announcement of a change, it is clear that at the beginning of most change all but the very few at the top who have had time to develop and engage with the change proposed are much more concerned

FIGURE 7.6   The process of engaging with change

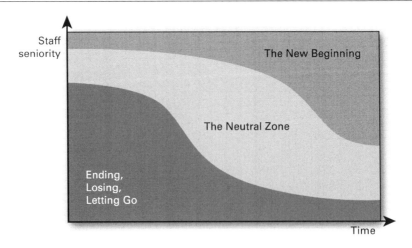

SOURCE: Good Growth Ltd, based on work of W Bridges

with what they will lose. At some point in the process, an organization is likely to have a significant proportion of people who are relatively emotionally disengaged – they neither mourn the past nor do they embrace the future. This is a time of the most risk, yet potentially, the greatest opportunity – effective leadership engagement here can take the change in new directions delivering even greater benefits; ineffective leadership engagement can generate rapid disillusionment and considerable loss of performance and ultimately talent.

One final point on the human aspects of change: behavioural economists argue that we need to understand the non-financial aspects of human behaviour in the context of delivering successful change. Many organizations in recent years have tried to incentivize changes through tying them to a financial benefit – applying neoclassical economic theory in the assumption that humans are rational and behave in a way to maximize their individual self-interest. While this 'rational man' assumption is a powerful tool for analysis, we know from Bridges and others that change isn't a rational process.

The New Economics Foundation is a UK think-tank that rejects many of the propositions behind neoclassical economics and highlights the main shortfalls in the neoclassical model of human behaviour. They have produced a useful briefing that combines behavioural economics and psychology to offer seven key principles that leaders should bear in mind when thinking through change.

These principles[36] are helpful to all leaders as they reinforce many things that nearly all management writers on change articulate from their own research:

- **Other people's behaviour matters:** people do many things by observing others and copying; people are encouraged to continue to do things when they feel other people approve of their behaviour.

- **Habits are important:** people do many things without consciously thinking about them. These habits are hard to change – even though people might want to change their behaviour, it is not easy for them.

- **People are motivated to 'do the right thing':** there are cases where money is de-motivating as it undermines people's intrinsic motivation; for example, you would quickly stop inviting friends to dinner if they insisted on paying you.

- **People's self-expectations influence how they behave:** they want their actions to be in line with their values and their commitments.

- **People are loss-averse** and hang on to what they consider 'theirs'.

- **People are bad at computation when making decisions:** they put undue weight on recent events and too little on far-off ones; they cannot calculate probabilities well and worry too much about unlikely events; and they are strongly influenced by how the problem/information is presented to them.

- **People need to feel involved and effective to make a change:** just giving people the incentives and information is not necessarily enough.

The leadership agenda

Part Seven: The development framework

What we have set out below is a leadership development agenda. This is a chance for you to think about your role, your ambitions for the business and how you can engage and empower people to deliver them. The digital revolution will keep going as the technology itself enables rapid innovation and evolution. This is a world where, possibly for the first time in history, governments, businesses and other organizations may never be able to catch up with the market as the connectivity offered by digital provides an opportunity for permanent disruptive change. Leadership in this environment is a very different challenge than leadership in a world where there is some chance of a leader being able to set the pace of change and so shape events.

Killer questions

About the e-commerce team

- What is the churn rate in your e-commerce team? How does it compare to other teams in your business and to anything you know about broader rates of churn in your sector?

- What does 'engagement' look like in your e-commerce team? Is it measured? If so, how does it compare to other teams in the business?

- Why do people leave? If your business does exit interviews, what are the most common issues and what 'motivators' are most regularly cited?

- How many new tools and techniques is the e-commerce team testing at any one time?

- How much time and resource does your e-commerce team allocate to keeping up to date with the latest developments?

- Who gets involved in the regular decision making in e-commerce in your business and how do they get involved?

About the business as a whole

- How clear are you about the purpose of your business and of your part of the organization? How clear are others?

- How difficult is it to get things changed in your business?

- In your experience, what happens when you have an idea? And what happens when other people have ideas?

- How much does your business operate with a shared language when it talks about e-commerce?

About you as a leader

- What drives your recruitment decisions? Expertise? Experience! Attitude! Which is the most important of these when you are deciding between alternative candidates?

- What do you do to support the development of the people who work for you? What expectations have you set for those in your team? How do you hold them to these?

- Do you scan the environment in the business more generally to assess for unforeseen implications of decisions you are about to take?

- How do you establish a common understanding before working on a problem?

- What is your personal approach to risk mitigation?
- How much thought do you put into helping others through change?

Leadership action

As with these suggestions in previous chapters, the priority and relevance of these questions will be determined by how you assess your own and more generally your organization's effectiveness. The following, however, may act as a good checklist:

- If churn is a big issue for you, then work out why, apart from telling you about the opportunity to earn more money, your digital staff are leaving and try and identify actions that can make these other factors less of an issue for those who remain.

- Establish a way of working that ensures that the e-commerce team do more than attend conferences and supplier workshops and that they are genuinely testing out alternatives to what they are doing today. This is critical in an immature industry.

- Check that all key stakeholders understand the language, the measures and what they mean – if they don't then do something to help them.

- Challenge your job and person specifications and test recruiting from outside the 'hot spot' of digital talent for good numeric skills, data handling and critical thinking.

- Establish a personal process for engaging people in change and try it out.

- Establish a discipline ahead of key meetings to ensure that everyone there has a shared view of the issues.

- Think through risks in what you are doing and how you can reduce them through ensuring clarity of what, how and measurement.

Notes

1 http://www.ibtimes.com/amazoncom-has-second-highest-employee-turnover-all-fortune-500-companies-1361257 [accessed 18 July 2014]

2 http://www.cips.org/Documents/Membership/Branch per cent20minutes/CIPS per cent20digital per cent20marketing per cent20buyers per cent20checklist per cent20one-pager.pdf [accessed 18 July 2014]

3 Bones, CJ (2007) Engagement is at the heart of successful M&A, *Ivey Business Journal*, January/February, Richard Ivey School of Business, London, Ontario

4 http://www.gallup.com/consulting/52/employee-engagement.aspx [accessed 29 July 2010]

5 Sirota, D, Mischkind, LA and Seltzer, MI (2005) *The Enthusiastic Employee*, Wharton School Publishing, NJ

6 The gap always shows that commitment is higher than engagement, suggesting that it is always easier to get people to 'like' working somewhere than it is to get them to 'engage' with the purpose of the organization to such an extent that they care for the outcome and operate in their day-to-day work such that their decisions consistently reflect what is best for the enterprise.

7 This is from an internal piece of work from 2004 led by Christopher Bones in his role as Group Organization Effectiveness and Development Director.

8 Sirota, D, Mischkind, LA and Seltzer, MI (2005) *The Enthusiastic Employee*, Wharton School Publishing, NJ

9 http://www.usatoday.com/money/economy/employment/2005-03-13-fired-usat_x.htm [accessed 30 July 2010]

10 For the 12 questions see: http://www.workforce.com/section/09/article/23/53/40.html [accessed 30 July 2010]

11 For a longer discussion of these trends and their implications for all organizations see Bones, C (2011) *The Cult of the Leader*, Routledge, London

12 http://news.bbc.co.uk/1/hi/uk/1657826.stm [accessed 30 July 2010]

13 Johnson, M (2004) *The New Rules of Engagement*, Chartered Institute of Personnel and Development, London

14 Monyagh, M and Worsley, R (2005) *Working in the 21st Century*, The Tomorrow Project, London

15 *Managing Tomorrow's Worker* (2005) Future of Work Forum, Henley Business School, Henley-on-Thames, UK

16 Monyagh, M and Worsley, R (2005) *Working in the 21st Century*, The Tomorrow Project, London

17 Collins, J and Porras, JI (2002) *Built to Last*, Harper Business Essentials

18 http://www.jimcollins.com/article_topics/articles/good-to-great.html [accessed 1 July 2014]

19 See http://www.fastcompany.com/magazine/04/hiring.html as one of many articles reflecting on successful company practices based on this approach

20 http://www.growingbusiness.co.uk/performance-or-attitude-what-s-more-important.html [accessed 1 July 2014]

21   Barsade, SG (2000) The Ripple Effect: Emotional contagion in groups,
     Yale SOM Working Paper No OB-01, available at SSRN: http://ssrn.com/
     abstract=250894 or doi:10.2139/ssrn.250894

22   Bones, C (2011) *The Cult of the Leader,* Routledge, London

23   Bradley, LM (2006) Perceptions of justice when selecting internal and external
     job candidates, *Personnel Review*, vol 35 Iss: 1, pp 66–77

24   Martins, P and Lima, F (2006) Applied Economics Letters, pp 1466–4291,
     vol 13, Issue 14

25   Herzberg, F, Mausner, B and Snyderman, B (1959) *The Motivation to Work*,
     John Wiley & Sons, New York

26   http://www.hrgrapevine.com/markets/hr/article/2013-11-29-top-reasons-
     people-quit-their-job-revealed[#].U8kyzoBdXIY [accessed 18 July 2014]

27   Stacey, R (2002) *Strategic Management and Organizational Dynamics: The
     challenge of complexity* (3rd ed), Prentice Hall, Harlow

28   Whyte, J (2003) *Bad Thoughts: A guide to clear thinking*, Corvo Books Ltd,
     London

29   Frankfurt, HG (2005) *On Bullshit*, Princeton University Press, Princeton, NJ

30   Enterprise Resource Planning systems – often referred to by their brand names
     (eg SAP or Oracle) – are used as the core platform for financial reporting,
     stock management, people management etc.

31   Dickens, C (1992) *David Copperfield*, Wordsworth Editions, Ware,
     Hertfordshire

32   We would like to recognize the work of Professor Eddie Obeng here in
     influencing our approach. He has used a very similar approach for some time
     that he describes as 'Issue Data, Question, Build'. We have developed this
     further in thinking about digital data and about the need to drive change and
     believe that creating shared issues through questioning helps leaders move
     back from implementation.

33   Adams, D (1995) *The Hitch Hiker's Guide to the Galaxy, a trilogy in five
     parts*, Heinemann, London

34   http://evigo.com/8296-uk-online-retail-market-15-building-growth-august-
     september/ [accessed 19 July 2014]

35   Bridges, W (2009) *Managing Transitions* (3rd edn), Nicholas Brealey
     Publishing, London

36   http://www.neweconomics.org/publications/behavioural-economics [accessed
     23 July 2014]

Digital leadership in practice

8

EXECUTIVE SUMMARY

What follows in this chapter are the thoughts, plans and concerns of business leaders, drawn from a range of sectors, and who are responsible in one way or another for exploiting digital as a route to market. These are senior people in medium- to large-scale organizations whose sectors are facing significant change as traditional products and services are transferred into a new channel, new products and services are created as a result of the new channel or disruptive competitors enter the market exploiting the new channel. They are talking here as leaders not as representatives of their companies.

We have selected these insights as they help to reinforce or expand key points we have made in the previous chapters and we have grouped them into sections each with a brief introduction.

Digital as a driver of growth

One of the many advantages of digital as a route to market is that it can help you connect more effectively with both the customer in the market and your own customer. Several of our leaders have spotted this opportunity. In motor retailing in the UK, Dews Motor Group has been seen by its manufacturing partners as a leading practitioner in developing the digital route to market in a sector that has traditionally been slow to pick up the opportunity. Here is Craig Hamer, Managing Director:

If you look at the motor retail industry, it's structured around a business model that succeeded and worked for the past 20 to 30 years. Then three to four years ago the industry started talking about a digital revolution and how we needed to move towards these kinds of activities. Everybody agreed but nobody really took action, or big enough action, to achieve it. So our strategy is to capitalize on a first mover advantage in the digital space for online motor retailing in the UK.

Speed is another perceived opportunity. Helen Brand, Chief Executive of the global body for professional accountants, ACCA, makes the point that as a global campaign channel digital can impact customers in the market far more quickly:

Marketing campaigns can be deployed much more quickly if they are specifically digital campaigns. Quite often campaigns link into all the traditional campaigns plus digital so I think that doesn't really add to the speed – it's just an extra channel – but when you have a pure digital campaign, that can get out there much more quickly and to many more markets.

A route to a more focussed customer engagement

For many others the channel offers the opportunity to understand the customer better and therefore engage both their own customers and customers in the market more effectively. Douglas Johnson-Poensgen was a managing director in Barclays Bank looking after the digital proposition for small businesses. He makes the point that digital provides businesses with an opportunity to become far more tailored in their communication with customers, moving from a strategy that resembled grapeshot to one more like a rapier:

Service providers can place an awful lot of information onto a screen which a customer just doesn't see. Or they can offer things that are relevant and targeted to the customer's needs, their lifestyle, the things that businesses like them are likely to be interested in at that point. For example, if you pay employer's liability insurance, that comes up for renewal once a year. As your banker, we know that you're paying it because we see the money going out of your business account every month. So why are we not offering a deal for such insurance in the run-up to renewal? All of that could be done digitally.

This focus on tailoring is echoed by Hugh Sturges, Managing Director of internationally renowned fine wine merchants, Berry Brothers & Rudd. They have been looking to ensure that their customer base information is closely linked to their e-commerce operation to support their interaction across channels:

> Part of our investment is in our own CRM system and linking that through to the e-commerce platform. Through that we can learn a lot more about the customer and about what the customer likes and doesn't like. This will enable us to tailor our offers much more closely. This can be used online, but I think this digital information should be used by businesses like us to encourage the right face-to-face conversations. I'm not a great believer in every time you walk past a shop, your phone buzzes and it tells you there's an offer inside; that would drive our customers mad. But if when a customer entered the shop, it popped onto the salesperson's screen that this person liked this particular wine, our shop staff could really engage with them by saying something like, 'Good afternoon Mr Smith, I notice that you've previously bought this wine from us a number of times, so I thought you might be interested to know that it's on offer at the moment and also that we have this very similar style that you might enjoy'. That would feel appropriate to me.

Zac Peake who is Commercial Director at UK Insurance broker A-Plan is a leader in a niche player whose route-to-market model is through a strong regional retail network with significant customer loyalty. He is seeing digital as the opportunity to engage other customers in the market who are looking for a more tailored service through the advocacy of their current customers:

> As a business we haven't traditionally done much by way of marketing. We have taken the 'build a good mousetrap and people will come and buy it' approach. This has served us quite well, but given the strength of our service offer and the strength of the advocacy and support we get from our clients, we are really missing a trick on the marketing side if we don't actively get involved in marketing in digital.

It is this provision of relevant information that is engaging Brett Aumuller, Director of Customer and Product Growth in satellite TV network, Sky. His concern is to ensure that they exploit the information available through the channel to ensure their proposition is communicated in the way the customer in the market wants to engage with it:

> I think digital is all about making sure, as we expand, that we can deal with an increased customer base and product base. Really, it's to align ourselves to how people are wanting to transact with Sky or how people are wanting to get more information from us.

Finally, a large utility company is looking to connect the channel with a product innovation: the smart meter. This combination is seen by one of their senior managers as a potential source not just of customer retention but also of a potential new revenue stream:

> Digital plus smart meters starts to enable customers to potentially understand better what is driving consumption in their houses and therefore gives them the information with which to make decisions on behaviour or what they purchase in terms of appliances, which may in itself lead to additional revenue streams for us which might not otherwise have been available.

An opportunity to introduce new products and services

All of our leaders operate in established industries where the route to market is driving transformation. As the route to market develops, digital technology enables these business leaders to introduce new products or services that will add value to existing and new customers alike. The fitness industry is a great example of both the disruption and the opportunity. David Langridge is the Group Marketing Director for global fitness club operator, Fitness First:

> The gym industry model, as we know it today, provides a high-repetition, non-competitive, low social reward, very individual experience and that drives only a certain type of person to stay as a member forever and ever. What we've had to do is turn that on its head. We are going to provide a digital platform that goes into the depths of human behaviour and supports the development of people's self-determination. It will provide autonomy through variety and choice, it will drive competence through education, information and understanding and it will provide social relatedness through friendly competition, social sharing and recognition.

Another example of a traditional industry where digital is enabling innovation is the utility sector. Here a senior utility leader is looking to turn digital information into a sales platform that in turn can drive innovation in services:

> We could, conceivably, provide you with information to understand what's consuming electricity in your house. It's a relatively small step to then giving you the opportunity to do something about it, for example insulation which we do a lot of at the moment – or it could be appliances or further information services. We could potentially charge for information as well, or the supply of things that you may put in your plug that may give you additional information.

Banking is undergoing a significant change in product and services. This is an industry with information about its customers which, if they can connect it to their activity and interests displayed in the digital channel, could enable a completely different level of service than many customers get today. Douglas Johnson-Poensgen thinks banking could get much closer to an Amazon-style interaction:

> The challenge of course is to reduce the cost of servicing for transactions as much as possible, but the other side of this is the degree to which – and we're on this journey now – we can maintain a relationship and proactively offer the right solutions to customers to encourage them to develop a deeper relationship with Barclays online. So, think of 'Amazon recommends' applied to Barclays. 'Can you do stuff like this?' and 'you might also be interested in this' or 'We noticed you were looking for such and such, how about this?'

The importance of learning about customers

All our leaders have recognized the importance of measurement and the ability the channel gives them to learn about their customers and customers in the market through a process of testing. Tete Soto, Online General Manager for Telefonica's UK subsidiary O2, sees this as a cultural challenge for the whole organization as much as a challenge for her e-commerce team:

> I am working to embed a test-and-learn culture in the business. In online we are doing a lot more than I was doing six months ago but I want to make that into a way of thinking not only for my team but for the whole organization. Doing more test and learn is an imperative in my business, but the real transformation only happens when the whole organization embraces it.

Sky's Brett Aumuller defines the building of this capability as important for the business as a whole and links the capability to test and learn to that of being able to execute change quickly so a business can benefit commercially from what it has learned in a test:

> I've certainly bought into the idea of test and learn. I think all good organizations and certainly relatively mature organizations like ours need to be flexible and need to understand what has worked well and what has not worked well. I think we are still on a bit of a learning journey with online and one of the main things we do need to develop is the capability to change quickly. Once we've learned, we may want to throw something out, do something different. We need to be able to do that quickly. Building that capability is important for us.

Konstantine Karampatsos has been Marketplace Manager for Amazon UK, Head of E-commerce Consultancy for Rakuten UK (Play.com) and Senior

Director for feelunique.com, an online beauty products retailer. He is a leader with real experience of how test and learn can drive superior business performance and makes the point that not testing and learning in a channel that offers that opportunity is counter-intuitive:

> For me you need to measure everything you do in the company in as much detail as you can. You need to agree what success looks like and understand how successful you are. Although in theory every executive will tell you they are doing just that, in practice they do not bother implementing it or they pick the metrics that always make them look successful.

For Helen Brand at ACCA this is as much about a cultural paradigm as anything else. In a global market with global competition and new competitors emerging from growth markets in Asia and South America, the key is to be agile and willing to consider changing anything and everything to be successful:

> We are experimenting and doing lots of different things. The key to all of this is to be agile enough to deal with whatever emerges. So you need both the technology and the people to not be embedded into one way of thinking or one particularly popular current channel or current framework. This is probably going to be key.

The challenge of changing customer behaviour

Whilst there are plenty of opportunities, there are challenges about moving online and moving customer interactions online. There are choices to be made about that which you believe is best done through 'self-service' and what is almost always better done in a direct conversation. This presents leaders with a dilemma of how to sustain customer relationships in a digital world. Douglas Johnson-Poensgen worries that banks could become like utilities rather than businesses that can add value:

> Of course you want to encourage those business customers to do as much business with the bank as possible. The challenge is that if your principal relationship with a customer is online and they simply conduct their transactions as seamlessly as possible, they start to see you as a utility and you don't necessarily have a relationship with them. So when they have requirements such as business insurance or perhaps even lending, they may not necessarily think of the bank as the first place to go.

Zac Peake's niche offer depends to some extent on the customer understanding the value to be added through a conversation that can make the difference between an insurance product that fits well and a standard product that may not deliver when it is required. They know that a conversation builds a relationship and they want to retain this part of the business model whilst recognizing the customer in the market is likely to start their search for insurance online:

> From our perspective it's about building that relationship and using that to retain you as a client and also to upsell and cross-sell – again that's much more difficult to do online. So that's why we want to transfer enquiries from online to telephone and actually a lot of other direct insurers and online sales are increasingly facing the same problem.

Our utility company senior leader knows that they could save time and money if their customers were able to engage online with issues such as the value of monthly payments that make up their annual plan. Finding ways that help both customers and the business was until very recently a big challenge:

> From time to time we change people's direct debits. Sometimes customers object to that and phone up and we have a 20-minute conversation with them explaining why changing their direct debit back again might not be a good thing to do. That's a lengthy call. Now they can go online where they can view graphs of their demand and see visually that if they set their direct debit too low, they will end up with a big debt down the line. It does allow them flexibility to move their direct debits by plus or minus 10 per cent and that works quite well.

Konstantine Karampatsos had to think through how feelunique.com helped their customers in a market where, once the product was opened, it could not be returned: beauty products. This had to drive innovation in product delivery such that the customer could return 'unsuitable' goods:

> The innovation here is making it extremely easy for them to return the products. We will send you very small samples to try on before you open up your make-up, because once you open the packaging you can't send it back. So you need to train the customers to be able to buy the same products online that they currently buy offline.

Finally, here is Helen Brand, whose global organization is recognizing that a single experience for every customer could well not work for those in specific groups or with specific needs:

> We have a very wide band of customers from a 14-year-old, potentially, through to a 65- to 75-year-old with very different customer needs. How do you meet

all those customer needs of investing in the younger end of the spectrum whilst maintaining the loyalty of your existing customers who will be expecting things to be done in a certain way? These are some of things we have been dealing with.

Talent is less about technical skills and more about business knowledge

This is a recurring theme for many of our leaders. They believe that whilst digital understanding and insight is important, commercial appreciation and business understanding is critical. Craig Hamer makes the point that the business knowledge explains why and therefore is likely to generate a better outcome:

> My technical and data person has already been in the industry eight years in operational roles. He's not just a young graduate who may be technically gifted but have limited knowledge of the commercial drivers in the business. He is someone who understands the commerciality of the business – the 'why' – and as such decisions can be made quickly covering all key aspects such as design, segmentation, customer experience and commerciality.

Douglas Johnson-Poensgen reflects on the need to build a much wider understanding of digital across the bank's staff as a whole with the argument that if staff didn't understand how to transact online how could they help customers:

> One of the reasons why Barclays instituted the programme of Digital Eagles was initially to help our own staff overcome their fear of technology. Any number of lovely people working in branches didn't themselves have smartphones and certainly didn't use mobile banking so how on earth can they show customers how to do it.

Konstantine Karampatsos argues that there is a gap between the technical and commercial worlds in e-commerce at present and that the bridge between the two needs to be the leader. It is the leader's job to ensure the two capabilities are pulled together into a coherent whole:

> A challenge is to find employees with industry and digital experience. You can have people in the boardroom who either know beauty or know e-commerce. The leader needs to bridge that gap, especially in terms of communications, because the e-commerce people don't understand the beauty specialists and the beauty specialists don't understand the e-commerce people. So it's a constant struggle. The e-commerce people know how customers behave when buying online, but they are not always aware of the particularities of the beauty

industry and its products. On the other hand beauty specialists, who may have been very successful selling products on the high street, struggle to understand how consumer behaviour changes when buying online. You need both aspects. It's not that one understands the customer and the other one doesn't. It's that they understand different aspects of the customer.

The leadership challenge is change

Every one of our leaders had a great deal to say about the importance and difficulty of getting their organizations to change. All express degrees of frustration with their organizations, they understand why the pace of change is as it is today, but all recognize that in an ideal world they would want to move faster. The utility leader we've spoken to sums this up for many:

> Are we moving fast enough? Probably not. The lack of speed is down to a team growing fast and trying to integrate itself. Budgets are limited and therefore even though digital has been prioritized that does not mean we can do everything and we are operating across an enormously broad range of customers which have different services and different propositions and then obviously we are trying to install smart meters across the whole country. There are many competing demands on us as a business and you can't address it all and that creates prioritization tensions.

In large global organizations such as banks the original business model makes the organization slower than are far more recent competitors. Douglas Johnson-Poensgen again:

> Organizations like Barclays face different challenges to banks like Fidor. These guys designed their businesses to work online whereas Barclays designed its business to work in the bricks-and-mortar world and has had to try and evolve its banking systems so that they interface and work effectively in a digital world. Many big traditional banks have struggled or slipped at various points on this journey.

O2's Tete Soto identified two challenges in change. The first is trying to be agile in a fast-moving market:

> The biggest challenges are twofold. One is just overcoming the inertia of any organization in the process of evolving to a mobile/digital first way of thinking. The second one is developing great customer experiences in a business of large scale at the pace that our marketplace requires. Getting things to market in a digital world – where customers' expectations are constantly rising and where there are over-the-top players developing wonderful digital propositions very

quickly – requires a very different approach to transformation for organizations that grew up in the offline world.

The second is about the impact changes in the market and technology are having on the way a business thinks about its current operating model which in turn is putting pressure on how the organization works:

> When you think about the digital and mobile ecosystems, the distinction between products, services and channels becomes very blurred and that creates a need for a different engagement model between your traditional product functions and your channel/sales functions.

Craig Hamer makes the point that there is also a generational issue for management as well in the customer base. The challenge of changing well-established ways of working in staff who have years in a job or within an industry cannot be underestimated:

> The individuals that now run these big businesses are by and large of a generation where they don't fully understand digital. The younger generation coming up – it's second nature to them and from my point of view, that's my biggest challenge. I've got staff here who didn't really use desktops until five or six years ago and suddenly I'm telling them to ignore the local newspaper, when they used to spend five hours every week sorting out their newspaper advert with their used car list in it. They are more comfortable doing that than actually sitting down for an hour and re-pricing all the stock on the web.

And then, of course, there's the technology

We have made the point that effective e-commerce is not so much a technology issue as a leadership one. Our leaders agreed but they still had these points to make about the technology challenges that they face today:

> I think the first hurdle is assessing and getting the right technology because new systems are always a difficult challenge for businesses to implement and so you want to make sure that you get it right.

> Hugh Sturges, BBR

> We have various systems, so anything we do online needs to make sure the back-end engines all tie in together. Quite often the time is taken making sure that customer transactions and data are tying into our CRM system and that all this works and doesn't break and that the user experience is as good as possible.

> Brett Aumuller, Sky

> Our client records are held in 70 different legacy systems in our branches. They are not integrated or centralized. We can't move those around and bring them

under one roof. That's a challenge. It is quite painful, and we are working on fixing this as we speak, but we don't have a CRM system or central e-mail capabilities. So there are all sorts of challenges that we face there.

Zac Peake, A-Plan

The leadership agenda

From these leadership insights we can draw a sense of a relatively consistent leadership agenda despite the differences in sector and size.

First and foremost, whether a business is in the forefront of sector change or trying to catch up with changes that are happening around them, this is a growth issue. Indeed for some it is rapidly becoming a long-term survival issue. Having a strategic appreciation for the current and projected change trajectory in your industry, a map of current and emerging competitors and an assessment of their performance is a real necessity.

Second, this is an organization challenge. Modern organizations need to be open to the voice of the customer and capable of responding to it. They need to be able to innovate, to test new ideas and to respond to results. Building flexibility and responsiveness into processes and cultures requires careful thought and significant leadership time.

Third, it is demanding a shift in thinking about talent and capability. Businesses need to invest time and resources in helping current digital immigrants become comfortable natives. They need to be innovative in how they build capability as reliance on the current supply levels in the market is driving up cost without improving performance outcomes.

If there is one word that keeps reoccurring in all these interviews and in the hundreds of conversations we have had over the past few years it is 'change'. Keeping pace with changes outside the business and establishing an acceptable pace of change inside the organization is a modern leadership preoccupation. The leadership metaphor that comes to mind is that of a surfer facing challenging conditions and potentially dangerous currents. In these circumstances success comes to those who embrace the waves and who have the capabilities to stay with the board whilst they look for the opportunities not just to keep afloat but also to move forward ahead of the next big wave.

The e-commerce leadership model

9

EXECUTIVE SUMMARY

E-commerce effectiveness will be a defining differentiator for competitive success over the coming years. Failure to get it right will hit revenue and profitability and over time may even lead to business collapse. To ensure effectiveness, whilst leaders do not have to be technical experts, they need to have a competent understanding of how the channel works and be able as a result to drive the best strategic choices for their business. This chapter summarizes the leadership agenda set out in Chapters 1 to 7 into a model for the management of e-commerce and summarizes the key choices that need to be made.

The e-commerce management model

Figure 9.1 shows the e-commerce management model that supports this book.

There are seven key elements to successful e-commerce. There are some strategic choices and some organizational ones. Most important of all are the choices that shape how a business attracts, engages and retains customers. We define these as:

- **Strategic purpose:** Being completely clear at every level of the organization on the purpose of the digital channel as a route to market. Whilst there will be other key needs, none of these are going

FIGURE 9.1   The e-commerce management model

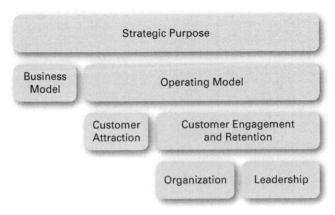

to be as important as the commercial goals of the business. This
clarity enables the proper placing of ownership in an organization
and the driving principle that gives e-commerce the lead. This
purpose should reinforce the commercial imperative such that
policies like 'brand guidelines' are established in the light of this
requirement rather than as present in many businesses in a silo from
where they are then imposed on the business with no thought for
sales execution online.

- **Business model:** A defined channel in terms of the proposition, the
  product portfolio and the platform – even if there will be stages in
  getting there, having a long-term ambition will help a business make
  the right interim decisions to support the long-term goal. A detailed
  definition of any fulfilment requirements and linkages through to
  back office and other systems such as customer relationship
  management (CRM). A clear set of longer-term goals for market
  share in the channel, revenue and margin. This provides the business
  context for how the channel will operate, the organization
  requirements and a leadership agenda.

- **Operating model:** The way in which the channel will work day-to-day.
  In Chapters 2 and 3 we introduced the principles that should sit
  behind the operating model in any business and explained how they
  can create the foundations of an operating model through the
  Customer to Action® process. However, we made the point that even
  if you adopt these, they need to be tailored and expanded such that

everyone involved in the channel, whether or not they are in the e-commerce team, understands how the channel will operate and the key processes that will drive this operation. This sets the standards and ways of working against which you can measure performance.

- **Customer attraction:** How you will drive traffic into the channel from online and offline marketing communications. Chapters 4 and 5 explained the key elements that have to be considered and reinforced the link to brand marketing in that it is important to align the brand experience with other channels and to be clear on the role and importance of social media.

- **Customer engagement and retention:** The manner in which you will 'sell' the proposition in the channel, convert interest into a completed transaction (sale or lead) and optimize the effectiveness of the channel over time. As we explained in Chapter 5 you need to be clear on the activities you want to see and the way in which you want to see them being deployed, including the importance of setting clear goals for conversion, ideally against the key customer segments in the market. It is also critical here to ensure you have a clearly defined approach to retaining customers and to any self-service aspects of the proposition.

- **Organization:** The resources, policies, processes and culture required to make the operating model work. As we discussed in Chapter 6, e-commerce doesn't require a huge headcount, but what it needs is commercially-minded people, passionate about getting it right for the customer, recognized and rewarded for their impact on both customers in the market and on their own customers. It will be important here to establish the culture the business wants to see and to understand the drivers behind sustaining that culture.

- **Leadership:** There are two aspects to this: first, the leadership required for the e-commerce team to be successful; and second, the requirement of leaders in the business to both understand and engage with the channel such that they can make sure that it is performing to the best of its capabilities. As we flagged in Chapter 7 here is the talent agenda and the need to understand how best to build capability from within as well as operating in the market to fill in capability gaps from outside. In addition, for many business leaders there is going to be a need to drive change through their current e-commerce operations if they are to become truly effective.

Leadership choices

Successful e-commerce is underpinned by a clear and shared understanding across the business of the choices made in each of these elements. These choices are leadership ones and should not be left to an e-commerce team to make for themselves. They will act as the drivers of investment in technology, people and activity and should define the context against which goals are set, standards established and performance measured and rewarded. Table 9.1 sets out the important choices to be made in each element and refers you back to the appropriate killer questions and leadership actions to support your analysis and prompt you as to the options available in your circumstances. These choices and the other actions set out in the book will help you establish and maintain an effective e-commerce function.

Final thoughts

We called this book *Leading Digital Strategy* because we think that digital presents far more of a leadership challenge to businesses than anything else. Every business is different but regardless of what every e-commerce team tells itself and its business leaders, the core processes and capabilities that make for an effective channel are the same, regardless of sector or size. What often makes it different are the choices leaders of individual operations make about how they think they need to work and the tools they think they need to support them.

We have spent our professional careers listening to individuals in businesses in which we have worked and with whom we have worked explain to us why they are different. In the vast majority of cases we think they are really deluding themselves and in the few places where there may be differentiation worthy of adjusting practice, it will be for 20 per cent of activity, not 80 per cent, With this in mind here are our final thoughts on the digital leadership challenge:

- **Become a champion of simplicity:** complexity is the enemy of an effective e-commerce operation. Challenge it in every aspect from processes and tools through to reporting performance.
- **Search out the voice of the customer:** ensure the customer is heard directly and responded to fully. Do not accept any proxy (however 'expert') and do not confuse focus-group outputs with real customer feedback given to your business at point of purchase or departure from your online store.

TABLE 9.1 The drivers of e-commerce success

	E-commerce Management Model		
Element	**Definition**	**Choices**	**Chapter**
Strategic purpose	The primary focus of the digital channel and the way in which it will be structured to meet other important stakeholder requirements	• Decide on the primary purpose of the channel and its link to overall strategic goals. • Decide on how to handle other important needs such as media or recruitment or shareholders • Decide on the ownership and ultimate decision-making process for the channel. Make sure you have clearly defined governance	1
Business model	The commercial model and the roles of other functions in enabling this and the key commercial performance metrics	• Confirm the product or service and the proposition that will be communicated to the market at large • Confirm whether the site will transact or generate leads or both. If both, what other channels do you need to work with to ensure a seamless experience • Confirm the platform requirements and if this requires a change, how the criteria will be judged in any alternative • Confirm the required links to ERP/back-office systems • Confirm the fulfilment model. This is just as important in service and lead-generating environments as retailing ones • Set margin goals and be clear on what the drivers of margin are and how you can test elasticity • Set revenue goals • Set market goals	1/2

TABLE 9.1 *continued*

	E-commerce Management Model		
Element	**Definition**	**Choices**	**Chapter**
Operating model	The core processes and capabilities required to make the business model work	• Define the end-to-end process that will be employed to drive growth and which functions/roles will be involved at each stage • Decide where you will deploy 'test and learn' and how this process will work • Establish the role of customer insight in decision making and how it is generated, reported and shared with the rest of the organization	3
Customer attraction	The generation of traffic for the channel	• Define the traffic strategy and resource allocation • Define the role of social media • Establish the link to brand marketing and the brand experience	4
Customer engagement and retention	The converting of traffic in the channel into transacting customers	• Set conversion goals • Set key performance measures for conversion • Define how the operation will work to optimize both engagement and retention • Establish a customer segmentation model for the channel and how it will be used to shape strategy going forward • Define how the operation will work to deliver customer service and support	4/5

TABLE 9.1 *continued*

	E-commerce Management Model		
Element	**Definition**	**Choices**	**Chapter**
Organization	The organization required to make the business model work	• Confirm performance management standards and process • Establish how performance will be linked to rewards and recognition • Establish the degree of cross-functional working and collaboration you will need in the business to deliver the operating model • Establish how to align activity across all channels and marketing • Decide on the standardization of language/terminology	6
Leadership	The leadership required to attain and sustain effective performance	• Decide on your communication and engagement approach • Review the overall employment contract and employee value proposition and look to change these if they are a barrier to recruitment and retention • Decide on how to ensure a focus on professional developments in the market and how these are spotted and tested • Establish a process for up-skilling of the whole organization in e-commerce • Establish a recruitment strategy that builds capability for the long term through a mix of 'buy' and 'build'	7

- **Look for hypotheses not theses:** hypotheses allow an e-commerce team to fail yet succeed. If they are built from a range of customer-authored inputs they are the most potent way we know of learning more about the customer in the market or about your own customer. Challenge theses when you see them: they are built to be endorsed. Often they drive individuals to adjust their parameters in order to ensure they are proven right. They drive tests that look to confirm, rather than tests that look to understand.

- **'Test and learn' at every stage:** every interaction with customers in the market and your own customers in the digital channel can be put to the test and in testing alternatives so you can learn more. Test to prove or disprove a hypothesis, not to find out whether one or other 'expert opinion' works best.

- **Place function over form:** whilst a beautifully designed website is aesthetically pleasing, it isn't a guarantee of commercial success. Indeed some very beautiful websites we have seen performed very poorly. Your website has to work for customers in market and your customers – not just for your designers or user-experience specialists. If it is not converting effectively then think about the customer agenda and how to meet it rather than a 're-skin' or a complete re-design.

- **Never think you've got it right:** as soon as you think you cannot learn from others, you will start to lay the foundations of under-performance. The world of e-commerce is one that is changing fast and new tools, practices and methodologies will evolve and supplant current ones. Keep a firm link to the outside world and don't rely on your agency relationships – they could well be out of date.

- **Stay ruthlessly commercial:** demand performance in commercial terms not technical ones. Be clear about revenue and margin and about return on investment for the channel. Link pay to commercial performance and recognize customer-centric behaviour. After all this will be the single most important channel for virtually every business over time, even if your customer chooses to transact with you in an alternative one.

At the heart of our thinking is the importance of testing to learn what works and what will be less effective in a fast-changing market. We believe that what you test should be based upon insight generated by engaging customers as they engage with you: in your sales funnel. Building a competitive edge in generating insight and testing effectiveness could create and sustain a significant competitive advantage. This is an organization challenge – aligning people, processes and technology in pursuit of growth.

Effective leadership in business creates an organization that stops guessing about its customers and starts learning from them.

GLOSSARY

A/B testing: A/B testing tests at least two versions of the same web page (version A and version B) to determine which one works best for the customer in the market.

Abandonment: The process of a session starting a funnel but not reaching a goal. A metric in analytics that can be measured by most analytics packages. Essentially the reciprocal of the overall conversion rate.

Above the fold: Used in website design and optimization analysis to refer to the portion of the web page that is visible without scrolling. As screen sizes vary drastically there is no set definition for the number of pixels that define the fold.

Above the scroll: See *above the fold*.

Ad: Advertisement using the online channel. These possess a hyperlink that links through to a target page on a website. They can take different forms such as videos, text and images. They are placed on other sites and search engine results pages. There are two mains reasons why people would create ads: to raise awareness or to drive people to a site and ultimately convert. Both types have different pricing models. They are known as cost per mille and cost per click, respectively.

Ad position: Position of a text-based ad on a search engine results page. The ad position is determined by the ad rank. High ad positions are sought because the higher the position the more chance some will click it.

Ad tracking: Ad tracking monitors the performance of advertising campaigns on the internet.

Affiliate: A site that highlights the commercial offers made by another company, by using banners, skyscrapers or text links. The commercial benefit for the display site is delivered through either a pay-per-click model or based on ultimate sales.

Analytics: The measurement of people on a site. Includes how they arrive, where they leave and what they did. Such data is normally presented in terms of sessions, users and page-views relating to particular pages. Users and sessions are normally reported against pre-set goals across the site as a whole.

AOV: see *average order value*

Attribution: The process of ascribing a particular direct response or sale against how the user arrived on the site. Often a setting to choose from analytics packages, usually between 'last-click attribution' and 'first-click attribution'. Sales/direct responses are singular. However, arrivals on site can be multiple (eg one may choose to visit a site through a number of mediums before buying). Analytics packages record all the visits and the mediums they used to arrive before converting. The choice is whether you attribute the conversion to the first or the last session. The alternative is attributing the conversion to the most expensive route.

Attribution rate: Shows the share of attribution and is calculated using the ratio between the total number of sessions and the total number of attributed sessions.

Average order value (AOV) or average ticket: the value of an average order within a period of time.

Banner: A rectangular element which contains an advertising message and which most often redirects internet users to a commercial website. Banners can be clicked on by users, and are either static or animated.

BID management: BID management involves managing commercial link auctions. BID management tools automate the cost per click of each keyword. Using a web analytics solution, coupled with a BID management tool to properly manage these links, helps businesses optimize their advertising investments.

Bounce: Sessions resulting in a page-view count of one or less where someone arrives on your site and leaves without any further recorded action.

Bounce rate: The number of bounces on a page divided by the number of entrances to that page.

Browser: An application designed to access the world wide web. The best known browsers include Internet Explorer, Firefox, Opera and Google Chrome.

Call to action: In marketing, a call to action (CTA) is an instruction to an audience to provoke an immediate response, usually using an imperative verb such as 'call now to find out more' or 'visit a store today'.

Campaign: A campaign can be an advertisement, e-mail marketing or partnership campaign, which uses e-mails to promote your products. Associated with conversions, campaigns are essential when it comes to analysing return on investment (ROI).

Cascading style sheet (CSS): This defines how HTML elements appear on a page. If used consistently, it allows you to control the appearance and layout of all the pages in a website in one single CSS file, eg headers are all the same size and colour.

Click-through or Click: A term used normally for advertisements or campaigns where it represents a single instance of a user following a hyperlink to another page or to initiate an action. In AdWords these are called clicks, which is confusing given that clicks can be associated in other metrics with broad user activity on a page.

Click-through rate/ratio: The number of click-throughs for a specific link divided by the number of times that link was viewed.

Clicks metric in analytics: In analytics, a click is a simple click of a mouse on an element within a page, even if that element has no link through to an action.

Consumer: This refers to people in the market who may or may not be shopping for your product or service.

Conversion: A user completing a target action.

Conversion rate: The ratio of conversions over a relevant denominator.

Cookie: A small string of text stored on a user's computer by a web browser. It consists of bits of information such as user preferences, shopping cart contents, the identifier for a server-based session, or other data used by websites to recognize visitors.

Cost per click: The cost per click-through on a paid ad (see *pay per click*)

Cost per mille: see *cost per thousand*

Cost per thousand: Cost per thousand (CPM) is a marketing term referring to the cost of a media vehicle reaching 1,000 members of an audience. The M in CPM is the Roman numeral for 1,000. A media program unit can be one print ad, one commercial, or one of any sort of advertising medium.

CPC: see *cost per click*

CPM: see *cost per thousand*

CSS: see *cascading style sheet*

CTA: see *call to action*

CTR: see *click-through rate*

Customer: This is the customer as purchaser.

Customer in the market: This is the customer as shopper, not yet committed to a purchase, but actively looking to complete a transaction. This term applies to both 'business to consumer' and 'business to business' markets and regardless of whether the digital channels aim to transact a sale or generate a lead.

Direct traffic: The number of sessions to your website that originated from users who a) clicked a bookmark to come to your site or b) typed your site URL into their browser. Direct traffic can include visitors recruited via offline (ie print and television) campaigns.

Domain: A domain name is a unique ID linked to an entity with computers connected to the internet. The system is hierarchical and can be used to define one or more sub-domains.

E-commerce: The activity that is responsible for commercial performance in a digital channel. This encompasses marketing in the channel, sales, promotions, new digital product development and channel performance measurement and improvement. It does not include responsibility for technology choices or management.

Entrance rate/Entrance to page-view ratio: The number of entrances to a page divided by the number of page-views of that page. Can be expressed as a percentage ie the percentage of page-views that were a site entrance.

Entry page: The first page of a visit.

Event: Any logged or recorded action that has a specific date and time assigned to it by either the browser or server.

Exact match: One of the match types that Google Analytics defines to identify a URL for either a goal or a funnel. An exact match is a match on every character in your search string from beginning to end with no additions permitted.

Exit page: The last page on a site accessed during a session, signifying the end of a session.

External referrer: Any site that links to yours.

Filter: A rule that includes or excludes specific data from reports. You can use filters to carry out actions like eliminating internal traffic from reports or to include only traffic to a specific subdomain.

Funnels: Series of steps a user completes to reach an end goal. Google Analytics allows you to indicate up to 10 pages in each funnel definition. Creating funnels can show you where sessions abandon the process during the path to conversion.

Geo-segmentation: Targeting information (user, population, category etc) based on geographical location.

Goal: A measure of something you want to track in Google Analytics that you define as a success. Goals must relate to a quantifiable action that your website's users take, such as product purchases, newsletter sign-ups or downloads. Goals are set up in Google Analytics to track conversions.

Goal conversion rate: The percentage of sessions in which a specified goal is completed.

Heat map: A visual representation of internet user clicks which is based on different intensity heat zones (ranging from blue to red).

HTML: Hypertext Markup Language. The main language that websites are written in which holds all the text, images and hyperlinks inside it. The HTML is converted by browsers into what you see on your screen. There are other languages that fit inside HTML that perform more complex functions including Javascript and Jquery.

Hyperlink: Any element of a website (button, image, text) that, once clicked, takes the user somewhere else (another part of the page, a different page, another website entirely) or performs a function (submits a form, turns of a carousel).

Impressions: Number of times a piece of content was delivered to a user's browser.

Internal referrer: A page URL that is internal to the website or a web property within the website as defined by the user.

Internet protocol: The term 'IP Address' is used to define a number which is given to each computer when it is connected to the internet. It is the fundamental communication protocol in internet protocol suite.

Internet service provider: An organization (usually a firm) offering a connection to the internet network.

IP: see *internet protocol*.

ISP: see *internet service provider*.

JavaScript: A computer programming language that is integrated into web page codes. It is used to measure the amount of traffic for a particular page.

Key performance indicator: A key performance indicator (KPI) is a metric that helps you understand how you are doing against your objectives.

Keyword: Represents terms typed into search engines by internet users.

Keyword searches: Actual keywords and phrases visitors typed into search engines to find our site.

KPI: see *key performance indicator*.

Landing page: A page intended to identify the beginning of the user experience resulting from a defined marketing effort.

M-commerce: Mobile commerce or m-commerce corresponds to the use of wireless technologies and the use of mobile phones for business purposes in particular. AT internet technology is used to measure the audience and performance of mobile terminals.

Macro conversion: A macro conversion is the primary conversion on a website, for example a completed sale on an e-commerce site or a completed lead generation form.

Micro conversion: A micro conversion relates to smaller engagements such as a newsletter sign-up or a user watching a product video. Micro conversions can often precede the macro conversion.

Mobile analytics: The measurement and analysis of data generated by mobile platforms and environments (applications).

Multivariate testing: A fine-tuning tool which involves testing a large number of versions of the same web page based on several variable criteria so as to determine which one will be able to attract a maximum number of visitors and generate the most sales. It requires a high volume of traffic to succeed.

New visitor/New user: The number of users with activity including a first-ever session to a site during a reporting period.

Organic traffic: Sessions to your website from unpaid organic or natural search engine results.

Original referrer: The first referrer in a user's first session, whether internal, external or null.

Page: An analyst-definable unit of content.

Page exit ratio: Number of exits from a page divided by total number of page-views of that page.

Page-views: The number of times a page is viewed.

Page-views per session: The number of page-views in a reporting period divided by the number of sessions in the same reporting period.

Paid traffic: This consists of users who come to your website from Google AdWords ads, paid search engine keywords and other online paid ad campaigns. When investing in an online PPC or other advertising campaign, this data will show you how effective your paid online marketing programme is.

Pay per click: Pay per click (PPC) (also called cost per click) is an internet advertising model used to direct traffic to websites, in which advertisers pay the publisher (typically a website owner) when the ad is clicked. It is defined simply as 'the amount spent to get an advertisement clicked'.

Platform: The technology used to support an e-commerce operation.

PPC: see *pay per click*.

Referrer: The page URL that originally generated the request for the current page-view or object.

Repeat visitor/user: The number of users with activity consisting of two or more sessions to a site during a reporting period.

Request URI: The string at the end of a URL after the '.com' in your web address.

Return visitor/user: The number of users with activity consisting of a session to a site during a reporting period and where the user also visited the site prior to the reporting period.

Revenue per user (RPU) or revenue per visitor (RPV): A composite measure of value of revenue per user within a period of time. It is calculated by dividing revenue by the number of users in a specific time period, RPU = (revenue for time period)/(users for time period).

RPU/RPV: see *revenue per user*

Scroll map: A type of heat map showing how far down a web page users scroll.

Search engine marketing: Search engine marketing (SEM) is a form of internet marketing that involves the promotion of websites by increasing their visibility in search engine results pages (SERPs) through optimization and advertising.

Search engine optimization: Search engine optimization (SEO) is the process of maximizing the number of users to a particular website by ensuring that the site appears high on the list of results returned by a search engine.

Search engine results page: A search engine results page (SERP) is the listing of results returned by a search engine in response to a keyword query. The results normally include a list of items with titles, a reference to the full version, and a short description showing where the keywords have matched content within the page.

Search referrer: An internal or external referrer for which the URL has been generated by a search function.

SEM: see *search engine marketing*.

SEO: see *search engine optimization*.

SERPs: see *search engine results page*.

Sessions: A period of time spent on your website by an individual. If an individual has not taken another action (typically additional page-views) on the site within a specified time period (typically 30 minutes), the visit will terminate by timing out. A session does not discriminate between several visits by one customer in the market or one visit made by several customers in the market. Also known as visits.

Single page-view visits: Visits that consist of one page-view.

Single-page visits: Visits that consist of one page regardless of the number of times the page was viewed.

Tag: An element which is inserted into each page that is to be measured so that its publication can be recorded. A tag is inserted into the page source code. It is used to generate a connection to the server which is used by a third-party measurement tool.

Tracking code: A small snippet of code that is inserted into the body of an HTML page. The tracking code captures information about visits to a page.

Traffic: The total number of sessions to your website. Within Google Analytics, traffic can be divided into multiple categories (mediums) including direct, organic and paid.

Uniform resource identifier: In computing, a uniform resource identifier (URI) is a string of characters used to identify a name of a resource. Such identification enables interaction with representations of the resource over a network, typically the world wide web, using specific protocols. The most common form of URI is the uniform resource locator (URL), frequently referred to informally as a web address.

Uniform resource locator: The URL is the address of your website (eg **www.mycompany.com**).

Unique page-views: Unique page-views represent the number of sessions during which the specified page, or group of pages, was viewed at least once. Multiple views of the same page and page refreshes are not included in this metric.

Unique visitors: see *users*.

URI: see *uniform resource identifier*.

URL: see *uniform resource locator*.

Users: Customers in the market who are visiting or have visited your website, ie the number of individual people (filtered for search engine robots) with activity consisting of one or more session to a site within a designated timeframe. Each individual is only counted once. Previously called 'unique visitors' within Google Analytics.

UV: Abbreviation of unique visitors (see *users*).

Visit duration: The length of time of a session. Calculation is typically the timestamp of the last activity in the session minus the timestamp of the first activity of the session.

Visit referrer: The first referrer in a session, whether internal, external or null.

Visitor: An individual who visits a website during a defined period. A visitor can make multiple visits and identification is based on the visitor's computer. A cookie helps determine whether a visitor is new or returning. Visitors are now called 'users' within Google Analytics.

Visits: see *sessions*.

Visits per visitor: The number of visits in a reporting period divided by the number of unique visitors for the same reporting period.

INDEX

Note: *Italics* indicate a Table or Figure in the text.